Roman Housing

Roman Housing

Simon P. Ellis

Duckworth

This impression 2008
First published in 2000 by
Gerald Duckworth & Co. Ltd.
90-93 Cowcross Street, London EC1M 6BF
Tel: 020 7490 7300
Fax: 020 7490 0080
inquiries@duckworth-publishers.co.uk
www.ducknet.co.uk

A catalogue record for this book is available
from the British Library

ISBN 978 0 7156 3196 6

Typeset by Ray Davies
Printed and bound in Great Britain by
CPI Antony Rowe, Eastbourne

Contents

Plates between pages 120 and 121

Preface

This book has been twenty years in the making. When I started my doctoral research on late antique houses in 1978 there were very few scholars working on either housing or related issues of social history. By the end of the 1980s articles had appeared by Andrew Wallace-Hadrill, Yvonne Thébert and myself. Roman social history was also starting to explore issues of the family through authors such as Saller, Dixon, Rawson and Treggiari.

It was always my intention to expand my thesis into a book, yet it seemed to me that the understanding of the early Roman period (especially outside Pompeii) was insufficient. In the 1980s I had explored the application of French social historians, family sociologists and town planners to housing in a body of largely unpublished work. It was only in the mid 1990s that the rise of a new generation of British scholars (in particular Sarah Scott and Ray Laurence) made me think that the time had come for this book. Mention should also be made of the refreshing new approach to Pompeii that has been the result of Andrew Wallace-Hadrill's work.

I would like to acknowledge the help of many eminent scholars throughout my travels in almost every province of the Empire during the 1970s and 1980s. Prime amongst these are my advisers and examiners at Oxford, Professors Mango, Frere and Harrison. Many ideas were also the result of discussions with friends at Carthage including John Humphrey, Colin Wells, John Hayes, Bruce Hitchener and Henry Hurst. In my travels abroad I had active support from many people of whom I must mention Noel Duval, Vladislav Popovic, Clive Foss, James Russell and Emilio Marin. I have also received more immediate help in compiling the book from Christopher Smith and Roger Ling.

Most of all I have to thank my family, my wife Mylène and children Emilie and Francis. Without their amazing tolerance in giving me time to write on top of a full-time job and moving house I would have been unable to form a single sentence!

November 1999   S.P.E.

Preface to the Paperback Edition

I am pleased that my publishers have seen fit to issue a paperback edition, which will make the book more widely accessible. Among peers who have commented on the publication, some have said that it talks too much about aristocratic housing, whereas others have said it does not say enough. It is thus appropriate that the text remains unchanged.

Montreal   S.P.E.
2002

1

Introduction

Houses are personal buildings, to which everyone can relate. We all need houses, and we all adapt our houses to fit our own particular taste. Today only the wealthy actively personalise the structure of the house by having it designed by an architect, but everyone changes the wallpaper or the carpets. These observations are just as applicable in Roman times as they are today. Nowadays we do not have pagan temples (though many public buildings imitate their architectural style), or amphitheatres, but we still live in houses.

This book provides the first empire-wide, overall introduction to Roman housing, covering all provinces and all social classes, from the origins of Rome to the sixth century AD. It introduces the student and the general reader to the Roman house in all its forms, and also to the particular problems of interpreting ancient houses. For the more specialised researcher it provides a wealth of comparative evidence from many different provinces. It presents new evidence in areas such as lighting and furniture, and constitutes the first statement of the overall place of the house in Roman provincial society.

The magic of looking at an ancient house is that we can feel an affinity with the family, or individual, who owned the building. The role of the individual in creating a house is both the greatest attraction and the greatest difficulty in studying Roman houses.

Consider the House of the Vettii (Fig. 1), one of the best known and most often visited in Pompeii.[1] No one who goes there can fail to be impressed by the secluded garden filled with greenery and sunlight, and the cool, richly decorated reception rooms opening onto it.

In the first century AD the house was owned by two brothers, A. Vettius Restitutus and A. Vettius Conviva. They were freedmen, that is ex-slaves who had gained their freedom, most probably either buying it from their master or being bequeathed it on his death. Either way they had been most successful, and were the owners of a very opulent house.

The house was entered through a short porch, which led to the *atrium*. This was a court with a rectangular opening in the ceiling. Rain falling through the ceiling was caught by a rectangular pool, the *impluvium*, in the centre of the room, and emptied into the cistern beneath. Private cisterns could be used to supply water for drinking, cleaning and indus-

1. House of the Vettii, Pompeii, Italy.

trial uses. Houses in Pompeii also had a piped water supply for drinking, and for fountains.

Walking straight through the atrium the visitor arrived at the *peristyle*. This was a garden area surrounded by colonnaded porticoes on all four sides. The garden of a Pompeian house[2] was often similar to its modern counterpart, with carefully chosen flowers or small box hedges. Interspersed between the flower beds there was garden furniture consisting of statues and fountains, a garden table or perhaps a complete dining suite.

In other houses, however, the peristyle could be devoted to industrial or agricultural activity. The secluded garden of the House of the Vettii with its statues is one of the marvels of the house.

As one stood at the exit from the atrium in the colonnade of the peristyle one would have seen three reception rooms. Two smaller reception rooms lay on the same colonnade that the visitor had entered, to the left and the right. The largest reception room lay open to view at the visitor's far right, at the end of the next portico.

This large reception room, the biggest room in the house, was richly decorated. Its walls were painted with deep red panels, separated by black borders. Every visitor, ancient or modern, has been and will be drawn to examine the exquisite frieze of miniature cupids at work, which runs around the central zone of the walls. The main function of this room was as a dining area, a *triclinium*. The guests reclined on their couches, set in a U-shaped arrangement around the back of the room. They would have looked out of the door down the length of the garden, with the heat slowly dispersing and the shadows slowly lengthening, a glass of wine in their hands.

To either side of this large reception room were retiring areas, commonly known as *cubicula*, where guests, or the owner and family, could go to sleep or sit in quieter discussion. The Romans slept or sat on couches, rather like a modern chaise longue, so that 'bedrooms' could be used for a variety of purposes. One room opened straight off a corner of the reception room. Two other 'bedrooms' opened off the adjacent small fountain court. This area was an elegant suite of reception rooms appropriate for formal receptions and intimate encounters.

In the two smaller reception rooms, near the atrium on the other colonnade of the peristyle, the large-scale mythological paintings of divine vengeance catch the eye. On the rear wall of the right-hand room is Ixion, who was tied to a wheel for daring to have an affair with Juno, Queen of the Gods. On the rear wall of the left-hand room is Pentheus being ripped apart by Dionysus' hounds after refusing to accept his love.

Two other groups of rooms should be discussed. To the right of the atrium, steps led down to several smaller rooms with a rougher style of decoration. These were the kitchens and the rooms where at least some of the servants lived. The furthest, darkest, room of this apartment was decorated with three simply depicted scenes of lovemaking. Yet even this more remote area of the house had a second smaller atrium court. This atrium was part of an earlier building, so it was easier to re-use it than to change the design.

Within this second atrium was a well-preserved *lararium*, the small shrine of the Roman household gods. A painting of the gods is framed by finely stuccoed miniature columns and pediment. The hearth was the traditional seat of the Roman familial spirits, and the usual location for this feature.[3] To this day 'larin' is the word for fireplace in the Venetian dialect.[4] If this area was truly for servants, they still had a reasonable standard of living, including several living rooms with painted walls, as well as the atrium court. These servants certainly lived better than many poor citizens of Pompeii, or provincials in other parts of the Empire. Perhaps the Vettii had some sympathy, remembering their own humble origins.

To the left of the atrium was a single large room opening onto the street. This was a shop. It was common for Roman aristocrats to build shops into their houses in order to provide rent to supplement their income, or to form a porter's lodge providing security and a doorman to announce visitors. In the House of the Vettii a separate porter's lodge was built next to the main entrance to the house.

Just behind the shop a staircase to an upper storey rose from the atrium. Few upper storeys are preserved in Roman houses, and it is important to remember them when considering houses whose physical remains consist of nothing more than foundations. Upper storeys generally copied the plan of the ground floor, so that the upper-floor walls would be supported by those on the ground. It is normally assumed that rooms on the upper storeys of peristyle houses were private suites and servants' quarters.

The modern visitor imagines how marvellous it would be to live in such an opulent house: the elegant lifestyle of the ex-slave brothers, the marble statues, the scents of the garden, the chattering fountains, and the colourful mythical events painted on the walls. Then one remembers the more sordid truths of Roman life: the cruelty of the amphitheatre and the lack of modern medicine.

This book is a scholarly work and so inevitably it will need to elaborate on detailed considerations of historical evidence, but it is also born of a deep love for Roman houses, and those feelings we all feel on entering the House of the Vettii. Many previous works on this subject have been concerned only with architecture, mosaics, or paintings. Here consideration will be given to a wide range of houses of the Roman period from imperial palaces to the smallest buildings. A holistic approach is taken, including some subjects, such as lighting, which have hardly ever received scholarly treatment. In this way it is hoped that some of the magic of the Roman house can be restored. The Roman house will be taken apart and pieced back together in a way never attempted before; from the building and its decoration, to the garden and its flowers, to the behaviour of the dinner guests and the way the sun set across the peristyle.

The object of this chapter, having set the scene, is to examine a few important preconceptions about Roman houses, to agree a definition of what a Roman house was, and so to lay the foundations for the main part of the book.

1. Roman houses: functions and inhabitants

The affinity we feel with the individual Roman can be misplaced. Although Roman houses were for living in, they functioned in a very different way from present-day houses. For example, the Roman aristocrat shared his house with slaves, servants and attendants. As a result archaeologists have often been at pains to look for servants' quarters, but historical sources show that they often just slept at the doors of their masters' rooms.[5] George[6] has correctly questioned all the assumptions used in identifying slave quarters: that slaves' rooms were badly lit, badly decorated, or located in separate areas of the house. Such rooms could be used for servants or slaves, but for example the Younger Pliny (*Letters* 2.17.7-10) had a suite of rooms in his villa that could be used for either servants or guests. Normally the approach in this book is to consider the archaeological evidence, which covers a wide area of the Roman world in depth, and then to add literary references, which are often anecdotal since the authors' concerns were not with domestic life. This, however, is one area in which archaeology cannot tell the whole story and we need to rely more on textual evidence.

Nowadays our conception of slavery is based on the history of the eighteenth- and nineteenth-century west. Rarely did Roman households have the same rigid divisions between slaves and the free-born that existed more recently in Europe and the USA. In Roman times, slaves who had gained their freedom could be very rich and powerful, rising to be important householders, such as Trimalchio in Petronius' *Satyricon* (32-49) – one of our most important sources on Italian housing of the first century AD. The House of the Vettii, with whose rich designs we began this chapter, was owned by just such a family of rich freedmen. But despite this, it is true that the majority of slaves were treated as simple property. They were bought, sold, and passed on to successors as part of the property associated with a house.

Houses were for business as well as domestic use. The house of the aristocrat was designed to be an office, the one-room house of the poorer classes also functioned as a shop or workshop.

In early Rome the aristocrat would expect to receive his most important friends in the early morning sitting in the *tablinum*, an important reception room near the main entrance to the house. Also in attendance would be his poorer followers, known as his 'clients'. The richer friends were bound to the aristocrat by agreements to support each other in obtaining lucrative posts or contracts. The poorer clients would be asking a favour from him to oppose the demands of a magistrate, or to support them in a quarrel. The aristocrat could, in return, expect their votes in local elections, or their physical support on the streets in clashes with political opponents. Such favours could put them permanently under an obligation to the aristocrat. For some clients their only source of income was the special payments or 'gifts' (*sportulae*) distributed by the aristocrat on such occasions.[7] By the late antique period the gathered 'clientele' of at least some aristocrats could even take the form of a private army.

Rich houses had many rooms devoted to specific functions relating to both business and pleasure, but amongst artisans it was common to have both living quarters and workshop in one or two rooms. The majority of shops which lined Roman streets were also houses. Often they had a separate workshop with a living room behind or above the shop, but sometimes they did not.[8] The shopkeeper had a hearth to manufacture pottery or work iron in one part of a room, and a bed in another. Such shopkeepers might have seemed wealthy compared to poor country peasants or urban vagrants, who may have lived in simple brushwood shelters.[9]

2. Interpreting the designs of Roman houses

The role of an archaeologist or historian is to look for patterns in the past. Thus variations in the design of Roman temples can be used to examine general patterns in society at large, in religion, culture or politics. In the case of houses there may be doubt over whether a particular architectural or decorative innovation is the result of individual taste, or the reflection of wider changes in society.

This problem is the main reason why no general books have been written on the Roman house for twenty years,[10] whilst books on Roman public architecture are relatively common. The earliest known occurrence of a new kind of painting or room design is often described as an innovation by the artist or patron, but the archaeologist always has to bear in mind that only a few houses are preserved out of the many thousands that once existed. A unique design could thus be the surviving representative of a widespread trend, or alternatively the product of an eccentric owner.

Even in the case of Pompeii, where a large part of the ancient town has been recovered, archaeologists are uncertain whether an innovation should be described as new to the Roman world or new to the Vesuvius area. It is to be expected that new designs in Pompeii were preceded by similar designs in the capital, Rome, which probably took the lead on cultural matters but where surviving evidence is weaker.

Under these circumstances it is hard to tell whether an individual house owner, or broad social pressure, is responsible for change. The historian or archaeologist wants to identify a change in society, but the specialist in housing can often see only an innovative individual.

To clarify these issues it is worth spending a few moments considering the design process for a Roman house, and the people involved in it.

The principal personality was the house owner. If the house was a new property he would influence the entire building process, gathering together architects and decorators as appropriate. If he had come into possession of an older property he would influence architectural changes and redecoration. The clearest expression of the influence of the owner on Roman housing is to be found in some North African mosaics which depict the owner himself and his estate.

The second most important personality was the artist or architect. While there can be little doubt that the owner, as patron, had the final say in any project, the artist as a professional could play a large part in guiding the owner's thought. Sometimes the owner may not have played a decisive part in the design process at all. He may have been disinterested and simply asked the artist to build according to the latest fashion, or he may have had so little knowledge of design that he let himself be swayed by the artist's ideas. On the other hand, the owner might have decided very firmly on his particular requirements and forced the artist to follow his lead. In the case of the African mosaics showing the owner and his estate, the artist may have suggested to the owner that such depictions were a very fashionable subject, or the owner might have decided that he wished to be personally depicted.

Stupperich and Ling have both argued, in papers written a decade apart,[11] that the classical education received by house owners in fourth-century AD Britain had a fundamental influence on mosaic designs. Stupperich argued that the mosaics of villas such as Keynsham[12] and Pitney had scenes which demonstrated a remarkable appreciation of classical mythology using rarely depicted characters such as Marsyas. He and Ling suggest that it was the influence of the owner that led to the juxtaposition of figured scenes which did not form a true mythological narrative. Ling[13] notes that at Room 12 at Brading three scenes relating to mystery religions were juxtaposed with a traditional illustration of 'amorati', and in Room 3 a Bacchic motif was arranged with a hunting scene. Such mosaics show those particular mythological episodes that interested the owner. It is difficult to provide conclusive evidence for the relationship between patron and artist for any particular design, but such ideas indicate the ways in which such partnerships may have operated.

Similarly Clarke has argued that the lack of unity in the painting schemes of the House of the Vettii at Pompeii is because of the owners' wish to pick images designed to impress rather than to follow a particular decorative scheme.[14] He identifies the iconographic theme of confrontation between god and mortal in the two lesser reception rooms, which has already been alluded to at the beginning of this chapter. He also identifies two lesser themes. One is the use of cupids in the main reception room, the atrium, and the peristyle. A second is the use of Priapic imagery in the kitchens, as well as a statue of Priapus in the peristyle and a painted image of the same deity in the entrance to the house.

Clarke associates this clash of themes with the freedman background of the Vettii, since freedmen were notoriously anxious to make an impression with their wealth. Indeed the painting of Priapus shows him balancing his phallus against a bag of money. This would seem, at least to modern eyes, a blatant statement of the origins of the owners' power. The lack of interest in a coherent decor should not, however, be pursued too far as a sign of lack of education. The decor may not have the depth of subtle allusion that one might expect from a traditional Pompeiian aristocrat, but the confrontation of mortal and god in the lesser reception rooms certainly sets a worthy moralistic tone. The other two themes have a much weaker role in the house. As Clarke says, no one could escape the Priapus in the main doorway, or indeed the statue which faced any visitor entering the peristyle, but though obvious, these two figures represent a small part of the overall decor. As far as the theme of cupids is concerned, it is not represented in the major wall panels. The main panel from the most important reception room is missing, so its role in the decorative programme cannot be assessed.

The decor in the House of the Vettii, as in the aforementioned British villas, indicates the influence of the owner on the themes of domestic decor. It shows that even in a wealthy Italian context less cultivated owners could be distinguished from the 'blue-blooded' in matters of personal taste. It also indicates the relative context of art, for if the House of the Vettii had been built in Roman Britain its decor would have seemed to attain the height of culture. Paintings and decor must be seen within the context of the ways in which such themes were transmitted from the centre of the Empire to the peripheral provinces. However, it is worth noting that when scholars have identified the influence of owners or patrons, it is often on the basis of their negative influence on artistic schemes. Cultured patrons would, no doubt, make positive contributions for artistic works, but the production of a highly cultivated piece is usually attributed entirely to the artist.

Much debate concerns the use of so-called 'pattern books'.[15] It is assumed that ancient artists had a store of stock designs, which they showed to prospective clients. Particular depictions of gods in certain attitudes occur in widely separated parts of the Empire. Images designed for one particular god are re-used to represent another personality, a different deity or a secular personage. Even the paintings in the tablinum of a rich Pompeiian house, such as that of Lucretius Fronto, the decoration of which is 'of incomparable refinement and beauty', re-use stock motifs derived from other types of scene.[16] Similarly geometric patterns used in mosaic design are copied or re-used in different designs of flooring.

There is little direct evidence for pattern books as documents, and some scholars consider that knowledge of designs was kept in the heads of master craftsmen, who passed on their experience to apprentices and colleagues.

Artists often formed 'workshops' in which several artists used similar patterns. Local mosaic workshops with local stylistic traits can be identified in every Roman province.[17] It is known that craftsmen did form into groups in Roman times, and particular groups of Arretine and Samian potters can be identified working from a single location.[18] However, it is uncertain how often local mosaic workshops represent several mosaicists working from a single site, or a number of craftsmen working across a particular area who simply shared a common tradition and experience.[19]

The use of pattern books and a standard repertoire of designs can be compared to the use of wallpaper and flooring catalogues today. Whilst in theory it might be possible to commission any design of carpet or wall-paper, in practice the choice is limited to conventional patterns and colour schemes. So also in Roman times, the owner and the artist were to some extent constrained by available materials, and by the conventional designs of society at large. Modern wallpaper is pre-printed, but Roman mosaics and paintings were usually assembled on site. Pattern books would there-fore have been indicative, rather than predetermining the final result. An exception to this arrangement were the centrepieces of some Hellenistic and Roman Republican paintings and mosaics. These were specially com-posed panels of particularly fine composition, known as *emblemata*, that were pre-prepared on plaster in the workshop and then slotted into place in the wall or floor.

This somewhat abstract discussion has now led us back to one of the central problems addressed by this book: the identification of general patterns and trends in Roman housing. Though houses represented the designs of an individual owner or artist, these two personalities were constrained by the conventions of society at large. Innovation was perhaps easier in housing than in public building, as a house was still primarily intended for an individual, whereas a public building had to be acceptable to the community as a whole. We are all aware how much controversy is stirred up by a radical post-modernist building in a major city today. Although it was in theory easier to innovate in housing, most people remained conservative in outlook, and innovation could be expensive as it often meant hiring leading artists or using new materials in untried structures.

In sum, a house represents the expression of an individual, but one that is heavily constrained by the conventions of the local community and society at large. In seeking to identify the general chronological and geographical trends in Roman housing we must tease out the role of the individual, and the role of society, in the design process of particular buildings.

3. Defining the 'Roman house'

What is a Roman house? This may appear a strange question, but it has caused real problems for archaeological studies. The nub of the difficulty is that the Roman world was made up of many ethnic groups, each of which had its own particular traditions of domestic architecture. In addition the

houses of the poor and the houses of the rich were often completely
different types of building.

In general terms, most citizens of the Roman Empire would probably
have come up with the same answer. The Roman house, which most
citizens of the Roman Empire aspired to, was one with a large richly
decorated reception room opening onto a central colonnaded courtyard or
peristyle. It is, however, difficult to go beyond this very summary statement. In North Africa, for example, during Roman times aristocratic
houses were often provided with two reception rooms facing each other
across the courtyard. Does this make the house African rather than
Roman? Should we say that the occupants were less 'Romanised' than the
inhabitants of Italy? If houses in Roman Britain had less splendid decora-
tions than those of Africa should we conclude that the British were less
'Romanised', poor, or just different?

Romanisation is a very much abused concept amongst archaeologists,[20]
but it conceals an important historical question. The debate about Romanisation is an attempt to establish the extent to which provincial subjects
of the Roman Empire wished to become like the Romans of Rome. Traditionally historians have held that citizens of the Roman Empire were
rewarded with privilege as they accepted the Roman way of life, and that
especially in Gaul and Britain the Romans deliberately encouraged people
to adopt the Roman way by building towns,[21] and granting Roman citizenship. Other scholars[22] have found evidence suggesting that provincials
retained many of their indigenous customs. They have interpreted this as
resistance to Roman culture and hence to Roman rule. It is likely that even
those who opposed Roman rule and culture would identify the owner of a
house with mosaics and columns as 'Roman' or at least someone who had
adopted 'Roman' behaviour.

The argument put forward in this book is that many people, probably
the majority, accepted Roman rule and the Roman way of life. It was
certainly the case that the more a provincial accepted the Roman way of
life, the better his chances for economic and social advancement.

Citizens of the Empire could in theory have adopted Roman architecture as a social convention, paying lip service to the state. This seems less
likely in the case of domestic architecture. Housing was a matter of
individual preference, and it is hard to imagine that a villa owner who
went to the length of having his own private baths, hypocaust central
heating, and very personal decoration on his house walls, was simply
conforming to society. By doing so he was conforming to Roman norms.
More importantly, he was also adopting specific patterns of Roman behaviour, bathing with his friends and holding Roman-style dinner parties.

In the Italian context the freedmen Vettii at Pompeii, like Trimalchio in
Petronius' account, had very definitely set out to adopt Roman behaviour.
They sometimes did so in an exaggerated fashion, cramming as many
cultural references into their conversation and decor as they could, rather

than building a clear narrative of cultural allusions (Petronius, *Satyricon* 34-5). Clarke[23] has shown how the wall paintings in the House of the Vettii do not follow any clear theme, whilst Trimalchio makes simple references to classical authors and myths rather than creating any deeper cross-linked structure of metaphor and allusion. Both the Vettii and Trimalchio had a wide-ranging knowledge of Roman culture. Any shortcoming in their knowledge was not through want of reading but more from their inability to restructure what they had learnt. Their aspirations to classical culture are clear, and their behaviour followed suit.

Of course Trimalchio and the Vettii were already irredeemably immersed in Italian Roman culture in a way that the inhabitants of Roman Britain were not, until at least the later second century AD, but given the extensive use of figurative mosaics with allusions to classical myth in the aristocratic houses of every Roman province, it is a reasonable deduction that the same process of socialisation was taking place throughout the Roman world. Many provinces maintained strong traditions of local culture, but at the same time domestic architecture indicates that Roman living habits were adopted. Even in the Greek-speaking east, housing adopted more of a Roman style.[24]

At the lower end of the social scale, rural peasants lived in wattle-and-daub huts with earth floors. Their contact with Roman culture may have been limited to trips to the market town, the use of coinage, and meetings with officials or other non-local visitors such as tradesmen. They could not have had a clear conception of the house of an Italian aristocrat, but they did know more about the local landowner in his rich villa or town house. It is possible to argue that peasants lived in wattle-and-daub round huts because they opposed Roman customs, but as in all ages it is hard to believe that if such peasants had been offered the chance to live in a richly decorated warm villa, many would have refused.

The definition of the Roman house can also be approached at an operational level, principally when discussing the villa. The popular understanding of a Roman villa is of a country estate with a richly decorated house. The most splendid villas were those placed on high cliffs overlooking the sea. Here the architects ran out long covered walks or *porticoes* along the cliffs with no other aim in mind than to present the owner with a fine view and a sheltered seat from which to contemplate it. This idyllic luxury is best known from the area around the Bay of Naples[25] where even emperors had such retreats. One of the most famous of Italian villas is the Villa Jovis at Capri (Fig. 2),[26] which may have been the retreat of the second Roman emperor, Tiberius, who reigned from AD 14 to 37. Commonly supposed[27] to have become obsessed by fear of assassination and corrupted by power, he left Rome and indulged in wild parties at Capri. The villa is located on the cliffs at the north-east promontory of the island, 334 m above the sea. The cliffs were overlooked by the main reception area of the villa, built in a semicircle some 25 m in diameter. This was entered

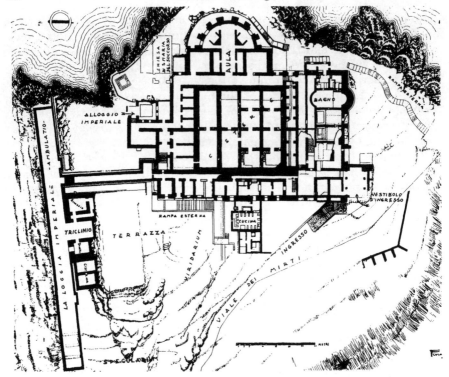

2. Villa Jovis, Capri, Italy.

by a long rectangular hall running up from the main courtyard to the west. The semicircular area at its far end was provided with two sitting rooms and windows looking out to sea.

The area of the central yard was occupied by four huge cisterns, with an overall surface area of 30 x 30 m. The dramatic location of the site, and the difficulties of water supply in Capri, precluded any running water. The cisterns would have been sufficient to ensure that the fountains ran continuously and to provide enough water for the whole imperial entourage. In addition there was a large kitchen with several ovens and plenty of space to prepare a large banquet. This building was situated in a more isolated position in case of fire.

The south side of the peristyle was taken up with the private baths complex, while the other two sides of the court were occupied by uniform ranges of stores and living quarters. However, the passageway on the west side of the central court continued further to the north to a rock-cut belvedere overlooking the north point of the island. Off the middle of this belvedere lay a reception room with an adjacent bedroom or retiring room on either side, as well as a purpose-built cistern for its own water supply.

The Villa Jovis is unsurpassed in its magnificent setting and architecture. Such villas certainly typify the popular view of the house of the over-indulgent early imperial Roman aristocrat. The Roman historian Suetonius says[28] that one day a fisherman climbed the cliffs of Capri to present the emperor Tiberius with an exceptionally large fish that he had caught. Fearful of assassination, and panicking at this breach of security, the emperor ordered that the poor man should have his face scraped with it. The fish scales, as intended, tore at the skin of the man so that he called out, 'Thank God I didn't bring Caesar the enormous crab I also caught.' Tiberius ordered that the crab be brought and the operation repeated.

The Villa Jovis might be considered a palace rather than a house. This is true in terms of its function, but from the beginning Roman palatial architecture was, as will be demonstrated later, intimately related to domestic architecture. The first Roman emperor, Augustus, always represented himself as first citizen rather than emperor, because the Romans were strongly opposed to the idea of a king. Augustus therefore impressed on the Romans that his palace was merely his house. Like the house of an aristocrat it had reception suites for business, but because Augustus was of higher rank than any aristocrat, his reception suites were correspondingly larger.[29]

4. Villas and farms

The majority of villas were as much working farms as countryside retreats, and certainly well below the standard of an imperial palace. Roman aristocrats of the first century AD, such as the younger Pliny, had villas from which they would idly contemplate magnificent views,[30] but they were also concerned to address the agricultural problems of the estate.[31] The agricultural role of a villa can usually be identified in the physical remains by the presence of agricultural tools and facilities for the storage of wine, oil or cereals.[32] Even town houses could have such an agricultural functions, as attested at Pompeii and at towns in Britain.[33] This book is concerned with houses rather than with the agricultural function. Although I will often make reference to rooms used for agriculture, I do not attempt any overall assessment of agriculture in the Roman period.

The balance between agricultural and leisure pursuits can lead archaeologists to classify a building either as a villa or as a farm. For some archaeologists any building with stone foundations and a rectangular plan can be called a villa. Such buildings can come closer to the agricultural than the leisure role of the house. I prefer to use the term villa for a rural house in the classical architectural style, implying that the building had, at least in part, a leisure function. The Romans themselves did not have a very precise definition of the word 'villa', but for modern archaeologists the use of a Latin word for a house must surely imply that the owner had adopted Roman culture, and we would expect a villa to produce evidence for portico columns or mosaic decoration.³⁴ In this way the word villa becomes associated with the concept of 'Romanisation', which has been discussed above. It also links the use of the word villa directly to owners with a certain social status who could afford both a degree of leisure and a degree of opulence.

5. Houses in literature

The most obvious place to look for the ideal description of a Roman house is in Latin literature. First, as in all areas relating to Roman architecture, we should turn to Vitruvius' *On Architecture*, which was written in Italy in the second century AD. Vitruvius does indeed have a great deal to say about the Roman house in his Book 8, and his work will be referred to frequently below. However, it does present a number of problems. There is some debate amongst scholars as to the degree to which Vitruvius was a practising architect. It was normal for the authors of Latin literature to be aristocrats with a penchant for letters rather than technical specialists. However one regards its author, Vitruvius' work is obviously not a technical manual such as we would expect a modern architect to produce.

Another problem is that most Latin literature was written by aristocrats at the centre of the Empire: Italy. Vitruvius knew little about provincial architecture, and may not even have mentioned important regional architectural styles within Italy. Considering that more houses were built in the rest of the Empire than in Italy on its own, Vitruvius may not have described the most common types of 'Roman' house.

In this book, as I have already stated, I describe a house as 'Roman' when it follows the central traditions of the Empire, and to this extent I follow Vitruvian principles, but it is worth noting at this early stage that Vitruvius should be treated with caution. Some of his ideas about Roman housing, being of a more theoretical nature, may not have existed in bricks and mortar. He may also not have included important architectural styles that were to be found in construction, but which had a less theoretical basis. As a Roman aristocrat, he would, for example, have found it beneath his dignity to talk about the housing of the humbler classes.

The second most influential ancient author to talk of housing is Pliny the Younger. In two letters (2.17 and 5.6) written at the very beginning of the second century, he gives detailed descriptions of two of his villas, at Tusculum and Laurentinum in Italy. Here we are on safer ground than with the 'architect' Vitruvius. Pliny is describing real houses, as they were used. The descriptions are not straightforward, however. Archaeologists have found it extremely difficult to reconstruct plans of Pliny's villas from his letters; time and again it has been found that the plan or architecture of Roman buildings cannot be reconstructed from literary descriptions alone. Authors always leave out details which were not relevant for their purpose. Pliny was merely giving an overall picture of the most impressive parts of the houses, not a precise room-by-room tour.[35] The fact that he does not mention the broom cupboard under the stairs does not mean that it did not exist.

It is tempting to assume that Pliny's villas were typical of those of every other contemporary Roman aristocrat. While Vitruvius was trying to give a broad description of the average Roman house, Pliny was describing the houses of a particular person. At the beginning of this chapter much emphasis was placed on the house as a reflection of the tastes of an individual owner or designer. Others' architectural tastes would have differed from Pliny's.

Pliny was describing his villas as they were in his lifetime. Houses before or after this might have followed different design principles. In his own lifetime Pliny might have changed the furniture in his rooms, or demolished and rebuilt part of the house. He did not set out to present precise architectural descriptions of his villas, but to impress his friends. The descriptions in the letters only apply to one time and one place – Pliny's house when he wrote the letter. In order to be sure that what Pliny described is more widely applicable it is necessary to find corroborative evidence, in the form of other texts or archaeological remains.

To readers who have studied historical technique, this treatment of Pliny may seem obvious in the extreme, but it is a particular problem for the study of domestic architecture. When an object is as dependent on personal taste as a house, the historian must require substantial evidence to put forward a trend in Roman architecture as a whole.

What has been said about Pliny applies to many other authors who make passing references to housing – Cicero, Martial, Petronius, Statius, Sidonius – to name but some of the more important. Some ancient authors comment on domestic architecture, and many more discuss behaviour which takes place in the domestic context. For the majority of them the setting of the house itself is incidental. They did not need precise description to communicate their message. They made assumptions and omitted details which would have been significant to us.

The most important author to talk about behaviour inside a Roman house is Petronius, whose description of Trimalchio's dinner party has been mentioned several times in this chapter. His *Satyricon* is a satirical sketch of society set in Rome during the reign of Nero. As a 'comedy of manners' much of the behaviour it describes is inevitably exaggerated, but it contains much fundamental information concerning Roman dining practices. This information is not simply window dressing to the story, as in the case of the letters of Pliny. Moreover Petronius' characters are forever engaging in overblown behaviour and exhibiting their foibles, so that this is one ancient text that is always a delight to read.

Some of the problems in attributing trends in Italian architecture to the Roman provinces have already been mentioned, and similar problems surround the attribution of Roman domestic behaviour to the provinces.

Dining habits and bathing are areas in which it is easier to prove the adoption of Roman behaviour by provincials, as these entailed particular features of architecture which can be identified in numerous houses.

Because of the problems discussed above, this book will rely more on material remains than literary descriptions, though the latter will be used to supplement the physical evidence. It is one of the glories of the Roman period that we can so often hear people talking about their buildings with their own voices.

Despite all these negative comments, some important points concerning the ideal Roman house do emerge from the literature. They give a sense of what a Roman aristocrat expected from a house, no matter what the architecture.

To begin with, he expected a view from the reception room. For a villa this meant that it should be sited in picturesque countryside. Views over the sea were ideal, and easily achieved in areas such as the Bay of Naples,[36] but views over estates were equally acceptable. Pliny was as happy to see the fields of his estate as he was to have a view of the sea. The importance of the view over the sea can be seen from the design of the reception rooms of the Villa Jovis at Capri. The late antique Gallic aristo-crat Sidonius was equally enamoured with the view from his villa.[37] In towns, house owners and architects were concerned to create views from reception rooms into the peristyle court, which often formed a 'pseudo-countryside' with plants, paintings and fountains.

Houses were also expected to show an appropriate balance between utilitarian considerations and luxury or display of wealth. Roman society was one in which social roles were very defined and everyone was expected to know his place. It was held that a house should not be more opulent than a man's social position required. An aristocrat had to have reception rooms which were of a suitable standard for receiving high status guests, though if such rooms were too ostentatious he would be thought to have put on airs. A lower-class Roman would be said to be acting above his station if he had anything more than the simplest reception room.[38] Freedmen such as the Vettii, or Trimalchio in Petronius' *Satyricon*, would have been criticised for having houses which were more opulent than their background as ex-slaves merited.

The ancient literature also makes clear the role of the house in both business and pleasure. The town house functioned as a centre for politics and commerce, while the rural house also functioned as a farm. These more mundane functions needed to be carried out in an appropriate context. Roman aristocrats were expected to devote as little attention as possible to the mechanics of business, and as much as possible to socialis-ing with their peers. Sometimes this could be achieved by isolating a particular part of the house for such functions, but more often they were isolated in time rather than in space. There was a time for business and a time for pleasure. This has often confused archaeologists and historians who have tended to try to associate different parts of buildings with different activities.[39]

6. The Roman vernacular

Thébert[40] argues that Roman domestic architecture had no vernacular, in that it was an architecture based on 'theoretical reflection' rather than following an unwritten or even unconscious local tradition. Vitruvius and other Latin authors certainly demonstrate the existence of architectural theory, but vernacular traditions did exist. Many different provincial styles of Roman architecture will be examined in this book. Thébert was writing about Africa, though he did explicitly apply his statement to all Roman provinces. Africa was subject to very strong Roman influence, but even here there were provincial styles, as he admits on the same page of his book.[41] Thébert's statement is only really appropriate when considering the aristocratic tradition of housing in the Roman period. Aristocratic housing did follow a theoretical model which contained elements of an ideal home. Discussion of such housing will be the subject of the next chapter of this book.

In the north-western provinces there can hardly be any doubt about the existence of a vernacular. In the smaller settlements of Roman Britain[42] it was common to find wattle and daub 'strip' houses. Each house had a narrow frontage onto the street, extending deeply away from it. The street frontage was the location of a shop, behind this were the living quarters, and behind this again there was sometimes a yard or workshop area. It is debatable how much such houses owed to a pre-existing Celtic tradition, but they undoubtedly formed the vernacular of Roman Britain, owing something to earlier pre-Roman building traditions, and yet representing a domestic architecture that was typical of the small Romano-British built-up village centre.

Such 'strip' housing, whilst in a vernacular tradition, can thus be said to have a clear association with the Romano-British, as opposed to pre- and post-Roman periods. It can then be termed an architecture of the Roman period, if not 'Roman housing'.

In the eastern provinces a similar strong vernacular tradition can be identified. Roman Syria, from the hills to the east of Antioch to the stony Hauran desert south of Damascus, contained many small villages of ashlar-built houses.[43] These were organised in a very 'un-Roman' and 'un-Greek' fashion with the living room above the workroom, and the bedroom above the living room, on three or more storeys. As in the case of the 'strip' houses of Roman Britain, these dwellings probably owe something to pre-Roman architecture, and yet their greatest *floruit* was during Roman rule. It will be argued below that they belong to a general vernacular tradition of Roman housing that can also be found in Egypt.[44]

These more lowly types of housing can thus still find a justified place in this book as housing intimately associated with the Roman period. As discussed above, since they were inhabited (after Caracalla's third-century AD citizenship decree, if not before) by Roman citizens, they at least deserve consideration as Roman housing. This hypothesis will be discussed in relation to the debate between town and country, or metropolitan and provincial styles. This debate is the subject of the third chapter in this book.

7. Chapter plan

Chapters 2 and 3 consider the range of architectural traditions across the Roman Empire and the forces that created them. It is impossible to cover all forms of Roman house design, so these chapters will inevitably be selective. Chapter 2 centres on the peristyle house, its origins and architectural development. The smaller 'middle-class' houses that still had mosaics and columns will receive less attention than the richest houses in the Roman world which demonstrate the leading edge of Roman aristocratic style. Chapter 3 redresses the balance somewhat by concentrating on 'non-peristyle' house types in the provinces. Here a selection is made on a geographical basis. Study is limited to those provinces where the local traditions of housing are best known, in particular the 'Celtic' world of Britain and Gaul, as well as the 'Semitic' styles of Syria and Egypt.[45]

Consideration will next be given to the interior details of housing. Chapter 4 gives a full account of the decor. The considerable artistic merits of Roman floor mosaics and wall paintings will dominate this discussion. Work in this area of study has naturally concentrated on the superbly preserved remains of the Vesuvian sites. Here it will be extended both geographically and chronologically to look at how the late antique cult of personality began to influence both media, and to question how far wall painting and decor descended the social scale. This chapter will also consider the use of fountains.

Chapter 5 will investigate furnishings, including furniture, lighting, and the garden. This is the most neglected area in the study of the Roman house, and will provide many new interpretations.

Chapter 6 will integrate the preceding chapters by examining the role of the house in society. This will include the family and the world at large. A considerable amount has been learnt about the Roman family in recent years, and the Roman house has become a central part of this evidence.[46]

The choice of sites and provinces in this book has been determined by two criteria. The first is the existence of a number of houses with particular characteristics. The second is the desire to balance description as much as possible between aristocratic and other forms of housing in the Empire.

One could write a book solely on the peristyle house and its development. This is not that book. The peristyle house still makes up a sizeable proportion of this work, and even then descriptions have had to be selective. Whilst mention is made of the many peristyle houses found in North Africa, I have had to provide a general typological description. It is still impossible to present a complete picture of Roman housing in North Africa as only a handful of major villas have been excavated. Many descriptions can be found in other works cited through the text. Some important examples of non-peristyle housing in North Africa are discussed in Chapter 3.

There is a similar problem with regard to the Roman houses of Italy. Discussions of Pompeii and Herculaneum can be found in every book on Roman housing. Their superior preservation provide much detail that cannot be studied anywhere else. They are discussed in this work, but selectively, so they may be compared with other houses.

Another remarkable unique Italian site is Ostia. The apartments of the city are discussed in Chapter 3, but much about the urban development of the city cannot be paralleled in other centres. It is an important site, but Ostian houses are not known archaeologically from other centres of the Empire, even though similar apartments are assumed to have existed in other large cities of the Empire.

Italy was the centre of the Empire, but the majority of the citizens of the Empire lived outside in the provinces. This book is more concerned with presenting an overview of the range of housing in the Empire as a whole. Provinces have been selected where the archaeological record is more complete. In France and Britain villas can be compared to town houses, strip houses and small farms. In northern Syria the magnificent peristyle houses of Antioch and Apamea can be compared with the villages of the limestone plateau that lay between the two cities. In both southern Britain and northern Syria there is a relatively complete picture of the whole range of housing that existed in the Roman period. In Britain this is the result of meticulous archaeological investigation over at least 60 years, whereas in Syria it is the result of extraordinary preservation and major excavation campaigns in two great cities.

No one person can possibly have examined every Roman house that has been uncovered. Any selection will and should depend on the areas of which an author has most expertise. The choice of provinces and sites, while reflecting the approach outlined above, will inevitably be a subjective choice. There are several sections in which detailed reference is made to British sites. Familiarity may be one reason for this, but Britain also remains one of the few provinces where there is a complete archaeological record covering every form of house, their contents and decor. The largest gap is the Balkan regions, for which I must confess I do not have a full grasp of all the housing types despite many visits. Nevertheless I venture to suggest that the reader will find that this work includes most types of Roman house that were found in the Roman world on all shores of the Mediterranean up to the frontier zones.

Similarly, although this book covers the whole Roman period from the seventh century BC to the sixth century AD, it is not possible to cover all provinces in all periods. Although the book discusses examples of houses dating from every century in the Roman period, there may be said to be a concentration on three critical epochs – the third to fourth century BC, the first century BC to the first century AD, and the fourth to fifth century AD. The first of these periods was that of the emergence of the Roman house in Etruria and Campania. The second period was the development of the newly conquered western provinces, when the impact of Roman control on a very different culture can be observed. The last period covers the short-lived renaissance of the late antique period, including the triumph of Christianity and the barbarian invasions. Other periods, most notably the second and third centuries AD, receive less coverage in this book, partly through a relative dearth of evidence, but more importantly because, though they saw important social developments, they were periods of less dramatic change in the Empire.

8. Chronology

Before beginning the detailed consideration of Roman domestic architecture in Chapter 2, a word should be said about chronology. For our starting point we have taken all lands as they come under Roman control, the slow expansion through Italy during the early Republican period, and the growth of Empire into the first century AD.

For the end point we take the middle of the sixth century AD and the reign of the Byzantine emperor Justinian. Justinian ruled Italy even though it had been sacked by barbarians several times in the fifth century AD, and the last Roman emperor had been deposed by the Goths in 476. For some time after provinces came under 'barbarian' rule people continued to follow a Roman way of life,[47] and it is in many ways the history of the Roman way of life that this book documents through the study of housing. To complete the story it is therefore necessary to follow the Roman house to the bitter end.[48] Until the end of the fifth century AD there still lived people, throughout Europe and the Mediterranean littoral, who would have known where to sleep and where to eat in a Republican house in Pompeii. It is likely that after the reign of Justinian no more Roman houses of this type were built, and people (apart perhaps from the Byzantine emperor himself) began to forget they had existed.

This change is much more important than whether barbarians or Byzantines ruled Europe. It is truly in the disappearance of the Roman house that we see the death of Roman civilisation and the end of the ancient world.

*

This chapter has served to introduce many of the themes behind this book. Subsequent chapters will deal with particular types of house in particular environments, but these themes will continue to emerge. Houses will be seen to reflect the degree to which provincials adopted the Roman way of life and changed that way of life through the history of Roman rule and beyond. Descriptions of houses will highlight how similar, and yet how different, Roman homes were to our own. Fundamental questions will be asked about what exactly a Roman house was and what it (or its owner) stood for.

2

Houses of Pretension

atria ...ambitiosa,
Martial, *Epigrams*, 12,68

It is first necessary to explain the title of this chapter, the significance of which may not be obvious. The topic of this chapter might be described as aristocratic housing, i.e. the housing of the elite.

So who were the elite? At Rome itself the elite could be said to be the senators, while in the provinces it could be said to be town councillors. The elite might also be understood to include rich merchants. Like many who had made their money out of trade rather than land, such merchants were originally excluded from high society in the city of Rome because wealth in land was regarded as the ideal for an aristocrat. The rise of the Roman emperors overturned some of this prejudice, since emperors could promote whom they liked on the basis of talent or money. Nevertheless, the ideal for an aristocrat remained wealth in land.

Archaeology encounters similar problems. It is of course extremely hard to be sure if a given house was owned by an aristocrat – unless, as occasionally happens, there is an inscription giving the rank of the owner. One can only assume that the biggest houses in any settlement belonged to the aristocracy. Such houses in the middle or high Roman Empire of the second century AD might be expected to have large areas of mosaic floor and a large open central peristyle, or colonnaded yard. However, many smaller houses had the same design in a more subdued style. Moreover, the grandest house of a distant province like Britain might not match up to an aristocratic house in Africa or Italy.

In domestic architecture it is not easy to identify an 'aristocratic' house, or to set an absolute standard on the characteristics of such houses. In this context the term 'houses of pretension' has a number of meanings. It continues to imply an aristocratic element in domestic architecture. It also introduces one of the major themes of this chapter, in the almost Dickensian overtones of pretension. I shall argue that, as proposed in the first chapter, the majority of citizens in the Roman Empire had pretensions to own a specific type of house – a peristyle house. This is a building with a large central yard or garden surrounded by four colonnades forming a peristyle. The owner of such a house was someone who considered himself a member of the aristocracy or upwardly mobile.[1]

The Dickensian quality of the title also draws attention to another aspect of Roman society which is of importance for this chapter. As in eighteenth- or nineteenth-century European society, there was little in the way of a middle class. The clearest distinction was probably between those who owned an urban house or a large classical-style villa, and those who owned no property or were small-scale agricultural plotholders. In this sense it is misleading to talk about an aristocracy when the major distinction was more between property owners and those who owned no property at all.

This chapter is fundamentally concerned with what is popularly regarded as the 'Roman house', in other words a house with mosaic floors, columns, and wall paintings. This kind of house was found in every province of the Empire, and to that extent can be seen as one of the unifying social forces in the Roman world. The presence of such a house in any settlement is enough in itself to make the archaeologist label the site as Roman. Like all cultural icons it went through a long development period during which the characteristics of the design became set. In order to determine those characteristics and how they came to be integrated into a house design it is necessary to study the origins of the 'Roman house'.

1. Origins

The Roman state was founded, according to legend, by Romulus and Remus in 753 BC. For much of its early history, until it became a world power after the Punic wars of the third century BC, its culture was influenced by the major powers surrounding it. The most important of these were the Etruscans and the Greeks.

The Etruscans to the north of the city were the most immediate external cultural influence on Rome's early history. They were a league of city states with a homogeneous culture and language. Rome was never an Etruscan city, in the sense that the majority of her citizens were not of Etruscan ethnic stock. Nevertheless, the sixth-century BC kings of Rome were Etruscan. Palace culture always plays a strong part in the formation of an aristocratic ideal. Social, and indeed economic, ties lead us to expect that many of the ideals of the later Roman aristocratic house can be traced to Etruscan influence.

Unfortunately the Etruscan culture is one of the least understood in the ancient world. Their writing system has only recently been deciphered, and Etruscan archaeology has tended to concentrate on cemeteries rather than settlement sites. It is therefore difficult to gain a clear idea of Etruscan housing.

One of the few Etruscan settlements to be extensively excavated is Marzabotto, near modern Bologna.[2] Excavations in the last century, which did not follow modern scientific standards, would seem to indicate that by the fifth century BC there were already houses with central courtyards and cisterns beneath to collect the water from the roof. Entrance-ways have been compared to the fauces of later Pompeian houses, and main reception rooms are said to resemble the Roman tablinum (see above). However, there is little sign of architectural embellishment such as columns or mosaics. It has been said that the central courtyard prefigured the Roman atrium, but there is little direct evidence, particularly as concerns the roofing arrangements for the central yards at Marzabotto. Vitruvius (*On Architecture* 6.3.1) ascribes a particular form of atrium to the Etruscans, but there is no surviving superstructure at Marzabotto against which to compare his description. At least one house did have a water tank in the centre of the courtyard, which could represent the typical impluvium of a Roman atrium (see section 2 of this chapter).

Mansuelli concludes that at Marzabotto there was 'not so much a precursor of the atrium, as a much older version of a true atrium'.[3] This is not the right approach. The real problem is that the true atrium as discussed in the ancient texts and identified by modern archaeologists at Pompeii dates from the third or second century BC. When considering the fifth century BC and earlier, we need to know much more about how the 'atria' at Marzabotto were used. Even if they were architecturally identical to the later Roman rooms, they may have served a general role of court-yard for living space, cooking, storage, and even as a potted garden, rather than the more specialised role of the later atrium, which will be discussed further below.

The architectural form of the courtyards at Marzabotto requires fuller explanation than is at present possible in the context of local culture in the fifth century BC.[4] They may indeed be the immediate precursors of the Roman atrium house, but it is most likely that they were not the same as the very specific Roman rooms, with a very particular function or func-tions, which were in use some 200 years later.

The Etruscans themselves were heavily influenced by the second major Mediterranean power with settlements within striking distance of Rome – the Greeks. The Greeks had founded a large number of cities along the southern Italian littoral. They had maintained important trading rela-tions with the Etruscans. The early Romans met Greek culture through the goods traded in the market, through direct encounters with Greek merchants and southern Italian settlers, and through Greek-influenced, Etruscan-manufactured articles.

Traditional Greek houses[5] were not architecturally elaborate. They had a central yard and a main reception room known as the *andron*. The andron was, as its name implies, a room for men (women in Greek society were not encouraged to show themselves in public).[6] The andron was normally located near the main entrance to the house, so that the men could entertain with as little disturbance as possible to the domestic arrangements of the women.

Some idea of Greek housing in Italy prior to the Hellenistic period can be gained from excavations at Megara Hyblaea.[7] The Archaic houses of this Sicilian colony consisted of small houses 15 x 15 m in plan. Three rooms opened onto one side of a courtyard. Most notable is House 30,11[8] where rooms were built around four sides of the yard, and which perhaps dates from the sixth to fifth century BC. One room with an *opus signinum* floor, of mortar and crushed pot, was located near the entrance in the corner of the house. Its position and flooring, unique in the house, identify it as the andron reception room.

All this began to change during the Hellenistic period inaugurated by the extensive conquests of Alexander the Great in the fourth century BC. Early Greek city states were run by citizen elites, but Hellenistic states were run by kings. Greek culture and middle-eastern culture merged in the Hellenistic world. Palatial traditions of architecture became the norm. For domestic architecture the result of this was the peristyle house. Colonnades were erected in the central yard of the house. Reception rooms became richly decorated with mosaics, wall paintings, and stuccoes.

Latin orators of the later Republican period, such as Cato and Cicero,[9] were worried about the over-exuberant influence of Greek Hellenistic culture, which they felt was having a bad influence on the traditional Roman modesty of life. In this debate the use of statuary and rich domestic architecture played its part. This is the Greek influence that features in most textbooks on Roman history, but it is important to realise that Hellenistic culture only began to take root at the end of the fourth or early third century BC. The Romans had had contact with Greeks from as early as the eighth century BC,[10] and the first Greek influences on Roman domestic architecture could predate the development of the peristyle house which was to become the ideal for much of the Roman Empire. For example, we may note that the Roman dining room was always known as the triclinium, after the Greek word for couch, *klinê*. Such couches were used for eating in a reclining position, a fashion that the Romans inherited from both their Greek and their Etruscan neighbours.

Finally, we should not forget other cultural influences. The Romans were surrounded by many Italic peoples from whom they drew cultural inspiration. To the north of Etruria lay the Celtic lands of northern Italy. Gallic armies from this area regularly threatened Rome. There is little apparent influence of these areas on the design of the aristocratic Roman house. There is a tendency, in studying aristocratic housing, to concentrate on the 'high' cultures of Etruria and Greece, but the potential impact of other peoples in the Italian peninsula should not be ignored.

R. Ross Holloway has provided a good summary of the influences in archaic Rome, based on the admittedly meagre amount of archaeological evidence available.[11] Trade goods and architecture (as well as the historical tradition of the kings) suggest that by 600 BC Rome was a relatively wealthy city in the Etruscan orbit. Despite this, the city maintained important connections with the culture of Latium. The strongest direct links were with the Etruscan city of Caere to the north, and Latin Lavinium to the south.

In Rome itself there are few traces of archaic housing. Potentially the most important domestic building is the Regia in the Roman forum,[12] which was maintained and revered in the imperial period as the ancient house of the kings of Rome. By the early sixth century BC a series of huts had been replaced by a courtyard building with a single range of rooms fronted by a portico. The Regia is very similar in plan to contemporary houses in Megara Hyblaea. Smith has shown how intricately the fabled houses of the kings of Rome were linked to religious ritual.[13] Religious and domestic associations appear inseparable, but architecturally the Regia is undoubtedly typical of what one would expect from an archaic house in Rome.

Elsewhere, in southern Etruria at Poggio Civitate (Murlo)[14] and Aquarossa, there is evidence for very large buildings with central yards of around 40 x 40 m. These were richly decorated with wall paintings and figured roof tiles in the Archaic Greek and Etruscan manner. Rooms surrounded the courtyards on all four sides and they were fronted by porticoes. Expert opinion is divided as to whether they represent early 'villas' of rich aristocrats or whether they were communal meeting houses for a family, or clan.[15] Considering their great size and rich decoration in comparison with the Regia and the houses of Megara Hyblaea, I am inclined to ascribe to them a semi-public function.

2. The atrium house

By the third century BC all these influences had crystallised into the 'ideal Roman atrium house'. This represents the chief type of aristocratic Roman house before the introduction of the peristyle and other Hellenistic influences in the third to second century BC.

The model for the atrium house took the following form. The main entrance passage, the fauces, led to the central atrium court. Most of the surface area of the atrium was covered by a downward sloping roof. The central part of the roof was open. The area of this opening corresponded to a low pool, the impluvium, in the centre of the atrium floor. The impluvium would normally have had a cistern below it to collect water from the impluvium, from the gutters of the roof over the atrium and other parts of the house.

There were two main types of atria, compluviate or displuviate (Vitruvius, *On Architecture* 6.3.1-2). A compluviate atrium was one in which the roof sloped down towards the central opening over the impluvium. This roof structure concentrated rainwater in the gutter over the impluvium.

The displuviate atrium, on the other hand, had a roof which sloped down outwards from the central opening, directing rainwater away from it. In a testudinate atrium there was no central hole in the roof, allowing upper-storey rooms to be built over it. Compluviate atria are divided into subtypes by Vitruvius. The roof opening in a Tuscan atrium was supported by beams stretching in from the walls of the room. In Tetrastyle and Corinthian atria the opening in the roof was supported by columns around the impluvium.

At the far end of the atrium was the main reception room of the house, the tablinum. The room was often completely open to front and rear, but this open aspect was limited by wooden partitions (see Chapter 5) that blocked the view into the atrium at the front, and into the garden (where this existed) to the rear. The tablinum was flanked by two other rooms, the *alae*, which were open towards the atrium. The alae were located on either side of the atrium, as were the bedrooms, the cubicula.

As we have seen, the dining room of the house was termed the triclinium, after the three dining couches which lay around the sides of the room away from the door. In these Republican Italian houses the triclinium normally lay off the side of the atrium close to the tablinum, often in the corner of the house. Under the Empire this room became one of the most important in the house, and is the easiest to identify in the archaeological record because of the traces of the couch settings, which were marked by a combination of a raised floor, a plain mosaic panel, a lowered ceiling or a different scheme of wall decoration.[16]

The tablinum and triclinium formed the reception suite of the house. The tablinum was originally the master bedroom and the storage area for the family archives (Pliny, *Natural History* 35.7, Festus 490), but early on assumed the function of main reception room. The house owner would sit ceremoniously in the tablinum during the early morning to receive guests and clients. The house owner was known as the *dominus*, after the house (*domus*). To his lesser business associates he was the *patronus*, after father (*pater*). To the family and household he was the *paterfamilias*, a term associated with strong legal controls over their behaviour.[17] The late Roman connotations of patron and dominus as lord indicate the 'high' attitude a traditional Roman house owner would assume on such occasions. When the house owner was absent his wife would often adopt the same position in the tablinum or the atrium, as *materfamilias*, to organise the running of the household.[18]

The atrium and tablinum also had a role in the display and storage of the family archives. It was customary to place large chests, *arcae*, containing the family treasures, at the sides of the atrium.[19] The shrine, lararium, to the family ancestors and the household gods, was often located in the atrium, or an adjacent room, as were the portraits of the family ancestors.[20] In later times the lararium was associated with the kitchen, because of the traditional association of the hearth with the central point for family life, and cooking was another traditional function of the atrium. It can be very difficult to locate kitchens in Roman houses of all periods. Sometimes food was brought in cooked, and portable braziers could easily be set up in different areas of the house.

Andrew Wallace-Hadrill[21] has reopened the debate concerning the origin of the atrium house. In particular he draws attention to a number of early Roman houses where there is evidence for a central courtyard, at the end of a long entrance corridor similar to the later fauces. However, in contrast to the atrium house there is archaeological evidence that these houses either had no consistent eaves or porticoes around the court or no central impluvium. The central court was thus completely uncovered and was drained either across the courtyard floor or by roof leading water away from the court.

The evidence for these developments is, however, somewhat uncertain. Rarely is sufficient roof structure preserved for its lines to be reconstructed. Wallace-Hadrill relies on housing at Pompeii, as re-examined by Nappo,[22] and erosion patterns on the court of a house at Cosa.[23] He produces examples of other houses where the central impluvium seems to have been a secondary feature, but the construction of the impluvium could have destroyed earlier structures in that location. He also uses the evidence of the housing at Marzobotto, discussed earlier in this work.

Wallace-Hadrill[24] is concerned to avoid discussion of an evolution for the atrium, but his extensive discussion of the unroofed central yard tends to plant in readers' minds the idea that this is the origin of the atrium. It is still appropriate to ask what led to the design of the first atria, as an architectural form. Wallace-Hadrill's examples of unroofed yards serve to demonstrate that, in the third century BC and before (if not throughout the Roman period), there was a large variety of courtyard houses, and it is dangerous to impose on them too much of a uniform model of social behaviour. Only when the architectural type is very closely paralleled, as in the case of the fully developed atrium house or the provincial peristyle house, are we on firm ground. As an example, already presented in this chapter, the houses of Marzabotto have central yards, but they must be interpreted in the light of Etruscan culture.

3. Distribution of the atrium house

It used to be said[25] that atrium houses were rarely found outside Italy. Today this is no longer accepted. The provinces in the eastern half of the Empire had been subject to Greek influence, and therefore maintained their own traditions, most notably the peristyle houses of Hellenistic tradition. On the other hand, few western provinces were actively developed before the age of Augustus, by which time the atrium house was beginning to seem old-fashioned. Where there are early settlements in the western provinces some atrium houses can indeed be found.

Ampurias was a sixth-century BC Phocaean colony at the northern end of the Costa Brava, near modern Barcelona. It was refounded as a Roman colony by Caesar. The houses known as House 1 and House 2 date from the second century BC.[26] There would appear to have been an atrium in House 1, but it does not seem to have been associated with either a tablinum or alae.

Often it is difficult to distinguish between an atrium and a peristyle. Both had a central open area surrounded by four colonnades. Only a small part of the atrium, immediately over the impluvium pool, was unroofed. In the peristyle the open area covered most of the courtyard. However, where the proportions of the room were ambiguous and the superstructure was not preserved it may be difficult to distinguish between an atrium and a peristyle.

In the case of House 1 at Ampurias the central open area of the 'atrium' was relatively small, but in the absence of a true tablinum, perhaps not small enough for us to be certain about its identification. The situation in House 2 is much less ambiguous as the house had both a tablinum and alae. In a later period it was extended further east and a peristyle was added.

The latest incidence of an atrium in Spain is said to be a late first-century AD house from Baetulo.[27] The plan of the house is only partially known from a small urban site, and the presence of either a tablinum or alae seems unlikely. Only three sides of the court have been uncovered. They do not include the reception facilities, neither do they include any entrance as characteristic as the fauces. The possible impluvium is large enough to have been the centre of a small peristyle.

So far, there would seem to be little certain evidence of atria in southern France. Vaison-la-Romaine (Vasio) was the centre for the Vocontii tribe who resisted Rome for much of the Republican period. An atrium has been claimed to exist in the House of the Silver Bust, which is said to date from the first half of the first century AD.[28] The house was entered through a monumental colonnaded porch. This immediately reached the putative atrium, which had twelve columns. A room behind the court was flanked by two corridors into the main house. The arrangement of room and corridors is reminiscent of a tablinum, but the room was entered by a regular door, whereas a tablinum should be completely open across the full width of the room. The atrium itself had such a proportionately large unroofed area and so many columns that it may be more correctly termed a peristyle.

A more convincing atrium is in the House of the Dolphin at Vaison. Here a tetrastyle atrium (one column at each corner) opens immediately off the street. There was thus no entrance corridor or porch such as one would normally have found in a Pompeian house. On the other side of the atrium there was a large reception room, fully open to the court like a typical tablinum. A corridor passed alongside the tablinum to reach the peristyle, as at Pompeii. There were no alae opening off the sides of the atrium court but, unlike many of the provincial houses that have been discussed, the atrium and tablinum combination is sufficiently distinctive to warrant the possible identification.

The House of the Silver Bust and the House of the Dolphin were both excavated just after the First World War, when excavation techniques were not well developed. Nevertheless the stratigraphy of the House of the Dolphin was studied by Goudineau[29] when he dug a large number of sondages in the early 1970s. These demonstrated that the house was first laid out, with its central peristyle, in the third quarter of the first century BC, but the atrium was not added until the late first century AD.

It might be expected that one would find atrium houses at another early tribal centre, St Rémy de Provence. Known in Roman times as Glanum, it was involved in Roman politics from an early date.[30] However, none of the recorded first-century BC peristyle houses had atria. The House of Sulla, for example, received its name from a threshold mosaic naming the owner. A graffito mentioned the Roman consuls for 32 BC, and several rooms were decorated with Pompeian-style paintings. The house had to make way for a basilica in 20 BC. The House of Attis is said to have had a tetrastyle atrium and impluvium. However, the supposed atrium had a proportionately large central uncovered area, and does not have a clear-cut arrangement for tablinum and alae.[31]

At Narbonne the well-recorded House of the Clos de la Lombarde[32] had an atrium-style court dating to the first century BC. The house had a deep entrance corridor like Pompeian examples, and the court had a definite impluvium pool. Beyond the atrium was a centralised reception room, which the excavators identify as a tablinum. This, however, backed onto the outside wall of the house. A triclinium lay to one side of this room, as in Pompeian houses. There were no alae and the peristyle lay to one side of the atrium.

Like many other houses, the Narbonne residence has several characteristics of a typical atrium court, but to fulfil the functions of a traditional Pompeian house it would have required additional facilities, or alterations in layout.

As far north as Bibracte, on the northern edge of the Massif Centrale, houses with courtyards were being built by 30 BC. The site was excavated by Déchelette in the last century, when a cluster of courtyard houses was found in the centre of the Iron Age *oppidum*. Excavations[33] of the 1990s have confirmed this dating, placing an *opus spicatum* floor around 30 BC, and a hypocaust in 15 BC. The plan of one house might even suggest an atrium/tablinum/alae combination. Such urbanisation does not seem out of place when it is remembered that Bibracte was one of the major pan-Gallic centres, and the base for several of Caesar's campaigns.

Although the first provinces of Africa were founded in the second century BC, no traces of atrium houses have so far been found there.[34]

Etienne has suggested that the proportion of covered to uncovered area in an African peristyle/atrium is related to the overall size of the room, and there is no reason to identify courts as atria.[35] This does not seem a conclusive argument unless one considers that the Africans held to a rigid standard of proportionality. Nevertheless, no African example of an atrium, tablinum and alae combination has yet been discovered.

Few atrium houses have thus been found outside Italy. They existed in Spain and southern France, but not in North Africa. In Spain and France sites are more poorly preserved and more such houses may exist. The absence of atrium houses from North Africa is surprising given that North African sites are better preserved, and though early houses may be buried beneath later settlements one would have expected some to have been uncovered.

It may be that in North Africa a strong tradition of aristocratic housing already existed before the Roman conquest and peristyle houses existed there from the third century BC onwards. Carthage presented a strong pre-Roman aristocratic tradition of housing in northern Tunisia. The area of modern Libya was also subjected to strong Greek influence from colonies in Cyrenaica.

Greek colonies also existed in Provence and had a strong influence on local housing. Perhaps the proximity of the area to Italy, its location on the route to Spain, and the presence of a larger body of Roman citizens resulted in an early influence by Roman domestic architecture. Frequent Roman involvement in Spain, and the lack of any competing aristocratic housing tradition in much of the country, may have led to the use of atrium housing there.

It would seem that atrium houses in France and Spain existed in those settlements with Greek influence, either colonies or Greek-style urban settlements. Their presence could indicate the early presence of Roman citizens in the principal urban settlements of the new provinces, or it could indicate growing acceptance that earlier cultural links with Greece were to be replaced by links with Rome.

4. The origins of the peristyle house in Roman architecture

The peristyle house became the dominant aristocratic house type across the Roman Empire. Although atria have been identified in houses of the second century AD and later, many of these interpretations are dubious, and the supposed atria are in subordinate positions to large peristyles which formed the central element of the designs. As Dwyer[36] has observed, the peristyle did not immediately supplant the atrium, but existed alongside it throughout the first century AD. Thus at Pompeii, whilst many aristocrats were able to include peristyles by buying up adjacent properties, they often maintained the atrium of their original properties as well.

Certainly it was easier to retain the atrium than to demolish and rebuild the whole property, but this also demonstrates that the atrium continued to have a meaning and a social role after the peristyle had been introduced.

Brief consideration should now be given to how the peristyle was absorbed into Greek housing. It is important to establish whether the peristyle influenced Greek housing in a similar way to Roman houses. This might indicate whether the Romans absorbed the peristyle directly through the Greeks or by another route.

At the small Sicilian Greek colony of Megara Hyblaea, excavations have recorded one true peristyle house, House 49,19.[37] The central court measures 17 x 11 m and had colonnades on three sides. It has been dated to the end of the fourth or the beginning of the third century BC. Another house, House 23,24 had a central yard of 23 x 16 m, with a narrow portico along one longer side.[38]

A similar picture emerges in other Greek settlements. Priene is a classic site for Hellenistic housing. The great majority of houses in the city were some 30 x 80 m in plan. The rooms opened off a central court rather than a peristyle. Occasionally the porch preceding the main living room had a column or two between it and the yard.[39]

Housing at Olynthus dates from between the late fifth century BC and the early fourth century BC.[40] Out of more than 40 houses only eight had porticoes. Four had complete peristyles, one had three porticoes, and three had two porticoes. At Olynthus, as at Priene and Megara Hyblaea, it would seem that peristyles were introduced in a fragmentary manner, by adding one or more colonnades to existing courts.

One of the earliest Olynthan houses is the House of the Comedians, dating to the late fifth century BC (Fig. 3).[41] These early peristyle houses show a number of characteristics that distinguish them from their later Roman counterparts. The House of the Comedians, in common with other Greek houses, had a peristyle covered with mosaic. The main reception room, identified by a mosaic and called the andron by the excavators, was located in the corner of the house, preceded by an anteroom.

The andron was commonly located near to the entrance from the street. It maintained this position no matter whether the entrance was from the north or south, whereas the main living room with adjacent bathroom was more commonly on the north side of the house. This would preserve it from the wind and give it a more sunny aspect.[42]

It would seem that in Greek colonies in Asia the peristyle was introduced at the end of the fifth century BC, and at Megara Hyblaea during the third century BC. The creation of colonnades was an essential feature. Often this meant omitting the front wall of a room where it opened onto the central court and replacing it with two or three columns. The peristyles, or partial peristyles, were as a result asymmetric and ill-balanced. It is noteworthy that the main reception room in the Greek house, previously the andron located near the main entrance, was now positioned at

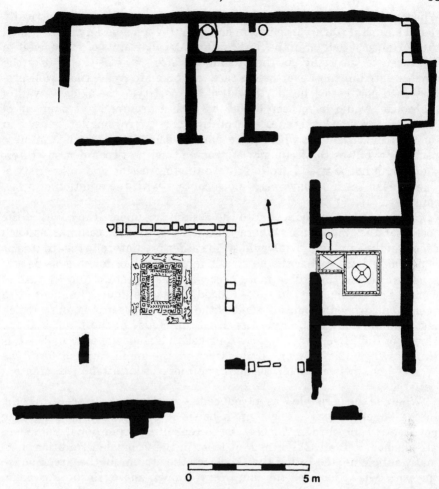

3. House of the Comedians, Olynthus.

the far side of the peristyle. This was not an attempt to create increasing privacy with increasing distance from the front door. On the contrary, it may be associated with a weakening of Greek principles of privacy which allowed guests to cross the house to reach the reception room.

5. Atrium and peristyle

In Pompeii, houses such as the House of the Surgeon and the House of Sallust continued to be built in the earlier atrium tradition during the third and second centuries BC. The first peristyles and porticoes would seem to have been more balanced than those in the Greek settlements.

Where columns were erected they tended to be arranged symmetrically round a central feature impluvium or garden. When a peristyle was added to the House of Sallust in the first century AD constraints of space led it to be placed to the right[43] of the atrium. Its size was close to that of the adjacent atrium, but nevertheless care was taken to create three well-proportioned porticoes. The fourth wall of the peristyle, the exterior wall of the house, would have been decorated with a 'trompe l'oeil' painting of columns and garden scenes. Naturally there were smaller houses in Pompeii and other sites where there simply was not room to put a complete peristyle,[44] but as the frequency of 'trompe l'oeil porticoes' demonstrates, the Roman house tried hard to achieve the impression of a full peristyle. The Greeks seem to have been more content with the addition of a few columns.

Columns were introduced into the atrium to support the eaves of the roof over the impluvium. Where there were only four columns at each corner of the impluvium, it would seem rather premature to regard this as a 'peristyle' type, rather than a simple introduction of columns as part of a general trend towards a more decorative architecture and the use of columns in a domestic context.[45] Indeed tetrastyle (four-columned) atria seem to have been popular in some of the largest houses of Pompeii which also had very large peristyles, such as the House of the Faun and the House of the Silver Wedding. By contrast, the House of Marcus Epidius Rufus, which had sixteen columns round the impluvium to form the largest atrium in Pompeii, seems to be more of an attempt to create a peristyle.

Whereas the peristyle was introduced as an element of the central court in the Greek house, in the Roman house it was introduced by adding porticoes to the garden, *hortus*, at the rear of the traditional Pompeian atrium house (Plate 2). It thus, at least in the Pompeian tradition, normally supplemented rather than replaced the atrium. In the Greek house the peristyle articulated the main central open space. In the Pompeian house it formed an addition to the reception space provided by the atrium. Whereas in the Greek tradition the peristyle was often entirely covered with a highly decorative mosaic floor, in the Roman tradition the peristyle was a garden. In later Pompeian houses such as the House of Octavius Quartio the peristyle became a deliberate attempt to bring a rural, villa-like, atmosphere into the town.[46]

Dickmann[47] has suggested that the Roman peristyle owes more to the Hellenistic gymnasium than it does to the Hellenistic palace. He compares the garden aspect of the Pompeian peristyle with the palaestra of the gymnasium. He notes that early peristyles at Pompeii had few rooms opening off them, except for one or two exedrae. This, he believes, underlines the common use of Hellenistic palaestrae and early Roman peristyles as areas for walking rather than spaces for giving access to apartments. Such an explanation does have the merit of explaining why peristyles

seem to have been more often taken on wholesale in Pompeii. His suggestion that the functional distinction between the Greek peristyle, used for
perambulation, and the atrium with its integral reception facility, was the
reason why the two courts were always kept separate at Pompeii, is an
attractive one. He does not explain how this distinction of function came
to an end.

Only in rare examples at Pompeii, where the atrium dons the aspect of
the peristyle as in the aforementioned House of Marcus Epidius Rufus, or
where the atrium area is foreshortened into a forecourt of the peristyle as
in the House of the Vettii (Fig. 1), is there a sign of the dominance of the
peristyle as realised in later imperial and provincial housing.

In architectural terms, there was a clear difference in emphasis between the atrium and the peristyle. The atrium had a vertical emphasis,
in which the opening in the roof mirrored the impluvium in the floor.[48] This
axis would be noticeable as rainwater and light penetrated the room. The
atrium has often been characterised as cavernous. It is a room that has
volume, in contrast to the peristyle, which has extension. Atria commonly
rose to two storeys with an internal balcony, whereas the peristyle was
always a horizontal space. It rarely rose to a second storey, and a two-
storey peristyle often appears as a balancing feat of two superimposed sets
of columns rather than a single volume. A colonnade will almost always
suggest horizontal extension through a multiplicity of columns – a forest.
Only when the columns are sufficiently high does it take on a marked
vertical dimension.

The introduction of columns has been seen by modern commentators,
and by the elder Pliny, as an attempt to introduce public architecture into
domestic buildings.[49] It is possible that, like Pliny, many Romans did see
colonnades as elements of public architecture in the Roman tradition, but
as examples in this chapter have demonstrated, columns were well established in Greek housing from the fifth century BC. As will be suggested
later in the case of the basilica, the Romans often reinvented architectural
elements in different forms of building.

In sum, the peristyle in Roman houses had a very different function and
architectural form to the atrium, as well as a very different function to the
peristyle in Greek houses.

6. The oecus

With the peristyle came the *oecus*, a reception and dining room which was
normally located off the peristyle (Plate 1) and usually in the middle of one
portico. The variations in the form of oeci are rather bewildering, and it is
often impossible to come to a precise identification of the room. Vitruvius
(*On Architecture* 6,3,9) mentions a Corinthian type of oecus with internal
columns that can clearly be identified in the appropriate position in the
House of the Labyrinth at Pompeii.[50]

Only one example of a Cyzicene oecus (Vitruvius, *On Architecture* 6,3,10) has been identified, in the House of the Dioscurii at Pompeii.[51] According to Vitruvius, it would seem to have been a double-sized oecus, with openings on all sides that could be covered over by folding screens or *valvae*. The latter are a frequently overlooked element of Roman domestic architecture to which we will often have occasion to refer.

The Egyptian oecus (Vitruvius, *On Architecture* 6,3,9) was an aisled-basilican room. It has been identified with a room in the House of the Mosaic Atrium at Herculaneum,[52] but this room is more likely to have been a grandiose tablinum since it opens onto the atrium rather than the peristyle.

The ambiguity in interpretation of the oecus in the House of the Mosaic Atrium is very significant. It is extremely difficult to confirm the existence of an oecus in houses of the first century AD and later outside Pompeii. Rooms in the normal location for an oecus will sometimes be explicitly identified by inscription as triclinia. It seems inescapable that, by the first century AD, there was some conflation of function between all three reception rooms in the Roman house – oecus, triclinium and tablinum.

This confusion is not helped by the fact that the oecus seems to have had a different form in the Greek tradition from which it was supposed to derive. Reception rooms in housing at Olynthus[53] were rarely centred on the peristyle, and at Delos were not completely open to the portico, as were their Roman counterparts. Hermansen[54] has voiced the opinion that the oecus was simply a reflection of the Romans' wish to apply Greek terms to fancy architecture. This is most probably the case, and it is significant that, irrespective of nomenclature, Greek and Roman reception rooms were very different.

The atrium continued to have an independent function when the peristyle was first introduced to Roman housing in the third century BC. It had begun to lose popularity to the peristyle by the end of the first century AD, suggesting, as in the case of the reception suites, that the need for an independent reception court had been lost. The loss of function for the atrium and tablinum must precede their increasing rarity in Roman housing. If a room type continues to have immediate relevancy to social life it will be built. Either the behaviour associated with the atrium and tablinum was no longer appropriate, or it could now be carried out in the new architectural forms of peristyle and oecus/triclinium.

For Wallace-Hadrill,[55] the decline of the atrium and tablinum is already visible at Pompeii. He notes how there is no tablinum in the House of the Vettii (Fig. 1), and the reduction of the atrium to more of a vestibule in the House of the Stags[56] at Herculaneum. He then suggests that the development of the single major reception room on the peristyle is 'an attempt to impose greater control on the exposure of the master to the public'. This is achieved by establishing a 'more private' room as the more prominent reception room. The private has become the 'public façade' of the aristocracy as a way of controlling the setting of domestic and business encounters.

This interpretation is definitely on the right lines, and it is possible to see this movement developing further in late antiquity, by the development of specific architectural forms for receiving guests. This line of argument requires further development with regard to changes in dining behaviour, which led the meal to move from the room adjacent to the tablinum, to the main reception room on the far side of the peristyle. It should also be noted that the setting of the oecus is more governed by the need to see out of the reception room into the peristyle (where guests could note the garden fountains and sculptures) than it is by the requirement to ensure privacy of the room at the far end of the house, as seen from the outside the room.

7. The expansion of aristocratic houses in the north-western provinces

The development of the peristyle house in Italy has taken Roman domestic architecture up to the end of the first century AD. Developments in the provinces should now be considered.

Architectural developments in the western provinces from the first century BC to the first century AD are of particular significance. From the point of view of the historian of Roman architecture, the more remote areas of the western provinces present something of a *tabula rasa*, in which many elements of Roman architecture were a complete cultural novelty. The west thus represents an opportunity to study Roman aristocratic housing in an environment which was less influenced by monumental architecture of an earlier period such as Greek, Hellenistic, or Semitic.

From the point of view of the European archaeologist, the existence of Roman domestic architecture in western Europe is a major point of debate concerning the extent of Roman cultural influence, or indeed the presence of 'Romans' in the newly conquered lands. The first of these Romans were of course soldiers in the Roman army. The provinces were subject to formal settlement of retired armies in the form of veteran colonies. Soldiers might settle as individuals in newly conquered provinces as garrison members married local women.

The first Roman colony in southern France was Arles, founded in 46 BC for veterans of the Sixth Legion. Part of an atrium house of the first century AD has been discovered,[57] but as with many urban sites there are no full plans of early houses. Excavation in modern towns is usually limited to small sites released for archaeological excavation before rebuilding.

One of the earliest colonies in Spain was that of Celsa, founded in 45 BC. For the archaeologist this site has the advantage that it was abandoned in AD 58, creating a very short time span for occupation, and a complete lack of subsequent building. The House of the Dolphins seems to have been constructed in the first century BC.[58] It had a triclinium with an opus signinum floor decorated in Hellenistic style with an inlaid outline picture of two dolphins. It appears to have been provided with an atrium and tablinum combination.

The remains at Arles and Celsa indicate that from the time of the first colonies in the western provinces, local visitors would have been presented with high quality examples of Roman domestic architecture.

From such examples Roman architecture may have begun to be adopted by local aristocrats, and Roman-style buildings began to appear in the rural hinterland. Keay[59] states that in southern Spain, in the provinces of Baetica and southern Tarraconencis, 'blocks of residential rooms decorated with simple mosaics set into pink concrete' began to be constructed in the first century AD. Pink concrete or opus signinum was a Roman invention, mixing brick into mortar to create a hard-wearing floor that was also waterproof for use in the construction of baths.

However, some peristyle houses clearly existed earlier. A good example of an early peristyle house has been discovered at La Caridad.[60] It had a central peristyle of eight columns, surrounded by a single range of rooms. There was a large oecus, or triclinium, off the side of the peristyle opposite the entrance. The floor of the oecus was covered with opus signinum, and had an inscription in the Iberic language mentioning a certain Licinius(?). Pottery from the site dates mainly to the second or first century BC with a few first-century AD sherds.

In Picardy, France, there has been considerable work on the development of Roman villas following the pioneering work of Agache[61] in the 1970s. Close study through prospection and excavation suggests a slow agglomeration of late Iron Age farmsteads into grand Roman estates. Examples can be found at Beaurieux les Grèves, Verneuil en Halotte, and 'Le Puits à Marne' (Roye)[62] where collections of small rectangular buildings had formed by the end of the first century BC.

In northern France peristyle houses were built in the major urban centres during the later first century AD. At Aventicum (Avenches) there was a particularly large house next to the forum.[63] The first major villas in northern France were built comparatively early in the first century AD, though significantly they were in the north-east towards the Rhine frontier. The major Roman military bases in this area seem to have provided a major stimulus to the local economy and the introduction of a classical Roman lifestyle. Wightman summarises:

> The date at which the truly luxurious house made its appearance is a vital and debated question. Growing evidence suggests that it was within the first century, if barely before the middle.[64]

The most important villa was Echternach,[65] built during the reign of Nero. Wightman[66] suggests that its remote location indicates ownership by a local Treveran. This is plausible, but at that period it should be assumed that the owner still had close business and social contacts with the military. Echternach had over 50 rooms, several of which had apses and mosaics. It stretched around three sides of a 40 x 70 m peristyle yard, and included a private bath suite. There was an exceptionally large, centrally placed, reception room. All this dates from the Neronian period, indicating, as Wightman[67] points out, a villa that was 'luxurious from the start', rather than the result of enrichment and agglomeration as in Picardy.

In Britain, St Albans was established as the Roman *municipium* of Verulamium by the end of the first century AD.[68] Although the first-century houses in the town do not show marked architectural pretension, it has been suggested[69] that the nearby first-century AD villa of Lockleys (Fig. 4) shows strong Roman influence through the use of an opus signinum paved triclinium and an external portico. However, it must be noted that Verulamium is the earliest of all British towns to exhibit strong signs of 'Romanisation'.

Britain also has its version of Echternach – the Roman villa, or palace, at Fishbourne.[70] Like Echternach, it is Neronian in date and has plenty of mosaic floors and an apsidal room. It is commonly identified as the 'palace' of the client king Cogidubnus; a reward for his help in the Roman conquest. It is becoming increasingly clear that its owner also had close contact with the military. A Claudian supply base for the invasion period is located nearby.[71]

At Gorhambury, a villa site near Verulamium, round houses of a pre-

4. Lockleys, Britain.

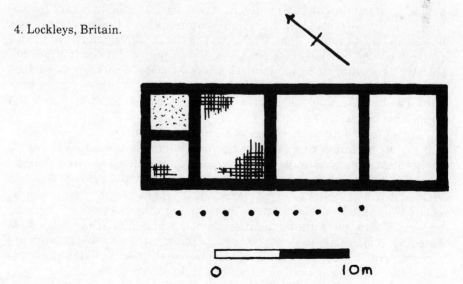

Roman kind coexisted in the same farmstead enclosure as a fully fledged villa with portico and mosaics, into the third century AD.[72]

The evidence of northern Gaul and Britain suggests that there was a slow introduction of the Roman lifestyle, not by imposition but by adoption, as and when the locals felt it was in their interests. The extraordinary luxury of villas such as Echternach and Fishbourne indicates that when there was a high degree of collaboration the rewards could be enormous.

8. Provincial and Italian houses of the High Empire

It is impossible to provide a comprehensive cover of all the hundreds of aristocratic houses that have been discovered throughout the Roman Empire, so it is necessary to be selective both in terms of houses and in terms of provinces.

In many provinces the evidence is limited to certain types of house. In Spain there is comprehensive evidence for villas, but less systematic evidence for town houses. In Africa there is considerable evidence for town houses, but little evidence for villas. The analysis can only be carried out for areas where there is comprehensive consistent coverage. Care should be taken in comparing provinces because the evidence may have been presented in different ways as a result of different methods of historiography and different approaches, such as the recovery of urban rather than rural settlements.

This section is mainly concerned with the second to early fourth century AD. Previously it has been shown how Roman housing developed in Italy during the Republican period, and how it expanded into the newly conquered western provinces from the first century BC to the first century AD. Now it is time to consider the High Empire, when Roman wealth and power was at its zenith. A relatively homogeneous development of aristocratic housing can be detected across the Empire during this period, though in the later third and fourth century AD certain changes associated with what historians have come to regard as 'late antique' culture took hold. The Late Antique will be considered in separate sections towards the end of this chapter.

Although modern archaeology is a scientific discipline, it is often difficult to date buildings precisely. Aristocratic Roman houses often attracted early investigators because of their colourful mosaic pavements. Roman mosaics have consequently been subjected to intensive study which has yielded detailed stylistic chronologies. Ideally, however, the archaeologist needs well-dated coins or pottery found in significant positions, such as beneath floors, or in the foundation trenches of walls. When a house is dated by mosaics alone it can be hard to tell whether the pavements are replacements of earlier designs, in which case they could date from some time later than the overall construction of the building.

9. The ideal type

The period of the High Empire saw the emergence of a dominant aristo-cratic house-type. It can best be described as an ideal rather than as the norm. It is an ideal because there is evidence that many landowners tried unsuccessfully to reproduce it in their own property. They failed because of lack of space or resources. It is not the norm because there was a wide range of variations in which the ideal house was in practice achieved.

The provincial ideal type consisted quite simply of a central peristyle flanked on all sides by ranges of rooms. The entrance from the street was in the middle of one range, and the main reception room was located in the middle of the opposite range. Bedrooms, secondary dining rooms, storage rooms, kitchens and secondary courts were all distributed around this basic arrangement, according to provincial traditions or individual taste. Sometimes, for example, there was great elaboration of the entrance. More monumental architecture could be used to emphasises its grandeur. Some-times a secondary court was placed near the entrance to provide a reception area which did not disturb the privacy of the main residential part of the house. Secondary courts can also be found towards the rear of the house where they have been interpreted as servants' quarters, or private areas for the family.[73]

Private baths, where they existed, were also commonly near the en-trance, or reception suite. It must be remembered that for the Romans, bathing was a social activity commonly undertaken with friends or busi-ness associates, so these rooms were regarded as rooms for public entertainment.[74]

10. Spanish housing of the second to early fourth century AD

With some notable exceptions, the majority of evidence for aristocratic Roman housing in the Iberian peninsula comes from villas.

A town house's restricted space limited the scope for architectural expression. The development of villas in almost all provinces of the Empire left no limit to the imagination of Roman architects, and it would seem that Spanish architects had the broadest imagination! The fuel for this imagination was probably provided by the wealth of Roman Spain (espe-cially on the south and east coasts) in wine, oil and minerals, as well as by the rise of Spanish citizens, such as the emperor Hadrian (AD 122-138), to the highest offices of state.

The villa of Torre de Palma in Monforte (Portalegre province, Portu-gal)[75] covered an area of 110 x 200 m by the fourth century AD. It had over 100 rooms, including two bath suites and a temple to Mars Ultor. The largest of three major peristyles (there were several other smaller courts) covered an area of 65 x 30 m. Late third- or early fourth-century mosaics celebrated the name of the owner, Basil, and named five favourite horses which he probably provided for races or amphitheatre shows in the nearest town.[76]

Architectural extravagances include the unique suite of six large apsidal reception rooms lining one side of a peristyle court at Dehesa de Soria, Cuevas de Soria (Fig. 5).[77] Such apses generally marked reception rooms in later Roman housing, but in this case it may be that they were bedrooms, or suites for retiring after dinner. Reception rooms, like the larger

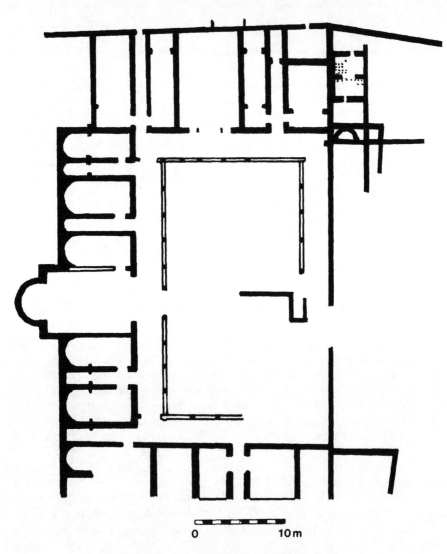

5. Cuevas de Soria, Dehesa de Soria, Spain.

central room in the group, usually have a wide doorway onto the peristyle, but most of these apsidal rooms were entered off side corridors. This arrangement seems designed to ensure privacy and limit the amount of light entering the rooms. The mosaics in the villa are all geometric designs, which are said to date from the second century AD, but such prolific use of large apsidal rooms is more likely in the fourth century AD. Geometric designs are more difficult to date than figured mosaics, and the pavements could recall earlier works in the buildings.

Another quite remarkable design is at Mexilhoeira Grande in the Faro province of Portugal (Fig. 6).[78] Here a single range of rooms forming part of a villa has been recovered, divided into three roughly equal separate areas. At one end there is a peristyle court with axial entrances from both sides of the range. At the other end the apartments are organised on either side of a long corridor which again crosses the range from one side to the other. The central part of the building is occupied by a hexagonal peristyle. Four separate rooms occupy the sides of the hexagon, while the other two sides are taken up by what appear to be axial entrances.

The hexagonal court and apartments recall palatial architecture in Rome itself, such as the Golden House of Nero, but even taking this into account the separate use of hexagonal court, peristyle and corridor seems like some bizarre architectural experiment in the use of space. The building is dated to the third and fourth centuries AD.

Atria have supposedly been identified at some of the Spanish villas such as El Faro (Torrox, Malaga), Pago de Bruñel Bajo (Quesada, Jaén) (Fig. 7),

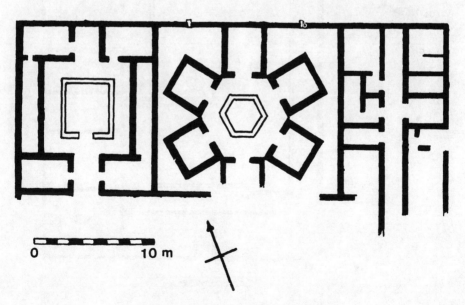

6. Mexilhoeria Grande, Faro, Portugal.

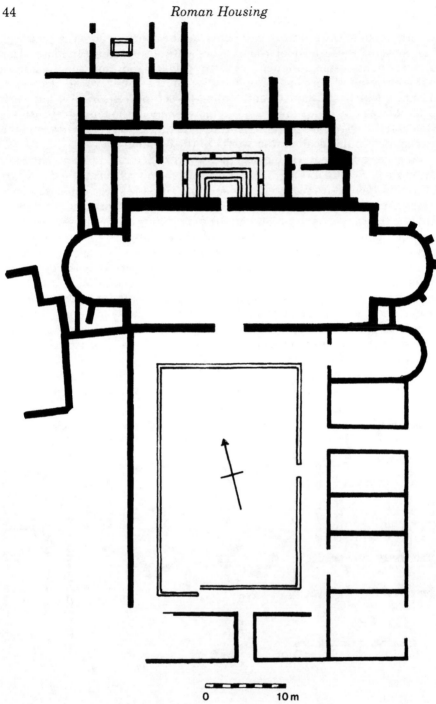

0   10 m

7. Quesada, Pago de Bruñel, Jaén, Spain.

and Torre Llauder (Mataró, Barcelona).[79] These rooms are in the appropriate position near the main entrance to the buildings, but they are not
associated with any tablina.[80] Given the high imperial date it is mo⁻
probable that these small courts were an aggrandisement of the entranceway. When set alongside the use of large reception rooms elsewhere in the
villa, the supposed atria would not have made an appropriately grand
impression on guests. Rather they functioned as a temporary waiting area
when a visitor first entered the building. Similar suites were also common
in Italian villas.

The largest reception room recorded in a Spanish villa seems to be at
La Olmeda (Pedrosa de la Vega, Valencia):[81] a rectangular room measuring
13.5 x 12 m. It was decorated with a mosaic showing Achilles at Skyros
and a hunting scene. A coin of AD 324-5 was found in the bedding of the
latter, providing a firm date for the reception suite. The location of the
main entrance to this villa is not certain, but a series of doorways in the
peristyle outside the reception room suggest it was built on the traditional
axial layout.

The reception suite was flanked to the south by two smaller side rooms.
This placing of paired side rooms beside reception rooms is common in
Africa, Gaul and Britain, but is strangely uncommon in Spain. There is
little evidence for the function of the side rooms, though they may be
assumed to have been used for food preparation. Their absence from most
Spanish villas could suggest different arrangements were adopted in this
regard, or they could just reflect a local architectural tradition.

One urban site from which several Roman peristyle houses are recorded
is Italica. The most interesting of these houses is the House of the Exedra,[82]
which had a long 37.5 x 7.5 m open area along the left side of the house when
viewed from the entrance. It is likely that this area was an open garden with
a beautiful apsed garden dining room at its far end. Such outside dining or
sitting areas are very common in Pompeian houses. The garden area gave
onto an underground portico, or *cryptoporticus*. Both garden and cryptoporticus looked out over the town walls near the outdoor dining room.[83]

The main dining room in the House of the Exedra was off the middle
right side of the peristyle, whilst the private baths, including a modest
pool, were at the far end of the house. These characteristics were shared
by other houses at Italica, most notably the House of the Peacocks. Water
display seems to have been common, as signified by the pools in the baths
area, and by the frequent placing of fountains in the peristyles.

11. Gallic housing of the second to
early fourth century AD

The houses of Gaul became increasingly sophisticated following their
early beginnings in the southern, Mediterranean, parts of the region.
Domestic architecture in Gaul seems never to have adopted the extrava-

gant architectural forms of the Spanish peninsula, but nonetheless both
urban and rural houses became larger and richer.

One of the most important centres of Roman Gaul was Lyons, established as a colony by Plancus in 43 BC as the centre of the provincial cult
of the Three Gauls under Augustus. It was a major commercial centre on
the Rhône river corridor, which linked the whole of Gaul from north to
south. Some 17 miles south of Lyons lay Vienne,[84] another colony of 43 BC,
founded by Mark Antony. The city probably formed a 'suburban' base for
local aristocrats, away from the busier life of the metropolis. Certainly
there were some remarkably grand houses there. The House of the Ocean
Gods was greatly expanded in Neronian or Flavian times. It had two
peristyles, a not uncommon local feature. Even the smaller peristyle near
the entrance had twenty-two columns and a large nymphaeum pool at the
far end. There was a large vestibule with a central circular pool. The larger
peristyle at the rear of the house had two small garden buildings at its
centre.

As far as rural housing is concerned, the villas traditionally cited are at
Chiragan and Montmaurin, on the northern edge of the Pyrenees.

Chiragan[85] reached the height of its prosperity during the second century AD. At this time the villa itself consisted of two great yards. An inner
one surrounded by four ranges of rooms formed the house itself. To the
south was a second larger yard; a common tradition for the western
provinces. The yard was formed by two underground porticoes, cryptoportici, which led down to the banks of the river Garonne. This second court
was apparently built at the beginning of the second century AD. During the
later part of the second century the villa expanded to the east with the
construction of a large bath house and a walled garden. The latter was in
the form of a semicircular enclosure with a pavilion at its apex. The
Romans enjoyed garden walks, interrupted by quiet discussions or meals
in such pavilions.

The most important part of the site was to the rear of the main house.
Here a long colonnade and a cryptoporticus led to a large number of
independent, simple, rectangular buildings, which were organised around
two large rectangular open spaces. These have been interpreted as agricultural buildings and houses for the workers on the estate. The whole
complex of villa and outbuildings was surrounded by an enclosure wall and
occupied forty acres.

The villa owner was a major local figure who also collected an edifying
set of statues, including the portraits of many emperors from Augustus to
Septimius Severus. Such sculpture collections are notoriously difficult to
interpret, but most likely reflect a desire to be associated with the imperial
administration, in other words the 'establishment'.

The villa at Montmaurin[86] has a beautiful symmetry of design. A large
semicircular portico, 53 m in diameter, formed the main entrance to the
building. Beyond this one entered the first of two peristyles. The first is

most likely to have been a public area, surrounded by reception rooms and storage facilities of a more agricultural character. It has been claimed that two large rooms on either side of the main entrance represent reception rooms for poor clients and richer friends. There does not seem to be much evidence for this assertion in the archaeology.

Beyond the first peristyle was a second, forming the main, private, heart of the house, and with two semicircular covered walkways to either side. A small stadium, or semicircular walled garden, formed the court for the bath suite, beside the outer peristyle. In the semicircular forecourt there was a small hexagonal shrine.

The symmetrical plan of the fourth century AD was the product of a long development of the site commencing in the first century AD.

12. African housing of the second to early fourth century AD

Virtually all the evidence for aristocratic Roman housing in North Africa comes from urban settlements. Ancient texts, illustrations in urban mosaics, and modern field survey all demonstrate the existence of large rural estates, but so far few have been excavated.

The urban development of housing in the second century AD is well represented by the study of Timgad, a veteran colony founded by the emperor Trajan (AD 98-117).[87] Each ex-soldier's house was a small square unit of 20 x 20 m. Into this were crammed some twelve to sixteen rooms, and a small central peristyle. A larger room dominating one side of the court was the reception room or triclinium.

It is very significant that despite the small space an effort was made to provide every house with both a triclinium and a peristyle – the essence of the true aristocratic Roman house. These houses have often been compared with the similar-sized barrack-quarters of army centurions. The size and regularity of plan do smack of a continuing 'camp' lifestyle, but the presence of peristyle and triclinium also indicate the desire to provide the ex-soldiers with something of civilian luxury. These architectural elements can be said to pick out the householders as Roman citizens and people of standing.

In the next two centuries after the colony's foundation, economic and social change affected the initial egalitarian settlement. Some houseowners at Timgad succeeded in taking over their neighbours' properties until, from an area of 20 x 20 m, the largest house in the city (House 11 – 'The House to the west of the baths of Filadelfes') had expanded to 40 x 75 m.[88] It now included two large peristyle courts and a private bath suite.

The plans of 27 individual houses are known from Volubilis, a city in the western part of Mauretania.[89] The houses date from the first or second century AD and were developed until the site was abandoned, perhaps in the fifth century.

The houses were generally entered through a triple-doored vestibule (Houses 2, 7, 8, 12, 15, 16, 17, 21 26), or a long corridor (Houses 4, 9, 13, 14, 18, 22, 23, 25). The central peristyle was not large, occupying about a quarter to an eighth of the total area of the house.

Many houses had a characteristic reception room which, rather than being at the rear of the house, was thrust forward into the central area (Houses 2, 6, 7, 8, 9, 12?, 17, 21, 25). This has the effect of leaving it almost free-standing, with corridors or open spaces on both sides. The bath suite was often situated in the area to the rear of the triclinium (Houses 2, 7, 21, 22).

African houses commonly had retiring suites of cubicula located, as those previously described in Spain and Pompeii, in more isolated parts of the house where there was less likelihood of disturbing the occupants.

A characteristic of some African houses was the presence of two reception rooms off different sides of the central peristyle (Plate 3). Sometimes they were on opposite sides of the peristyle, as in the House of the Frescoes at Tipasa (Fig. 22).[90] More frequently they were orientated at ninety degrees to each other – as at the House of the Peacock and the Domus Sollertiana at Thysdrus (El Djem),[91] or the House of the Cascade at Utica.[92] Secondary triclinia, or oeci, are found in houses in other provinces, but they are usually of much smaller dimensions than the principal reception rooms.

13. The Aegean

Whereas in the western provinces new settlements, or settlements re-planned on Roman lines, were common, in the east most of the major centres had a long history as Greek or Hellenistic cities. On a cultural level the language of the western aristocracy was definitively Latin, but in the East the language of high culture was Greek.

This situation creates great problems for the archaeologist examining domestic culture. Eastern aristocrats continued to use Greek architectural elements and patterns of behaviour long after they had become part of the Roman Empire. Eastern cities had commonly been founded by the fourth century BC, and continued to exist up to the eighth or ninth century AD. Large areas of ancient sites such as Ephesus and Pergamon were mostly excavated or 'cleared' in the nineteenth century when archaeologists were less interested in housing, and precise dating on the basis of pottery and coin deposits was rare. During their long occupation houses could be adapted from very early buildings, room arrangements could be gradually changed, and old-fashioned rooms could be redecorated with new mosaics, wall paintings, or even colonnades.

As a result, though there are a large number of houses which can be dated to the Roman period, there are fewer that can be precisely dated within it. The typical aristocratic house in a prosperous eastern city could incorporate architectural elements separated by over 1,000 years. It is difficult to say whether such a mixed-style house was Greek or Roman, and even more difficult to date all the elements of its composition without detailed archaeological investigation.

The reasons for the conservation of Greek architectural elements or the adoption of Roman ones can be obscure. It may be that maintaining the structural integrity of the house forced an owner to maintain a Greek-style reception room long after such rooms went out of fashion. It may be that, in the cramped urban space in which he was constrained to build, it was impossible for him to produce any other kind of design. He may have decided to enliven an antiquated reception suite with a new style of floor mosaic, or it may be that an earthquake forced him to replace it.

All this serves to illustrate how, from all the famous ancient cities of the east, so few houses are useful to the discussion that follows.

During the second century BC, at the same time as Mediterranean-style housing was beginning to expand in the western provinces of the Roman Empire, the Aegean island of Delos was beginning to reach the height of its power. Delos flourished from the second to the first centuries BC.[93] During much of this time it was an independent state, though it had a community of Italian traders and was an ally of Rome.

The houses of Delos[94] show strong Greek Hellenistic traditions, which are interesting to compare with contemporary western Roman houses. The site is of prime importance in the archaeological record. Houses at Delos had peristyles covered in mosaic rather than given over to gardens. The main reception room, commonly described in modern texts as an oecus, was located on the central axis of the peristyle, like western Roman houses rather than the Greek houses at Olynthus. The reception room had three doors, making it more open than the Olynthian andron but not as open as the Roman oecus or tablinum. The decorated panel of mosaic in the Delian oecus, as at Olynthus, was placed centrally within the room. This associates it with Greek dining practice in which the couches were placed around the edges of the room, rather than the Roman practice of placing them in a tightly drawn U arrangement. Moreover the Delian oecus was provided with two side, or retiring rooms. As has been noted in the case of the House of the Vettii (Fig. 1), Roman houses had similar retiring rooms, but they were not usually directly accessible from the main reception room.

The House of the Trident (Fig. 8)[95] is a typical Delian house. A deep entrance corridor similar to a Pompeian fauces led to the peristyle, the centre of which was decorated in mosaic. Off the far left-hand corner of the peristyle was an alcove like one of the pair of Roman alae. The oecus was placed on the central axis of the house beyond the peristyle, but whereas a Roman oecus would normally have been deeper than it was broad, the opposite was true at Delos. The central decorative mosaic in the oecus was surrounded on all sides by a plain border some 1 m wide, which formed the

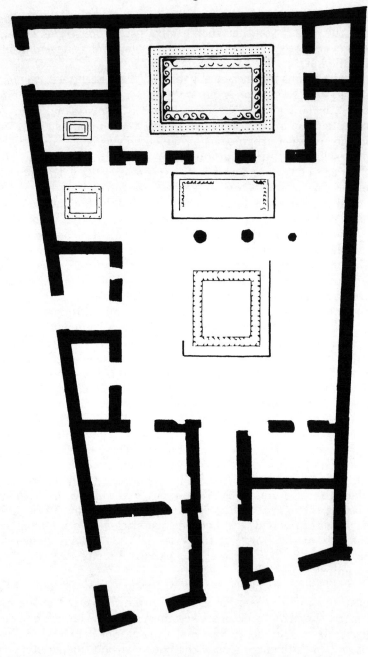

8. House of the Trident,
Delos, Greece.

0   ·   10 m

setting for the dining couches. There were three doors into the oecus from the peristyle. The central doorway was wider, but did not open up the major part of the room to the exterior, as it would have done in a Roman house. Lastly, in Greek Delian fashion there was a small retiring room off one side of the oecus.

The significance of Delos is to indicate a continuing diversification of Greek and Roman housing during the period in which, to Roman eyes, Greek influence in Rome was seen to be increasing. This also demonstrates that, as far as everyday culture was concerned, there was very little change during the establishment of Roman political control in the east. This is, as has been seen, in marked contrast to the situation in the western provinces.

Very few houses in the Greek-speaking eastern provinces of the second to third centuries AD have provided complete plans. However, some fragmentary and often poorly dated examples suggest that by this time houses had begun to take on a more 'Roman' appearance. Partial plans of Roman housing at Thasos,[96] and the better documented House of Dionysius at Paphos in Cyprus,[97] suggest that, at least in the Aegean, peristyle houses now had more of a Roman-style garden court than the earlier mosaic yard. The peristyle of the late second-century House of Dionysius contained a central pool. Many rooms in the house had rich mosaics, which in a Delian residence would also have covered the peristyle. The peristyles of the houses at Thasos were stone flagged. The use of small peristyles in such modest houses seems more characteristic of Roman provincial housing than of the preceding Hellenistic period.

Furthermore, the House of Dionysius at Paphos had a conventional Roman-style reception room, a triclinium. It is large, 11.5 x 8.5 m, and located on the central axis of the house, entirely open to the adjacent peristyle. The room was paved in figured mosaic whose panels significantly formed a U shape around a central motif. This U shape is the Roman arrangement for dining couches, rather than the Greek fashion as exemplified at Olynthus and later Delos, where mosaic panels demonstrate that couches were placed around all four sides of the room.

A fragmentary plan of a house at Naoussa[98] in Greek Macedonia includes a typical Roman-style bedroom suite. The cubiculum can be identified by the single plain white mosaic of the couch setting. Like many such suites in the west,[99] it was located in a slightly secluded position off one corner of the peristyle. Although the cubiculum is traditionally identified as the bedroom, it may be better described as a retiring room, which could be used for sleeping, eating, or reading, alone or with a companion.[100]

It may be objected that these few houses might simply represent Romans resident in Greece. Similar arguments have been proposed to explain Roman influence in other provinces, particularly Gaul and Britain. It would seem somewhat invidious to try to separate out 'Roman' and 'provincial' in the later second century when the Empire had been under central political control for some four hundred years. Having said this, clearer unequivocal evidence of Roman housing in the Aegean during the period of the 'High Roman Empire' is definitely required.

14. Villas in Italy from the Imperial period

The houses of Italy have been left until last in this list of provinces. This is because it was useful to examine the wide range of provincial types before looking back at the centre of the Empire where one would expect to find the residences of the richest aristocrats in the Roman world.

This section will be concerned with villas because during the imperial period houses in the city of Rome were dominated by a very different form, which is best considered in the context of urban settlement in the next chapter.

The prime characteristic of the general layout of aristocratic villas in Roman Italy was the use of extensive terraces, or yards, surrounded by porticoes. Such structures did exist in some provincial villas but seem to have been more common and more elaborate in Italy. Villas had been sited on slight rises in the ground since the Republican period. These rises were accentuated to create artificial terraces supported by extensive buttressing. Underground porticoes could be created in the terraces with windows looking in through the buttressed terrace wall. The letters of Pliny[101] provide much testimony as to how Roman aristocrats liked to walk about these terraces contemplating the view and talking to friends.

At the beginning of this century Ashby[102] recorded several large villas in the vicinity of Rome. The villa of Centroni[103] consisted of several terraced enclosures or 'platforms', each 50 x 60 m in area. One platform has the long narrow characteristic shape of a walled garden with a polygonal end, and these were often set out in the shape of a Greek 'stadium' running track.[104] Another villa of similar design was Sette Bassi. Here the central buildings were arranged on a terrace of 315 x 200 m. This formed part of a larger complex with several other separate terraced buildings nearby.

Similar terraced villas are known from other parts of Italy. At a villa attributed to the poet Horace in Licenza,[105] a neat symmetrical design incorporated a terrace of 50 x 80 m. In the centre of the yard was a large rectangular pool. The residence, at the far end of the yard, had reception suites arranged around a central fountain court, similar to an atrium. At Sirmione,[106] the whole villa, attributed to the Augustan poet Catullus but dating to the second century AD, is raised onto a high platform overlooking Lake Garda. A series of porticoes and suites take advantage of views outward onto the lake and internally onto the central gardens (Plates 4-5). Whereas at Licenza the apartments lay entirely at one end of the terrace, at Sirmione they were around all four sides of the peristyle.

Many of these grand villas of Italy were founded in Republican times, and it is possible that some of these rooms had their origins in true atria of the Pompeian type, but by the imperial period many of them do not appear to have had the function of traditional atria. It is significant that, in the Villa of the Mysteries at Pompeii in the first century BC, the peristyle precedes the so-called atrium which has no side rooms (alae)[107] as at Licenza.[108] Another example was found in a villa on the Via Nomentana near Rome.[109]

True atria seem to have persisted in villa architecture until the second century AD. One with alae and a tablinum existed in the villa of Sette Finestre[110] in southern Tuscany. Here it is noticeable that there was no traditional corridor beside the tablinum through to the peristyle. Anyone passing from the atrium to the peristyle would therefore have had to pass through the tablinum, disturbing whatever activity was going on there. For this reason one might suggest that even here the atrium and tablinum did not fulfil their traditional function. It is uncertain whether the principal entrance to the villa was through the supposed atrium or, like the Villa of the Mysteries, through the peristyle.

Another true example of an atrium was discovered at Este,[111] where a nearby room in the complex dates its continuing use, like Sette Finestre, to the second century AD. The atrium at Este was entered directly from the street, and was provided with alae and tablinum.

There were of course many different types of house and villa in Italy, many of which were nowhere near as opulent as some of the villas that have just been described. The purpose of this section has been to draw out some images of the character of the major senatorial houses at the height of the Empire.

15. Palatial architecture in the early Empire

After the expulsion of the kings in 510 BC, Republican Rome had an aversion to all things regal. It has already been noted in this chapter how the Regia, the ostensible house of the kings of Rome, was little different from the average house in the contemporary Greek colony of Megara Hyblaea. Coarelli[112] has associated the Regia as part of the same complex as the *domus publica*. The latter was the traditional residence of the Roman chief priest, the *pontifex maximus*. The domus publica, at least in its later development was a traditional atrium house.

The first emperor, Augustus (27 BC – AD 14), was always at pains to avoid being seen as a king, so when he was offered a 'palace' he decided to continue to live in his own house and simply adapted part of it to meet his public duties. As Cassius Dio says,[113] he turned down the traditional public residence of chief priest in 12 BC, and instead made part of his house state property.

The house of Augustus, and that of Livia his wife, like those of many Republican aristocrats, were on the Palatine hill in Rome, and it is from the Palatine that we derive the word 'palace'. It may be no coincidence that Augustus, in replacing the house of the chief priest, was effectively moving the ritual associated with the rulers of Rome from the area of the Regia to his own house and the Palatine. By not taking up the residence of the priest near the Regia he avoided the label of king, but by moving the traditional priestly functions to his residence on the Palatine he was maintaining the ancient traditional link between 'royalty' or authority and domestic life.

The only residence preserved on the Palatine from this period is the so-called House of Livia, which contained a rear area with 28 cubicula surrounding a central court over two floors. At the other end of the house three large reception rooms opened onto a court.[114]

The distinction between palatial and domestic architecture, seems to have been almost deliberately blurred by Augustus. From earlier parts of this book it will be clear to the reader that every Roman aristocratic house had a public role in the reception of guests and clients, and as a centre for business negotiations. In many ways Augustus' decision regarding his own house was a reflection of society at large. Other aristocrats needed to receive their associates; Augustus needed to receive foreign kings.

What applied to Augustus also applied to imperial officials. Governors of provinces, financial procurators, legionary commanders did not normally have 'palaces' or offices from which they worked. Instead they lived and conducted business from buildings which followed the traditions of domestic housing. This makes it practically impossible to identify the seat of administration in any town. Archaeologists have often labelled houses as 'of the Governor' or 'the Bishop's Palace', but there is rarely evidence of this role. The houses have been identified as palaces because they were the largest excavated on the site *up to that time*. However, the richest local aristocrats could be wealthier than the provincial governor or any member of the town council, so that an exceptionally large house might not even belong to a local administrator.[115]

This is not to say that true palatial architecture did not exist in the Roman world. It has already been observed that domestic architecture of the late Republic was becoming more splendid under the influence of the newly conquered eastern provinces. It did not take long for this to reach imperial circles. Successive emperors enlarged Augustus' house on the Palatine. Reception rooms became larger and grander, as did porticoes and entranceways.

It would take a separate book to present the palaces of the Julio-Claudian emperors in all their detail, taking into account work on Hellenistic palaces and textual references.[116] The main purpose of this book is to look at domestic housing, and the Julio-Claudian palaces will mainly be discussed in relation to domestic architecture.

The so-called *domus Tiberiana* (named after the second Roman emperor, Tiberius, who reigned AD 14-37) on the north-west part of the

Palatine is incompletely known. It seems to have included several large peristyles and a major reception suite at the northern end of the complex. The use of peristyles with reception suites on their further side is certainly a characteristic of domestic architecture, but can also be found in many public buildings such as baths and fora, where a *palaestra* for public gatherings normally preceded the main buildings – the baths themselves, the temples, or the senate house.

The domus Tiberiana appears, on the face of it, to be the first Roman palace which took the more general repertoire of domestic architecture and enlarged it to grandiose proportions, incorporating elements from public architecture. However, Tamm[117] pointed out that there are no textual references to the domus Tiberiana before the Flavian period; moreover he considers it unlikely that Tiberius would have been the one to break from the Augustan precedent of basing his residence in a recognisable, if somewhat enlarged, Roman house.

The culmination of early Roman palaces was the famous Golden House (*domus Aurea*) of Nero (AD 54-68),[118] which stretched from the Palatine to the Esquiline hills, a distance of some 1.5 km. The main buildings were set out in the early part of Nero's reign as the *domus Transitoria*, but the fire of AD 64, which he was rumoured to have started for this purpose,[119] provided the emperor with the opportunity to extend the complex. Many parts of the house are still preserved beneath later remains, most notably the Baths of Trajan.

The domus Aurea certainly incorporated some architectural elements recognisable in domestic architecture. There were large rectangular reception rooms, axially centred on peristyles. There was also a large number of apsidal rooms. The apse made a natural focus point at the back of the room, and thus could be the setting for a favoured statue, painting, fountain, or even a throne. While apses were plentiful, it would seem that the domus Aurea did not make use of them with a basilican space, as an explicit throne room.[120]

The normal use of large open reception rooms can be compared with the use of more intimate dining and retiring suites in the domus Aurea. Some mention has already been made of the grouping of two or three cubicula, as bedrooms or retiring rooms, in a separate suite. Such suites existed on a more lavish scale in the Neronian palace. Most notably, four or five large rooms with niches for couches were grouped around polygonal courts. These suites could have been used individually for smaller-scale dinners, or collectively for a large gathering. A reception in the large rectangular traditional oecus/triclinium might well have been very formal. The dividing of such a gathering into smaller parties in adjacent suites created a more intimate atmosphere.

In size and extravagance the domus Aurea can only be described as 'over the top', and it caused resentment amongst the landed class in Rome for the way the emperor had expropriated their land to build it.[121] Nevertheless, it demonstrated how impressive palatial architecture could be, a point that was not lost on Nero's successors.

Vespasian (AD 69-79), who succeeded Nero and established the next Flavian dynasty after the fighting of the 'the year of the four emperors' in AD 69, was a notably modest ruler. He did not develop the palaces and is noted for receiving guests in his bedroom. It was left to his younger son, the tyrannical Domitian (AD 81-96), to complete the development of the Palatine palace at the end of the first century.

Domitian's palace[122] was built on the eastern half of the Palatine. It was organised around three large peristyles. Most of the public reception rooms in the palace appear to have been built around the north-western peristyle, which was surrounded by porticoes of Numidian yellow marble columns. The walls were covered in Cappadocian gypsum which had a highly reflective surface, creating a 'Hall of Mirrors' effect. A large square room with a shallow apse at its far end was centrally located on the southern side of the peristyle. It was completely open to the peristyle, through an colonnade of six columns of Egyptian granite. Further frequent openings along the sides of the room gave access onto garden areas with central oval pools. This arrangement can immediately be identified as a dining room or reception room of the oecus/triclinium type. Conventional houses can be identified in which dining rooms were open to gardens and pools.[123]

Another large rectangular room at the opposite end of the peristyle was entered by two very large doors, one at each end of its façade. The interior of the room was decorated with a complex architectural façade of Phrygian marble columns and niches. It has been identified as an audience chamber. Although it had one large shallow niche, the room does not appear to have been focused on any particular location for a throne. It may instead be considered as a room in which those wishing an audience waited to be summoned.

Doors opened up to right and left at the far end of this richly embellished hall.

The left-hand door led into a basilican structure with a large deep apse at one end, and colonnades of Numidian marble. This is the most likely candidate for the imperial audience chamber, where Domitian could appear in state on his throne in the apse. In this room were discovered two colossal black basalt statues of Hercules and Apollo.[124] The introduction of the basilican form into the palace was a step away from domestic architecture. One basilican room has already been mentioned in the House of the Mosaic Atrium at Herculaneum, but examples dating to the first century are rare.

The right-hand door led into a large room generally known as the 'Lararium'. In fact there is no evidence for any religious association, and the function of the room is unclear.

All the last three rooms described, basilica, audience room, and 'lararium', could also be entered from an external portico, or corridor, which ran round the outside of the buildings from the main entrance for this area of the palace to the west of the peristyle. To enter the peristyle at this main entrance one passed through a domed vestibule.

The eastern half of the palace, thought to have been the private apartments, was entered from the south through a more conventional rectangular vestibule, though this was set in a semicircular exedra behind the Circus Maximus. A similar semicircular entrance has already been mentioned at the villa of Montmaurin in south-west Gaul, and a fourth-century example from Piazza Armerina in Sicily is discussed in Chapter 5. Such semicircular colonnades were a popular way of framing a grand entranceway. If these were the private apartments they certainly did not have a private entrance. Indeed the entrance on this side of the palace is more monumental than that to the so-called public rooms to the west, already discussed above.

On leaving the semicircular portico visitors passed through a lower peristyle surrounded by a variety of rectangular and apsidal suites, which was presumably used for informal political discussion. Staircases then rose up the Palatine to the upper peristyle. To the left a large rectangular vestibule served to create the link to the 'public' wing, while to the right an oval vestibule with internal colonnades overlooked a large garden area in the form of a 'stadium' running track. Such stadium gardens, as we have seen, are not uncommon in regular domestic houses, and we have even noted one in an urban house, the House of the Exedra at Italica in Spain.[125]

On the south side of the upper peristyle, and therefore above the entrance at the base of the hill, were two semicircular porticoes fronting open suites with views over the Circus and the city. Similar pavilions were described in Chapter 1 at the Villa Jovis in Capri.

Like the domus Aurea, the palace of Domitian adapted a number of features commonly found in Roman domestic architecture, thereby preserving the link between house and palace established by Augustus. The overall plan of Domitian's palace with its succession of peristyles and reception suites was more typical of regular domestic architecture than the domus Aurea. It is notable that the 'public' wing of Domitian's palace was more conventional in its layout, with one main axially-placed rectangular reception room. The eastern 'private' wing is more reminiscent of late Pompeian housing and villas, in that it incorporated extensive gardens and open pavilions.

One word of caution should be sounded. Although it is certain, from dated brick stamps, that this palace was largely the work of Domitian, it continued to form the principal palace of the emperor in Rome throughout the Empire. During this period it was embellished and adapted by numerous rulers, and archaeologists have yet to write the definitive history of the building.

For further development of palace architecture during the High Empire we can turn our attention to the villa of the emperor Hadrian (AD 117-138) at Tivoli, 20 miles to the east of Rome.[126] The design of the villa was enlivened by an amazing arrays of architectural novelties. The pavilions of Domitian's palace have been compared with those of the Villa Jovis which is attributed to Tiberius. This form of villa architecture emphasised the view from a portico or salon which overlooked the surrounding area. The architecture of Tivoli takes to its ultimate development another characteristic of the villa form; the ability to create an extensive landscape of architectural fantasies.

There were two enormous water features. In the centre of a huge peristyle, with internal and external porticoes surrounding an area of 232 x 97 m, was a large pool or rather, an artificial lake. It is nowadays known as the Pecile. A second 119 m long narrower pool, sometimes thought to be a representation of the Nile, is known as the Canopus (Plate 6). At its head was a nymphaeum with an outdoor dining area, while along the sides were a number of exotic statues. A third smaller pool was positioned in a peristyle known as the 'fishpool quadroportico'. Whether or not the pool held fish, its principal role was decorative, to create an atmosphere, rather than for rod or net.

The Romans liked to have extensive walled gardens round which they could walk with their friends. There was a stadium in Domitian's palace and there was a similar building at Tivoli.[127] The large-scale use of water, and Nilotic imagery are common to several palaces and rich villas. Lavish use of water helped to create a rural atmosphere and emphasised luxury. Egyptian motifs symbolised the exotic, and commonly consist of water scenes (the Nile including the swamps of the Delta), with crocodiles and hippopotami. These could be represented as motifs in mosaic, or as at Tivoli by pools and sculptures.

Two of the most remarkable suites at Tivoli are the Piazza D'Oro and the 'Maritime Theatre'.[128] The former included an octagonal court graced by gently curving porticoes, creating a star-shaped plan. The latter was a circular porticoed island surrounded by a water-filled channel, and served by wooden bridges (see book jacket). It was presumably a tranquil area to which the emperor could retire undisturbed. In the way that they adapt Roman architectural forms to a completely new context, these two buildings are generally regarded as the most original architectural features of the palace, and remain very impressive today.

The palace at Tivoli also included more conventional apartments, large apsidal reception rooms, and two bath suites. The extraordinary architecture of the villa is rightly celebrated as one of the masterpieces of the Roman period. However, there is a temptation to overstress its unique qualities. It should be remembered that Hadrian was born in Spain. Spain has already been singled out in this work for the remarkable architectural qualities of its villas. Tivoli should also perhaps be seen as what a

Spaniard could do when provided with the unlimited resources of the imperial throne.

16. Late antique palaces

From the third century AD Roman society underwent a profound change. Elements of this change may have had their origins earlier in the second century, but their effects were felt at the end of the third century, which saw a breakdown of political stability and military security in the Empire. There was a succession of short-lived emperors and at the same time barbarian tribes from outside the Empire pressed on its borders. At the end of the third century this led to the establishment of an increasingly autocratic centralised government under Diocletian and his successors. This autocratic style of rule was to have a profound influence on the special structure of the aristocracy and their houses.

At the same time there was a move from a formal state religion, whose only requirement was that citizens followed its rituals, to more personal religions whose adherents were required to follow a certain moral standard in their everyday life.[129] These religious movements culminated in the adoption of Christianity as a state religion in the early fourth century AD under Constantine the Great. Christianity had an important impact on domestic life, most especially on personal comportment and relations between the aristocratic patron and his clients.

The economic and political instability of the period have made it very difficult for archaeologists to date buildings to the third century. The basis for this statement is very complex, and requires considerable discussion beyond the scope of this book. In simplified terms, third-century coinage became debased, and long distance trade was disrupted, leading to a dearth of the artefacts that archaeologists use for dating. At the same time political and economic problems made it less likely that anyone would have the wealth to build a substantial new house.

Stability returned at the end of the third century, and it is to this period, and the subsequent peaceful Constantinian period of the early fourth century AD, that the first 'late antique' remains belong. The new mood is reflected by the palace of the emperor who made this stability possible, Diocletian (AD 284-305).

Diocletian has the remarkable distinction of being the only Roman emperor to retire. He reorganised, or perhaps more correctly in modern business parlance re-engineered, almost every aspect of the Roman state, including the economy and the administration. He left a 'college' of four emperors to succeed him.

Diocletian was a 'hard man' with a soldier's background. Not for him the luxurious villa. His retirement palace at Split[130] on the Dalmatian coast was a fortress looking across the Adriatic towards Italy. It formed a rough square 200 m on each side with four large rectangular corner towers. On entering the palace from the coast one passed through a basilican hall or reception area into a domed vestibule. From here steps rose to the higher ground level in the centre of the palace.

The steps led to the 'peristyle', with two temples to the left, and to the right the massive octagonal mausoleum of the emperor. This 'peristyle' was a long narrow space. It has been called a 'basilica discoperta', or unroofed basilica,[131] and like a basilica may have held a tribunal for addressing the assembled local people or imperial staff. The possible tribunal was a raised platform above the passage up from the entrance at the lower level. The floor of the 'peristyle' was lowered to provide an intermediate level between that of the entrance and the interior of the building. The most appropriate architectural term, peristyle or basilica, need not concern us here. The space could even be designated a forum as it had a tribunal and was used as a meeting place. The Romans adapted architectural elements to a variety of building forms and functions. Suffice to say it was a central square surrounded by colonnades, where all those in the palace could meet.

Many of the apartments in the palace were on the upper storey, and are preserved on the southern, seaside, façade. They included a bath suite and a true basilican reception hall. There was an open walkway along the top of the walls, recalling the pavilions of Domitian's palace and other seaside villas such as those in Capri. The location of the reception suite on the upper floor, with a grand staircase from the main entrance below, also recalls Domitian's palace.

One of Diocletian's immediate successors was Galerius (AD 305-311), who chose to build a similar palace to Diocletian's in a more remote part of the Balkans, at Gamzigrad (Fig. 9)[132] close to the Danubian frontier of the Empire. Whereas the interior of the palace at Split was entirely built up, at Gamzigrad there would seem to have been much open space in the interior of the massive fortress walls. This open space allowed Galerius to have a more conventional villa design for his palace. There was a regular domestic-style peristyle with a large apsidal reception room off one side, an adjacent public reception suite with two huge apsidal rooms, private baths, and a long corridor entranceway that probably served as a way to queue and sort visitors according to rank. There were also two classical temples at Gamzigrad as at Split.

It is noticeable that the bath suite at Gamzigrad was formed from two clusters of small circular chambers, allowing small groups of bathers some privacy. This is a typical reflection of growing late antique 'pudeur', which turned its back upon earlier Roman communal bathing. Nevertheless baths, and group bathing, were still part of Galerius' reception facilities.

Diocletian's palace was a hybrid architectural form. Aspects of it can be related to basilican buildings, imperial mausolea, and terraced villas overlooking the sea. It may have borrowed from domestic architecture, but it does not fit the overall design tenets of Roman housing. It is significant

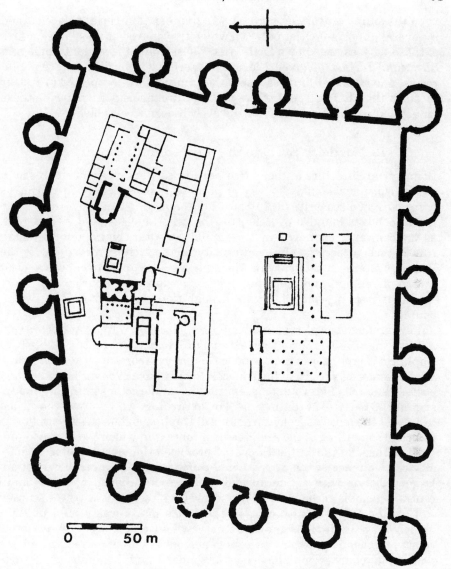

9. Palace of Galerius, Gamzigrad, Serbia.

that the other contemporary, securely identified, imperial palace reverted to the conventional form of a villa.

Despite the profound changes brought by Diocletian, palatial architecture never shook off the overall form of domestic housing. When Constantine founded Constantinople such traditions continued into the Middle Ages in the palace of the Byzantine Emperors.

In the fourth century emperors had a number of imperial palaces based in several important cities between which they moved as need arose. Parts of these palaces are known from Trier, Thessalonika, Constantinople and Sirmium.[133] They involved the use of peristyles, basilicas, ceremonial rooms, and attached circuses where the emperors were expected to appear to start the chariot races. However, the archaeology of none of these palaces is sufficiently known for the overall design to be clear.

18. Northern Syria in the third to sixth century AD

Domestic architecture of the fourth century saw an enormous increase in the conspicuous display of wealth and status, especially in Syria, as witnessed by discoveries at Antioch and Apamea.

Antioch was founded by Seleucus, the general of Alexander the Great, as the capital of his new kingdom in 300 BC. After coming under Roman rule it rose to become the leading city of the eastern provinces of the Roman Empire, in rivalry with Alexandria in Egypt. Antioch was a great centre of religion and learning, pagan through the suburban shrine of Apollo at Daphne, and Christian through the patriarchate of the Syrian church.

Few archaeological remains have been discovered from Antioch itself, but in the 1930s there was extensive excavation in the suburb of Daphne.[134] Daphne was the residence of many important local aristocrats, as in the case of several suburban sites which have been discussed. Many eastern suburbs like Daphne seem to have undergone significant expansion in the early fifth century AD. The excavators were mostly concerned to recover the mosaics from the houses at Daphne, but on the way they also recorded something of the architectural context in which they were found.

The House of the Buffet Supper[135] produced the most detailed archaeological sequence of the excavations. During the fourth century it had a large peristyle with a fine apsidal dining room aligned with the main central long axis of the house. The mosaic from this room will be discussed in Chapter 4. In the fifth century the whole house was rebuilt at right angles to its original orientation. The new house had two large peristyle courtyards. One to the north-west opened onto the main street. At a later date some rooms seem to have been extended into the middle of the yard. This is quite a common phenomenon in urban houses occupied over a long period. The peristyle had to be used when there was little room for expansion at neighbours' expense. An axial reception room with typical side rooms lay off the second peristyle. Although the main access was from the main street, a side street lay adjacent to the south-west side of both peristyles. There was a nymphaeum next to this street in the inner peristyle, and given the restricted space along these western street frontages it is likely that other rich apartments lay opposite the fountain to the north-east. A fountain was often used opposite the main reception room to form a 'rural' view for the diners; a particularly fine example from Apamea will be discussed later in this section.

A number of smaller houses were also recorded. Surprisingly, small yards fronted by single porticoes are much more common than complete peristyles, though the fragmentary nature of many house plans makes it difficult to piece together the full picture.

The House of the Boat of Psyche was a small rectangular house some 15 x 15 m in size. A short entranceway was flanked by a cubiculum and a room of indeterminate function. The entrance led into a small central courtyard. A second cubiculum lay to one side of this, while to the other was a triclinium. The triclinium and cubiculum opened onto a narrow portico fronting an elaborate nymphaeum that formed the far end wall of the property. All the rooms to which functions have been assigned had rich mosaic pavements. These date the house to the third century AD, which is somewhat earlier than the majority of Daphne residences.

The House of Menander had a small central court with a portico on its south side. The main entrance to the house took the form of a corridor which joined the east end of this portico. To the left of the entrance, near the street, there were rooms which seem to have formed two private apartments, comprising two cubicula and two larger reception rooms. On the far side of the court a narrow oecus gave a view onto a second court through a colonnade along one side. Against the far wall of this second court was a nymphaeum fountain. The mosaics in the House of Menander suggest a date in the fifth century.

The House of Dionysius and Ariadne, of the fifth century AD, has similar dimensions to the House of the Boat of Psyche. It appears to have had two intercommunicating reception suites, side by side, opening onto a portico. This was a typical arrangement, in which the larger room (with the eponymous mosaic of the house), was the dining suite with the smaller as a retiring room or cubiculum. The main entrance, however, rather than entering the portico in the normal fashion, took a circuitous route to enter the dining room through its rear side-wall. A further entrance passed through some poorly decorated rooms (perhaps service rooms) to enter the dining room through its rear wall.

Still near the Orontes river, but some 70 km to the south, lay Apamea, another very large city of the eastern provinces. Significantly, as will be shown in the next chapter, Apamea was separated from Antioch by a highland plateau, where there were many villages with well-preserved houses of a very different architectural form. Excavations at Apamea have uncovered a number of very large peristyle houses dating, in their preserved form, to the sixth century AD.[136]

In contrast to Antioch/Daphne, these houses all had the conventional form of a large peristyle with a reception room on the main axis of the house. These reception rooms were of an exceptional character. They were often as large as 10 x 20 m (the largest recorded in this book), and have several doorways from side rooms. Normally one would expect one or two doors on each side of the room, but the largest room in the House of the Consoles (Fig. 10) had seven side doors, while the largest reception room in the Building of the Triclinos had five or six side doors, as did the reception room in the House of the Capitals with Consoles. The large numbers of side rooms could suggest that the main room had a slightly different function to the reception rooms in other parts of the Empire. It is interesting to note that the House of Pilasters had a typically large reception room which was almost two-thirds the size of the adjacent peristyle. It might be normal amongst urban Roman houses from Pompeii onwards to sacrifice space for the sake of having a large reception room, but it is rare to find such a massive room in this size of house, especially in an urban context where space was at a premium.

Almost every one of these houses had a large fountain or nymphaeum in the courtyard. In late antiquity these commonly took up the whole of the rear wall of the peristyle. They were often decorated with niches, and presumably rose high enough to house statues, like their public counterparts. The House of the Capitals with Consoles had an exceptional nymphaeum. It was located at the end of the peristyle just opposite the reception room, and is formed by two large niched basins, separated by a walkway into the garden beyond. The arrangement for the ideal late antique dining room was a huge theatrical salon, with the dining couch at the far end. Diners would look down the richly decorated room to see garden greenery and a wall of cascading water on the opposite side of the peristyle. This arrangement will be invoked throughout this book in consideration of decor, furnishings, and social meaning.

Occasionally in these eastern houses the reception room had an apsidal end. At Antioch an apse was added to the reception room of the House of the Phoenix in the fifth century AD.[137] The Building with the Triclinos at Apamea had two apsidal reception rooms, one on the middle of each peristyle axis. Each apse housed a stibadium, a semicircular dining couch which replaced the rectangular arrangement of couches from the end of the third century. Not all aristocrats had apsidal reception rooms, but from the fourth century they were common. They were in vogue, but not an absolute requirement of aristocratic society. Sometimes the apsidal dining couches were used in rectangular rooms. This can be demonstrated, for example, in the House of the Buffet Supper at Daphne, where the location of the stibadium is marked by a semicircular mosaic floor panel, which will be discussed in Chapters 4 and 5.[138]

The aristocratic houses of Antioch/Daphne and Apamea provide a good sample of housing in the two greatest cities of northern Syria from the third to the sixth century AD. The Antiochean houses demonstrate that even in the richest city of the east housing did not slavishly follow the regular peristyle form. The reception suites at Daphne often seem to be more tucked into the corner of the house than centralised on the peristyle,

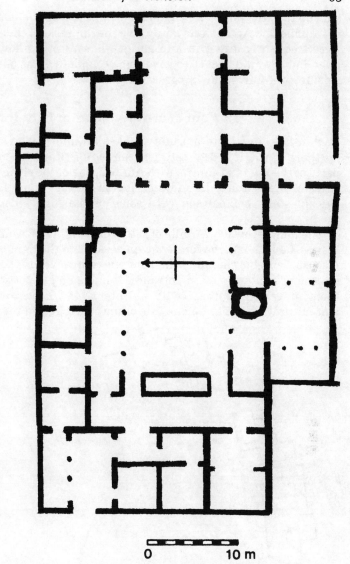

10. House of the
Consoles,
Apamea, Syria.

0   10 m

and the reception room in the House of Dionysius and Ariadne communi-
cated directly with the adjacent cubiculum. It is tempting to ascribe these
characteristics to the Greek traditions exemplified by Olynthus, but this
would seem unlikely given signs, discussed below, that in Greece itself this
tradition had broken down by the second century AD. Given that Antioch
is now covered by the modern Turkish city of Antakya, further evidence
may not be forthcoming.

Before the Apamea houses had been studied, Stillwell[1:39] had identified a trend towards larger reception rooms in the Daphne houses. The houses in Daphne and Apamea certainly give the impression that reception rooms were frequently larger in late antique houses of the fourth century and later, but it would be nice to have some complete plans of earlier houses at Apamea to confirm this progression.

19. Fourth-century villas in Britain

Roman Britain in late antiquity makes an informative comparison with northern Syria. It is interesting to compare Britain, as one of the remoter parts of the Roman Empire, with Antioch, one of the richest, most cultured cities of the Empire. In addition, fourth-century AD villas in south-west Britain stand comparison with some of the highly developed villas of Spain.

The fourth-century AD villa of Littlecote (Fig. 11)[140] would at first appear to have had a fairly conventional appearance in the light of other buildings discussed on this chapter. It had but one central yard. The main house was located opposite the main entrance. It had a single portico, with a square room at each end that could be interpreted as a tower. There were agricultural buildings on one side of the court, but on the other side was a

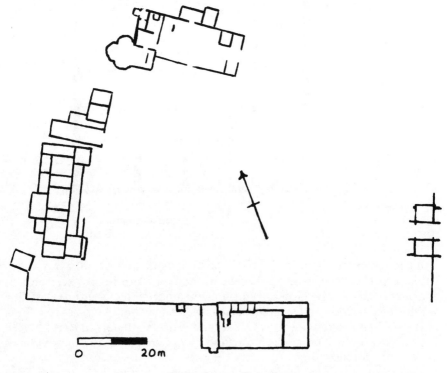

0   20m

11. Littlecote, Britain.

smaller yard and a triconch, or tri-apsidal, hall, decorated with a rich mosaic of Orpheus and the beasts.

It can be demonstrated that this was a formal dining suite, typical of many late antique houses in the Mediterranean provinces.[141] Such rooms were often located to one side of the main building. This allowed them to be entered independently, so that dinner guests or retainers would not disturb the main residence. Early Roman dining rooms of rectangular form had used three banks of dining couches arranged in a U. It was natural, following the introduction of the semicircular couch at the end of the third century AD, to use three such couches, which gave the room the three-apsed shape.

The apsed dining room seems to have appeared in Romano-British houses at the same time as it appeared in the Mediterranean provinces at the end of the third century AD. Thus aristocrats in Britain were adopting the latest domestic fashions as quickly as those at the centre of the Empire.

The Littlecote reception room was decorated with a mosaic of Orpheus. Another characteristic Orpheus mosaic decorated the reception room of Woodchester,[142] one of the most splendid British villas. Although the room is rectangular rather than apsidal, it was 14 x 14 m in area and had four internal columns, making it reminiscent of Vitruvius' basilican Egyptian oecus. The main reception room of Woodchester was located on the central axis of the villa, which had two courtyards following the conventional pattern of an inner domestic court and an outer court surrounded by agricultural buildings. Other fourth-century villas in Britain, such as Bignor[143] and Chedworth, also had two courtyards and single-apsed reception rooms.

More unusual architectural forms are also found. At Keynsham[144] there were suites based around hexagonal rooms at each end of the main range of a courtyard villa. The hexagonal room to the left was the central room of a private bath suite, but the room on the right gave access to three dining suites, one of them apsed. The location of this room can be compared to the Littlecote triconch and similarly represents a formal dining room. A close parallel is provided by the villa at Mediana near Niš (Fig. 29),[145] which as Roman Naissus was one of the principal imperial residences during the fourth century. An octagonal reception suite in Britain existed at the villa of Great Witcombe (Fig. 12).[146]

It would be incorrect to claim that late antique villas in Britain had all reached the high architectural level of those in other provinces. Rich reception rooms, double courtyards, and polygonal rooms were rare. Nevertheless, it is true to say that the richest late antique houses in Roman Britain were comparable to aristocratic housing in the other provinces. A Mediterranean aristocrat would have felt at home in the Littlecote reception suite, whilst a visiting Spanish magnate would have been impressed with the hexagonal suites at Keynsham, which would not have been out of place in the richest Spanish villas.

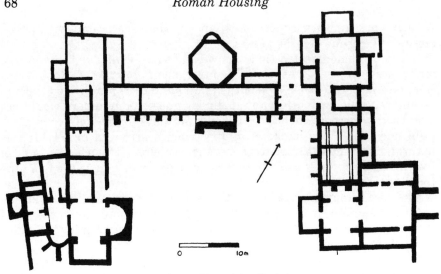

12. Great Witcombe, Britain.

20. Currents and trends in Roman housing

This chapter has examined just two types of houses that were common in
the Roman period – the atrium house and the peristyle house. A rough
chronological framework has been adopted. This has brought out a number of interpretations.

The development of the traditional atrium house, primarily associated
with Pompeii, has been examined. It has been suggested that caution
should be exercised in assuming that rooms identified as atria, and dated
to before the second century BC, had the same function as the classical
Pompeian atrium. Doubts have also been cast on the identification of some
tetrastyle courts of the first two centuries AD as atria. Their location in
relation to other parts of the house has suggested that they may have had
a different function to the Pompeian atrium.

The growth of Roman-style housing in the western provinces has shown
that by the first century AD the elites were highly Romanised. It has been
suggested that the speed of Romanisation was determined by whether
local elites felt it was in their interest to adopt Roman houses and
behaviour. There are suggestions that in the east Greek domestic styles
were more persistent and only changed by the second century AD. Areas of
Greek influence in the western provinces may have led the introduction of
the atrium and other elements of Roman housing.

In the second to third century AD the story is one of unity in diversity.
All provincial elites favoured peristyle housing. Urban houses had one, or
if they were exceptionally large two, peristyles. Villas had similar large
peristyles, or porticoed courtyards. There was normally one major recep-

tion room located on the central axis of the house off the inner peristyle or
yard. The lack of atrium, or specialised reception room, at this time
suggests that the single large room acted at the same time as dining room,
a room for receiving visitors, and perhaps as an office.

It has been shown how, following the decline of the atrium in the first
to second century AD, there was no specialised reception room until late
antiquity, when formal reception rooms and audience halls came into
vogue.[147] At present the loss of the atrium cannot be easily related to any
decline in the role of formal receptions in Roman society. One possibility
would be to associate the change with the decline of the traditional Roman
aristocracy during the early principate of the first century AD, but the
evidence for this hypothesis is not very strong. Atria are found well away
from the city of Rome which formed the base for the traditional Roman
aristocrat. The use of atria also declined somewhat later in the first
century AD, whereas civil war had reduced the number of the Republican
aristocracy well before the middle of the first century AD.

On the other hand, the reintroduction of a specialised reception room
can be associated with the more autocratic nature of late antique society,
in particular the way in which the aristocrat needed to receive clients and
wield wider power from his own home.[148] It has been accepted that the
preference for the oecus over the tablinum was due to an interest in using
more private rooms for public receptions. The late antique use of audience
halls would then be a reversal of this process, as a return to the use of a
more public reception room closer to the entrance of the house.

It would be wrong to identify provincial 'types' of peristyle house. There
was a wide range of variations on the basic peristyle type. Variations grew
up in each province, but the fundamental prototype remained strong. A
Roman aristocrat transposed from one province to another would have had
no problem in finding his way around a house in another province. Some
characteristics may be ascribed to one province or another, some may be
ascribed to several provinces. In the case of African urban housing and
Spanish villas, there is a fairly complete picture of the evidence, but in
other provinces not enough complete houses have been uncovered for us
to be certain of the general picture.

The geographic distribution of particular architectural characteristics
is also uncertain. For example, in the Former Yugoslav Republic of Macedonia there are many late antique peristyle houses, which have fountains
in the middle of their triclinia.[149] It is not, however, known how far back
into the Roman period, or how far in geographic terms, such fountains
were characteristic.

The importance of the central reception room, and peristyle, can be
gathered from the design principles used. Darmon[150] has shown how the
House of the Nymphs, at Neapolis (Nabeul, Tunisia) was given a carefully
constructed polygonal peristyle, which made the irregular space seem
rectangular when viewed from every portico. Smaller houses were often

given two- or three-sided peristyles, allowing the other sides to be com-
pleted as a 'trompe l'oeil' with half moulded, or painted, columns on the far
side of the garden or yard. Examples of this at Pompeii included the House
of the Priest Amandus (insula 1,7,7),[151] and the House of the Tragic Poet
(insula 6,8,5).

The peristyle and reception rooms interacted to create important views
across the house for dinner guests. Clarke[152] has shown how, at Pompeii,
room orientations were adjusted, intercolumniations were aligned, and
major art works were sited to build views and draw the gaze of the
spectator through the house.

Significantly, these broad design principles applied in every Roman
province, and can be applied to elite housing from the first to the fifth
century AD. In fifth-century AD Roman Gaul aristocrats like Sidonius
Apollinaris struggled to maintain the Roman culture exemplified by their
houses in an area increasingly under the political control of Franks and
Visigoths. In the east, housing in cities such as Apamea continued to be
built in the common vocabulary of the peristyle house until the mid-sixth
century AD. Social and economic change meant that fewer peristyle houses
were repaired, and more aristocrats could not afford to keep their opulent
lifestyles.[153] When the Byzantine Empire re-emerged after the internal
and external struggles of the seventh to eighth centuries, the peristyle
house had gone for ever, preserved only as an anachronism in the architecture of the imperial palace at Constantinople itself.

*

This chapter has concentrated on the architecture of aristocratic housing.
It has indeed concentrated more on the plans of houses than the compo-
nents of their decor such as columns, marbles, mosaics and paintings.
Nevertheless, a number of important points have been established.

As far as origins are concerned, there remain many questions to be
resolved. Although the Romans may have believed they owed much to the
Greeks, Greek architectural elements were not employed in a Greek
manner within the Roman house.

Roman-style housing was quickly adopted in the western provinces
during the first century BC, and functioned as an instrument of accultura-
tion. By the second century AD local provincial traditions of housing had
emerged, and patterns of Roman housing had begun to affect the eastern
provinces.

Through all this time the room functions mutated with changing lifestyles. The Greek reception room with its concentric couches was changed
to the Roman triclinium with its three couches focused opposite the
doorway, and in late antiquity a semicircular arrangement was adopted
which withdrew to the far end of the reception room. Further consideration

of this change in behavioural patterns will have to wait until other forms of housing from the Roman period have been examined in Chapter 3.

Conclusions

The origins of the atrium peristyle house remain obscure. A considerable amount of further archaeological evidence will be required to establish the architectural form, and more importantly the use, of reception facilities and courtyards in Roman houses before the third century BC. It has been suggested that there were notable differences in the way that peristyles were used in Greek and Roman housing, and that Greek housing first incorporated isolated colonnades while Roman houses first incorporated complete peristyles as secondary courts.

The initial introduction of Roman housing styles into the western provinces may have taken place through Greek milieux in France and Spain, while in other areas the advent of the Roman army was the instrument of Romanisation. The existence of a few extremely rich villas, such as Fishbourne and Echternach, in the frontier zone of the north-west provinces during the Neronian period suggest that the Romans rewarded significant local aristocrats with the construction of very large houses. The archaeology of military colonies, such as Timgad in Algeria, also suggest that army billets were consciously adapted into Roman housing, which also will have influenced the surrounding settlements.

An Empire-wide tradition of peristyle housing had been established by the end of the first century AD. In the first and second century AD each province developed its own housing characteristics. The chief characteristics of peristyle housing in the High Empire – a peristyle, and a reception room opposite the entrance – are well known, but there are many other less well known characteristics which we have identified in several provinces. They include the use of paired side rooms next to the main reception room (Africa, Britain, Asia and Syria). Fountains are common opposite the reception room (Syria, Africa) especially in late antiquity. Roman domestic architecture emphasised the importance of having a view of the fountain, or garden, from the dining couch in the main reception room. Many aristocrats looked for more private suites, or gardens, where they could sit or walk with their friends. Characteristics limited to particular provinces include 'pseudo'-atria of the early imperial period (Italy), garden terraces (Italy and Spain), and twin reception rooms (Africa).

From the end of the third century AD, profound social change and a more autocratic government meant that the house increasingly became the base from which an aristocrat personally controlled a large group of adherents who were economically, socially and politically dependent on him. This required more elaborate reception facilities such as audience chambers and large formal dining rooms. The *stibadium*, a semicircular dining couch previously used for open air dining, became the fashionable dining facility, and spread from Britain to Syria before the end of the third century. It would seem, from limited evidence in Asia and the Aegean, that by this time the remaining traces of Greek domestic architecture had disappeared.

It has been emphasised that a Roman aristocrat's house was also his place of business. Business and domestic life were so intertwined that it is impossible to find a house that did not have a business function or vice versa. Offices and industrial buildings, as will be seen in the next chapter, did not exist without domestic facilities. The relationship between domestic life and business is also the key to understanding Roman palatial architecture. For Roman emperors and officials, their house was their 'palace'. Even the most extravagant emperors, Nero and Hadrian, built palaces that developed the domestic form.

3

Town and Country

In the preceding chapter much was made of the peristyle house as the ideal residence for the Roman elite in every province. However, the provincial elites were always a small minority of those living in the Roman Empire, and there was a wide variety of house types to suit all tastes and pockets. This chapter will discuss these other types of housing. Particular attention will be paid to their distribution to consider to what extent such house types should be considered local to one province or part of a wider trend.

The other important aim of this chapter is to compare urban and rural housing. Traditionally rural housing is associated with agricultural pursuits, and urban housing with trade and artisanal work. Columella (*On Agriculture* 1.6.1) distinguishes between the agricultural parts of a villa, and the residential, or urban, quarters. Archaeologists have followed this distinction in trying to distinguish rich luxury villas from those that were working farms.

In fact such distinctions are hard to justify in the majority of cases. Artisanal or 'industrial' activity was not limited to towns, nor agricultural activity to the countryside. At the individual level the house and household had to function as a unit, and it is wrong to separate out the leisure of the aristocrat from the economic production that supported his lifestyle.

1. Urban housing

It will be convenient to define certain characteristics of urban housing. The majority of the populace in Rome were not lucky enough to be landowners, and could not afford a peristyle house. Undoubtedly, suitable land for development could command a high price. As the population rose with the acquisition of the Empire, they were forced into denser housing and built apartment blocks. The occupants of these buildings were tenants of more wealthy, often unscrupulous, landlords.

Thanks to the excavations at Ostia, one of the ports of Rome, we do have a clear conception of one type of apartment, the so-called *cenaculum* or *medianum* house. Hermansen,[1] almost despairingly, captures the difficulty in applying the conventional names for the rooms of a peristyle house to the apartment form.

We have then, two different sets of names for two different Roman habitations. For all that we know it is wrong to use the word tablinum to speak of apartments and it is equally wrong to speak of atrium in Roman apartments. The tradition supplies different names.

The remains at least are fairly explicit. The archetypal Ostian apartment consisted of four or five rooms. One of these rooms was an enlarged corridor which linked together the other rooms of the long narrow apartment. This enlarged corridor is normally called the medianum. The medianum was the common location for exterior windows, so that it provided light and air for the other rooms as well as access.

The apartment was entered from a shared staircase. The entrance passage wound around a sizeable room at one end of the medianum. Moving down the medianum one might pass one or two smaller side rooms, before reaching the largest, best decorated room in the apartment. This room can undoubtedly be paralleled with the principal reception room of the peristyle house, the oecus or triclinium. The room has the same relative location as the reception room – at the furthest end of the residence – and comparable decor. The fact that the reception room in these apartments was sometimes as richly decorated as the triclinium in a peristyle house demonstrates that apartment tenants could still be people of some means.

Hermansen[2] identifies the medianum as a dining room, after a reference in the Gospels (Mark 14:15). It is certainly dangerous to equate any domestic function too rigidly with one room; use of houses is after all a matter of personal taste as much as of social convention. Nevertheless, the last chapter should have made it abundantly clear that if there was one room in the house which deserved to be classed as a dining room it was the main reception room. Eating was inextricably linked with entertaining at Rome, and if the medianum was used for eating then it was a distinction such as we might make today between using the dining room and having a tv dinner. Hermansen himself states (p. 22), that the medianum was where the cooking took place; normally in a brazier. Cooking never took place in the richly decorated triclinium, because of smells and smoke. The medianum in an apartment was more suitable for cooking because it was the best-aired room. It was not suitable for a formal dinner.

Given that we have correctly identified a reception room and a kitchen, it is most likely that the largish room at the opposite end of the medianum was the master bedroom. This is a suitable location as it would have been useful to guard the front door in view of the reduced security in apartment blocks, and the absence of the rich Pompeian's porter. The location would also have provided a rapid exit in case of fire, an ever-present risk as there was no upper-floor water supply.[3]

The adjacent House of the Graffito and the House of the Yellow Walls form convenient examples of medianum-style housing at Ostia. The two apartments lay back to back. The House of the Graffito faced east onto the Street of the Vaults, that is, it was from this side that light and air entered the medianum. The House of the Yellow Walls faced west onto the court-yard of the Garden Court, or Insula.

Built between AD 123 and 128, the Garden Court[4] is one of the most remarkable examples of Roman urban design. A large rectangular area about 100 x 120 m in size was ringed by apartment housing to make a huge 'garden court'. In the middle of the court rose two independent apartment blocks containing at least thirteen apartments. In between the free-standing apartments and the outer ranges of the court were eight fountains.

The designer of this area clearly had an appreciation of the problems of apartment living, with which we have become familiar since the 1960s. The presence of fountains demonstrates that the internal court was to provide the apartment dwellers with much needed open space, whether for watering their horses, domestic cooking, or artisanal activity such as iron smithing.

Studies of 1960s apartment housing have amply demonstrated the need for architectural design to create 'defended space' around apartment blocks. Research has demonstrated that when the space around high rise housing is not clearly defined it can create a hostile no-man's-land where crime and mugging become common. It would not be correct to push this analogy between modern skyscrapers and Roman houses too far. It is, though, reasonable to assume that the Roman designers appreciated that, by creating the outer range of buildings around the court, the inner space would be secure and private. The study of atrium and peristyle housing in the previous chapter has shown how the Romans appreciated the privacy of an internal court.

The Garden Court was entered from the east by a wide entranceway flanked by two lodges; their presence in itself is an indication of the perceived need for security. The House of the Yellow Walls and the House of the Graffito were adjacent to this entranceway. Their front doors opened in front of the north lodge, off a small yard or turning area. The House of the Yellow Walls[5] was on the left (Fig. 13). A staircase to the upper storey rose to the right of the vestibule. Crossing the vestibule the visitor reached the central medianum, which was almost square in shape, creating a court rather than a corridor. Three large windows lit the medianum from the west. The same arrangement lit reception rooms at each end of the medianum. Two cubicula lay off the side of the medianum opposite the windows in the centre of the apartment block, and thus were lit only indirectly.

The main reception room in the House of the Yellow Walls lay at the far end of the medianum. The central panel of the floor mosaic was slightly off centre. This allowed it to align with a large arch at the far end of the room. It also formed a passage along one side of the room, which entered the dining area through a smaller doorway. The dining area was paved in

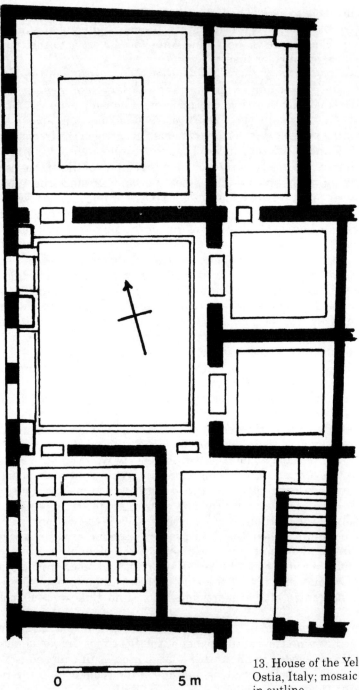

0   5 m

13. House of the Yellow Walls,
Ostia, Italy; mosaic panels shown
in outline.

plain mosaic, as was common with spaces frequently used for furniture settings. A door at one end of the area led to one of the cubicula.

It is interesting to note that many of the doorways between rooms had sockets for door pivots. By contrast, there were no doors between the vestibule and the staircase, between the vestibule and the medianum, or between the medianum and the smaller southern reception room. This may suggest that the latter room was more of a public space than the main reception room, which could be closed to the gaze of inquisitive visitors. The lack of doors in the vestibule suggests that the upper storey above the house formed part of the same property. The house had good, if not high quality decoration, and the owners may have been rich enough to house some servants on the upper floor.

The adjacent House of the Graffito[6] was smaller than its neighbour. The vestibule was a corridor no wider than the staircase to the upper floors which flanked it. The medianum was a corridor 3.7 m wide and 10.5 m long, in contrast to the neighbouring apartment's 7.5 x 7.5 m square room. The two cubicula and reception rooms were located in a symmetrical position to those in the House of the Yellow Walls. The smaller reception room in the House of the Graffito was markedly smaller in size than its counterpart in the neighbouring apartment, even though the medianum was on a much reduced scale. The main reception room did not have the arched dining area of the adjacent apartment, but it did still have three windows onto the street. The reception room at the other end of the apartment was small and had only one window.

In contrast to the vestibule of the House of the Yellow Walls, the vestibule of the House of the Graffito was probably common property. A setting for a door between the vestibule and the medianum suggests that it was at this point that the apartment began. The vestibule was probably a public stairway and, in contrast to the House of the Yellow Walls, the upper floor or floors formed one or more separate properties.

It is not surprising that the House of the Yellow Walls, which obtained its light from the secluded Garden Court, was designed as the larger, richer apartment, while the House of the Graffito, whose windows opened onto the noisy, less secure street, was the smaller. There were nevertheless many Ostian apartments smaller than the House of the Graffito. Its main reception room had a mosaic floor and its walls had coloured paintings. It should also be noted that to the rear of these two apartments, and forming the north-east corner of the Garden Court development, was a conventional peristyle house, the House of the Muses.

The significance of the Ostian apartment is that it forms a specific housing type recognised by ancient Latin authors, and yet distinct from the atrium or peristyle house. Even within the mainstream tradition of Roman housing there was room for a number of different types of house. It was a specifically urban design and not amenable to use in the rural environment as was the peristyle type.

Medianum-style apartments have not been recognised outside Ostia and Rome. There are, for example, many cities in Roman Africa where substantial areas of urban housing have been uncovered, but there are few signs of the medianum. Perhaps African cities never achieved the high land values that are one of the conditions for high density living. African tastes, and a hot climate, may also have militated against the close atmosphere of the medianum.

2. Shops and taverns

Another type of urban house with well-defined architectural characteristics was the shop, or tavern/bar. It may be considered that it is wrong to classify a shop as a house, but this would be a mistake. Aristocratic houses were as much a place for business as a residence, as we have seen, and shops were as much residences as businesses. Sometimes shops formed part of a larger business, like our chain stores or franchises. Sometimes the shopkeeper had a separate house in another quarter, or was merely the counter operator for an absentee owner. However, archaeology suggests that a large proportion of shopkeepers lived on the premises.

The most common form of Roman shop was a two-room apartment. The front room on the street was of course the shop itself, which was often provided with a stone counter in the main façade of the building or inside the shop itself (Fig. 14). Sometimes business was conducted outside from a permanent stone, or temporary wooden, street-side counter. Shops without counters might have been like a walk-in display case, as in many Middle-Eastern bazaars.

Behind, or above, the shop itself was the second room of the apartment, which functioned as living quarters, stores, or a workshop, or all three. Often potential domestic hearths are found here alongside industrial debris. The shopkeeper, and his family or assistants, could curl up on rough mattresses anywhere on the premises. At Pompeii there is sometimes archaeological evidence of the bed's location in the form of a 'bed niche'. This consisted of a shallow cut into the walls around the corner of a room. The dimensions of the object pushed into this recess, are just the size for a bed or couch.

It was common throughout the Roman world for aristocrats to establish shops flanking the entrance to their rich houses. Such shops were almost certainly owned by the aristocrat and leased out. In late antiquity it became common to build a line of shops along every main street, where they were fronted by colonnades. The building of such colonnaded streets may have become a social convention, creating an active city centre and encouraging commerce. For the builders of large public buildings, and private house owners, one suspects that the shops also formed a useful way of defraying construction costs with rent payments.

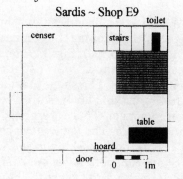

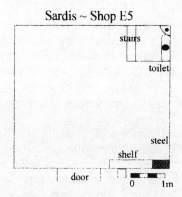

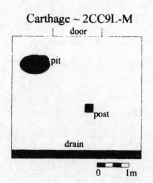

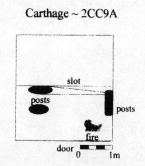

14. Schematic plans of late antique shops at Carthage and Sardis.

A good example of Roman shops, to which discussion will return, is the line of 32 that fronted the gymnasium and synagogue at Sardis in the early seventh century AD (Fig. 14, Plate 7).[7] Much of the furniture and merchandise in the shops was caught in a fire and preserved for modern archaeologists. The shops included a wide range of industries: eight dying or fulling establishments, three bars, three glass makers, a locksmith and an ironmonger. There were also five shops which had no distinguishing signs of trade. They may have been purely residential accommodation, or offices for those working in service industries, such as scribes or notaries.

Shops could often form part of larger commercial premises. Many cities had formal market places. These consisted of courtyards surrounded by shops, as at Wroxeter in Britain, or Thuburbo Maius in Tunisia.[8] It is perhaps more dangerous to ascribe a residential function to such complexes. The right to use them may have been rotated through the local businesses, or the shops may have been purely commercial.

Shops may also have been the fronts for larger residential property. Hermansen[9] identifies a small bar on the Via delle Corporazioni at Ostia (2.6.5) which had a staircase to an upper-floor medianum apartment. In a similar fashion, successful businessmen may have maintained shops attached to their rich houses. Fullers and bakers in particular might have large artisanal and residential premises, with different rooms devoted to different aspects of their trade. The smell of baking, or the noxious substances used in dying, would have pervaded the whole house and neighbourhood.

Shops are very important for a balanced picture of housing in the Roman world. They are the smallest easily distinguishable residential units, and as such provide important evidence for the range and scale of housing. It is also important to remember that shop keepers were not necessarily poor. Bars in Ostia commonly had mosaic floors, pictures and inscriptions, which afforded the opportunity of an additional sales pitch (see the Caupona of Alexander Felix, which is discussed in Chapter 4).[10]

Shops were the smallest recognisable residential unit, but they were not the bottom of the housing ladder. In many large Roman cities it was common to find people sleeping in the streets or under the street porticoes. A large solidly built masonry or brick shop, with lighting and water, could also provide a better residence than the rough lean-to of a rural estate worker.

3. Other urban house forms

Apart from the aristocratic house, the apartment block, and the shop, there were a large number of other kinds of urban house which cannot be easily classified. The extensive published plans of many classical cities show smaller houses with irregular layouts organised around a courtyard or corridor. Unfortunately they have not attracted as much attention as the larger properties, because they rarely have mosaics or fine architecture.

The existing remains are usually the result of centuries of adaptation rather than constructions of a single period. Their original appearance cannot be reconstructed and it is therefore problematic to consider their architecture as deriving from any uniform tradition. Nevertheless, it is important to illustrate the full diversity of Roman house forms by presenting a few better known or better published examples.

The House of the Prince of Naples, at Pompeii, is an interesting example of a non-standard house which has been well documented.[11] It serves to demonstrate that even at Pompeii there were many houses that did not follow the idealised atrium/peristyle model. The house had a short fauces leading to a small but regular atrium. The atrium was the only standard element of the house. The area to the rear of the atrium was divided into two, destroying the usual axial symmetry of fauces, atrium, and centralised tablinum. The reception room is the left-hand room of the pair, while the right-hand room is a kitchen. The left room was completely open to the atrium and thus may be identified as the tablinum. Both rooms had rear rooms. The left-hand room, behind the tablinum, was a cubiculum, while the room to the right, behind the kitchen, could have been the larder.

A door from the left-hand side of the atrium led to a communicating space in the form of a portico. The portico looked over a garden area at the rear of the house. Windows from the tablinum and the rear cubiculum also overlooked the garden. Two rooms opened onto the portico. The furthest room from the atrium was the dining room/reception room with a large 2 m wide doorway. The adjacent room was a plainly decorated store room or service room, one corner of which was occupied by an external stair from the street, leading to the separate upper floor apartment.

A small room had been constructed within the portico. This is a common feature in Pompeii. It is tempting to see it as a later addition making space in a cramped position when expansion was necessary. However, in this particular case, the decoration of the whole house is of a single scheme, and the main door to the triclinium respects the front of the room in the portico. Indeed the triclinium door is also aligned to an intercolumniation of the portico.

At 225 m² the House of the Prince of Naples is in the third quartile of Wallace-Hadrill's sample of Pompeian houses, and close to the average property area of 271 m².[12] It is thus not particularly small, and the high style decor in the reception rooms suggests that its owner was not of the poorest class. Its design incorporates all the elements of the traditional aristocratic house. Tablinum, atrium and triclinium are all recognisable, though only the atrium had the standard form. The house plot is 15 x 15 m square, which would surely have been large enough to create a more standard arrangement. At the very least the tablinum could have been centred on the fauces atrium axis. It would seem that the house was the product of an original architect or owner.

Another major class of more modest housing has been identified through excavation in Pompeii during the 1990s. Nappo[13] has demonstrated the existence in Regio 1 of several extensive but simple houses, with central courts and large rear gardens, which were built at the end of the third century BC. He defines four types, of which two clearly had a court rather than an atrium, one had a small Greek-style 'pastas' yard with a pool. A fourth type had a central court of similar proportion to an atrium, but without an impluvium. More detailed stratigraphic evidence would be desirable to demonstrate that, in the examples he gives, the impluvium was definitively a later construction. Of the two types with central court, one had a tablinum, and the other features a triclinium. The tablinum can be identified by its characteristic broad entrance, and the triclinium by the niches for couches.

These house types are extremely important. They demonstrate the existence in Pompeii of houses which do not use either atrium or peristyle, and yet do have traditional reception facilities, whether they be tablinum or triclinium. In the case of the tablinum they would seem to demonstrate that it was not necessary for it to be preceded by an atrium, although without an atrium the precise identification of a tablinum may be questioned.

Many houses had a much more irregular layout, which does not allow easy identification of room function or the social class of the owner.

A full insula (city block) of housing is preserved in the centre of the city of Utica, the ancient rival of Carthage. At the centre was a typical peristyle house, the House of the Cascade, while there were three smaller peristyle houses in the adjacent plots. Towards one end of the insula there was a very different kind of house known only as 'Lot 11' (Fig. 15).[14] This was organised around a 13 x 1.5 m corridor. The threshold block at the entrance to the corridor indicates that it had a locked door, forming a single house, or group of apartments. At the far end of the corridor was a small 2.5 x 3.5 m yard containing a well or cistern. An overflow, or collection pipe, led from the cistern along the corridor to the street. It is most probable that this flagged cistern court was not roofed and formed a light well for the surrounding rooms.

At the street frontage there were two or three shops. Doorways from the larger shop to the left of the corridor led all the way back to the central court, suggesting that this belonged to the principal owner of the building. There may have been a separate four-room apartment off a corner of the court. A door led to a square stone-flagged vestibule. This gave access to an isolated store room and a suite of three adjoining spaces. The vestibule led to the central space. On one side of this was the largest space, separated from it by a large opening, which suggests the room was a triclinium or reception room. On the other side of the central area a

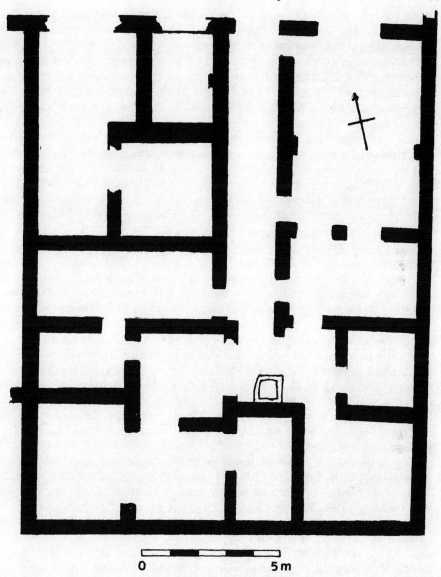

15. 'Lot 11', Utica, Tunisia.

regular doorway led to the third space in the suite, which could have been a cubiculum.

It is not possible to establish the structural history of the building, but fragmentary pavements and finds sealed beneath them suggest that the room arrangement dated to the first century AD when the insula was first planned. The building occupied one of twelve regular 'lots' within the insula, which included five peristyle houses and other forms. It indicates, as does similarly located housing at Pompeii, Ostia and elsewhere, that the Romans mixed housing of all classes.

The House of the Painted Vaults at Ostia[15] followed the same design principle as Lot 11 at Utica. It was built in the early second century AD, on the other side of the street to the House of the Graffito described at the beginning of this chapter. Ten rooms were divided five each side of a central corridor. There were external doors at each end of the central corridor, but the west range which faced a main street also contained a vestibule with a major entranceway. This was flanked to the south by the best decorated room in the house, which was probably the main reception room. A geometric black and white mosaic is flanked to the south by a plain panel which probably marked the location of the dining couch. Four other rooms, two on each side of the corridor, had mosaic floors, while the east range also contained a kitchen area. At the north end of the east range a room with yet another external door held a stair to upper-storey apartments.

The profusion of external doorways makes it difficult to determine how many apartments existed on the ground floor. The exterior door to the stair certainly suggests separate properties upstairs. It is however clear from the ground plan that the House of the Painted Vaults lacked the medianum normally regarded as characteristic of Ostian apartments.

On the northern edge of the hill city of Djemila (Arabic for beautiful), adjacent to the baths of the Capitolium, lay a small house known as the House of the Brick Walls,[16] with a good view down towards the city walls. Its seemingly unremarkable name results from the fact that almost every building in the city was built of stone. The house in question occupied the north half of a group of two similar properties, and consisted of only five ground-floor rooms.

The external walls of the house were of the normal *opus africanum* masonry style, which consisted of regularly spaced columns of upright stone blocks with small-stone masonry between them. Only the internal walls were of brick. The main entrance to the property led straight into its largest room, 4 x 6 m in plan. Here there was a very solid, brick and stone-treaded, staircase to an upper storey, which may have formed a separate property. This is suggested by the fact that there was only one narrow doorway out of the stairwell, and it was provided with a door.

The doorway led into a room with mosaic covering two-thirds of its area. The mosaic was a coarse imitation of a marble floor such as one would find in the reception room of the richest late antique houses. A single column on the edge of the mosaic suggests that the mosaic was roofed over but that the remaining third of the room was another light well. Crossing the light well one reached the remaining three, somewhat nondescript rooms of the house or apartment.

Here we have a small apartment house, perhaps the ground floor of an

Ostian-style apartment dwelling. However, even in this restricted space
the owner found the resources for a mosaic and a one-column 'portico'.
Despite the fact that the room with mosaic was entered direct from the
'stairwell', there can be little doubt that it was a reception room, the decor
of which was by no means inferior. The mosaic cannot be securely dated,
but its coarse style and the brick walls of the room would well fit the fourth
or fifth century AD.

Despite the irregularity of these houses there were two particular
architectural characteristics which they had in common. They all incorporated an internal court, and they all had a main reception room. Lot 11 at
Utica and the House of the Painted Vaults at Ostia were both organised
around a corridor. Lot 11 also had a small courtyard, as did the House of
the Brick Walls at Djemila. The reception room of the House of the Brick
Walls had a small mosaic, and the reception room in the House of the
Painted Vaults was also recognisable from its mosaic.

A wide range of other house types with irregular courts or corridors, and
reception rooms with rough mosaics, stone flagging, or some other architectural embellishment could be added, and some will be discussed in
other parts of this book. The need for a central yard and a more ornate
reception room indicate how these two elements of the peristyle tradition
were regarded as the most important attributes of a house. These houses
show how these particular spaces were interpreted when restrictions of
space, or finance, made the full realisation of the 'ideal' peristyle type
impossible.

4. Housing in the urban context

The previous sections have concentrated on housing from major classical
cities. These cities ranged from the capital to a provincial centre such as
Djemila. They can all be classed as 'planned' cities.[17] Planning does not
necessarily mean that they all had regular right-angle, or Hippodamian,
street grids. Rather it means that space in the urban layout had been
allocated for large public buildings. The main streets were usually provided with colonnades. Though the topography of the hill on which Djemila
is situated gives the city a rather irregular form, the major axes are clear
within the street plan. Within the contours of the hill the majority of
buildings are located within densely built rectangular blocks.

This can be contrasted with 'unplanned' development, where the location of buildings was controlled more by individual owners than by the city
authorities, or where the town councils did not adopt any particular
guidelines for patterns of land use. In a planned city the land available to
any particular owner was predetermined and restricted. Building regulations[18] were less of a problem than the need to take account of
infrastructure and adjacent properties. Infrastructure can be availability
of piped water, or the need for shops to be built on the street.

The influence of adjacent buildings on house design is best illustrated by the House of the Ass at Djemila.[19] The house was extended around the back of a temple in the late antique period. An apsidal reception was built on one side of the temple, and a bath suite on the other. There being no room for a garden, a nymphaeum with three niches was built within the reception room itself, up against the back of the temple sanctuary. To enter the reception room a 4 m wide corridor had to be built from the street, squeezing between the original house and the temple. The insertion of a nymphaeum into such a restricted space illustrates its importance for the 'ideal' type of reception room.

Whenever urban land values rise housing responds, either by rising in height, as at Ostia, or by squeezing into all remaining free space – a process known to modern planners as 'infill' and 'town cramming'.

5. Towns in the north-west provinces

Roman towns in the north-western provinces are often known only from fragmentary remains. The majority now lie beneath modern towns, where only partial plans of buildings are recovered during rescue excavations. Some of the most important western towns, such as Trier or London, may have been as densely inhabited as cities in North Africa, Italy, or the eastern provinces. Here, as has been demonstrated, there was a great density of housing laid out in regular rectangular blocks. Urban land was at a premium and house designs were compressed into any available space.

Near-complete plans of some towns in the north-western provinces have been recovered, usually through aerial photography. They have often produced a different picture to Mediterranean cities. Buildings are often distributed more sparsely amongst the city blocks. Large open spaces result, which have been interpreted as agricultural land, associated with farm buildings within the urban circuit.

Of course the inhabitants of Pompeii also worked on what may be described as 'agricultural' pursuits, most notably at the Garden of the Fugitives and the House of Octavius Quartio.[20] However, these agricultural plots were contained within regular urban garden or 'hortus' plots. In north-western towns the areas were extensive enough to be considered as open fields, and the associated buildings spread out, rather than restricting themselves to a compact urban form.

Silchester,[21] tribal capital of the Atrebati in southern Britain, is a good example of such urbanism. Only two blocks immediately to the west of the forum showed the slightest signs of being completely built up. The vast majority of the insulae had large areas of open space. A large number of buildings lay on alignments that did not relate to the main street grid. An earlier street grid on a different alignment has been proposed but it is unlikely that any urban grid could explain all the variations in alignment.

Amongst the buildings at Silchester it is still possible to identify a number of large houses with central courts and peristyles, but the most regular urbanism was found along the main street into the town from the west. From the west gate to the centre of the town this street was lined almost continuously with 'strip properties'.

The 'strip' building has been found in most towns of the north-western provinces, and is sufficiently defined to be recognised as a specific type of urban house. The house was long and narrow with one narrow end fronting the street. The street frontage consisted of a shop or public area, behind this was a living area, and behind this again was a yard or workshop. The shop can sometimes be identified by its sales goods, or evidence of artisanal activity. The living area can be more difficult to identify with absolute certainty, but normally presents the appearance of domestic arrangements. This might include domestic hearths or occupational deposits. The yard at the rear can often be easily linked with a workshop on the basis of a smithing hearth, a large oven, or other 'industrial' feature.

A good example of his kind of development from north-eastern France is at Bliesbruch,[22] where a long street fronted by many such properties has been subjected to several years of excavation.

The growth of such towns and housing can also be closely followed at Besançon.[23] From around 120 BC to AD 1 the site in question was covered by a number of two-room wooden houses, following the orientation of the road through the area. By AD 15 many of them had masonry foundations. Soon after, but still before AD 50, a full urban fabric had developed with a street portico, a courtyard house, and narrow alleys between the smaller house/shop frontages. The resulting development was similar to the (admittedly wooden-built) dense line of shops recorded in Britain at Verulamium, before the Boudiccan destruction of AD 60.[24]

The strip housing of the north-western provinces is a very interesting architectural form. It might be thought to have originated in pre-Roman urban settlements of the *oppidum* type. Oppida such as Bibracte, discussed in the previous chapter, were the true towns of the pre-Roman period, with a dense occupation of rectangular buildings. The strip house is nevertheless characteristic of the Roman period. To that extent it should be regarded as 'Roman' housing – that is, housing of the Roman period, rather than housing that can be linked with classical culture per se. Subsequent sections of this chapter will examine housing in the eastern provinces which is equally Roman by date, but not apparently Roman by culture.

Such towns approach the limit of the definition of urban form. A settlement, even if enclosed with a city wall, that included open fields and farms cannot readily be accepted as urban. Admittedly towns such as Silchester were provided with a wide range of public buildings, including forum, basilica and public baths. It is likely that, at least for part of the

Roman period, such towns had a true urban or market economy, operating as a central place for the surrounding area. On the other hand, from the point of view of domestic architecture the housing often had more in common with rural housing than compact urban dwellings.

6. Trade and industry in Town and Country

It is traditionally assumed that Roman aristocrats did not indulge in trade. Excavations like that at Sette Finestre,[25] where a rich villa can be closely linked to pottery production and long distance wine trade, have largely dispelled this notion, but the study of Roman domestic architecture still suffers from this prejudice. The point has been made before in this work but deserves to be stressed again at this juncture. No house functioned purely as a residence and there were few if any purely commercial buildings in the Roman world. This has several implications for the debate of urban as against rural houses.

A rich house of the Pompeian type is almost always seen as a rich habitation, in which its business role is secondary.[26] A poor 'strip' building is seen as 'artisanal' with the owners fighting to create enough domestic space to raise a family. This is a false dichotomy. For householders at both ends of the social spectrum business was inseparable from family life. It is therefore wrong to interpret any house as rich or poor because it would appear to have more or less of a commercial function. Senators may have claimed an independence from trade, but in practice one suspects that the attraction of an increased income was enough to make even them dirty their hands.

For the same reason it is also false to distinguish a house as urban or rural on the basis of its 'artisanal' function. Agriculture, and some degree of artisanal pursuit, say smithing or baking, took place in a wide spectrum of urban and rural properties. The business role of a politician was as much required from the village elder as the urban elite.

A rich urban house, as against a rural village 'hut', does certainly represent a social distinction. The picture of a Roman aristocrat as a landowner with no interest in either agricultural work or trade is a myth projected by Roman literature. It may even be true to say that the majority of Roman literature, with a few notable exceptions, was written by those aristocrats who were the least likely to 'dirty their hands' and thus had every interest in perpetuating the traditional myth.[27]

Exposing this error helps to clear the air of the debate about urban and rural lifestyles as this work moves on to consider the houses of the Roman countryside. Despite many archaeologists' attempts to distinguish between urban and rural housing, there was but one difference – space. It was lack of space, owned or occupied, that generally restricted the architecture of the urban house. Functionally there was little difference between town and country. Both urban and rural houses had an economic function. If the owner had sufficient status then a larger proportion of his house might be devoted to leisure, or would be richly decorated. The greater the wealth or status of the owner, the more resources he had to devote to leisure, and the more need he had to entertain influential guests.

7. Villages

By villages I will understand small clusters of houses that would normally be thought of as forming a community, and yet which have no major Roman public buildings, especially a forum which would indicate formal municipal status.

There will be an overlap between villages and small towns. Villages, like towns, can be planned or unplanned. They may have grown according to a premeditated conception, or in a more organic fashion, whereby, following population growth and migration, further houses were added as infill. If a village has a dense clustering of buildings it may be that the houses take on the compact forms of urban houses. This classification is not based on a strictly theoretical approach, but that would require a considerable depth of analysis and this work is concerned with houses more than with urban form.

It will be convenient to begin with some villages of the eastern Mediterranean.

8. Syrian villages

In the previous chapter allusion was made to the villages of the limestone plateau between Antioch and Apamea. Work in this area in the early part of this century, by Butler[28] and later by Tchalenko,[29] discovered a large number of village houses preserved to a height of two storeys. This house type was further recorded by Butler throughout much of Syria and especially in the stony Hauran desert on the border between modern Syria and Jordan. The preservation of all the buildings was little short of amazing, with buildings complete up to their rafters and boundary walls still at their original height. Since the beginning of the century many of the sites have deteriorated, but there are still buildings whose preservation can be absolutely startling.

Dar Kita[30] was a typical settlement, of about twelve houses (Fig. 16). There was no clear plan to the village, which was organised around a number of open yards. Many of the buildings had dated inscriptions posted above their main entrance. The earliest was of AD 295/6, ten others date to the fifth century AD, and one from a church was of the sixth century AD. Two houses, 3 and 4, had peristyle courtyards, but the majority consisted of single ranges of 5 x 5 m square rooms fronted by a portico.

This was the characteristic house form of the area. The width of the room was determined by the limited length of the rare wooden beams that

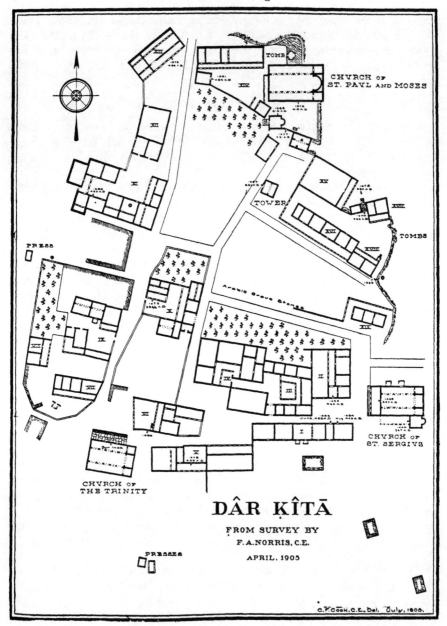

16. Village of Dar Kita, Syria.

could be used to support a roof. Usually each square room was spanned by a single arch, so that the rafters needed to be 5 m in length, or half the dimensions of the room. The walls were built of dressed stone blocks. The villagers were skilled masons who often added mouldings to windows, and inscriptions or symbols over doorways.

The majority of the square rooms did not interconnect. This makes it very difficult to tell whether a single long range of six rooms, such as Building 16 at Dar Kita, represents a number of apartments, or shops.

At Dalloza[31] in northern Syria a single house occupied an area of 20 x 25 m. The front half of the house was taken up by a walled yard, with two two-storey towers, one in each corner. They may have been watch towers. Exterior windows were small, but not noticeably defensive in nature. At the rear of the yard was a two-storey portico in front of the main dwelling. On each floor were two large 10 x 10 m rooms, and a narrower 5 m wide room which could have been roofed in a single span. Behind these rooms was a long covered storage area across the back of the house. The room contained a cistern.

The house at Dalloza is not definitely datable, but is assumed to be fifth-century. It is chiefly remarkable for its fine preservation and architectural detail. Next to each ground-floor door was a small niche that may have contained a water jar, or an oil lamp. The lamp was effectively the light switch to be used for lighting the main lamps of the room; a lamp was found in a similar niche at the House of Bronzes at Sardis.[32] Water jugs were found in similar niches at Medinet Habu, where excavators assumed that they reflected the Middle Eastern tradition of hospitality to visitors.[33]

Another important single house is recorded from Il Medjdel in southern Syria (Fig. 17).[34] It had a single large square room on the ground floor. The rear wall consisted of an arch over a low wall topped by seven stone basins. Beyond this arch was a narrow rear space. It is assumed that this ground-floor room was a stable, but it is also comparable to many subdivided houses of the late antique period (as described in the final section of this chapter). The upper-floor main room was subdivided into four. Large arches joined three of the four spaces, leaving one small 2 x 2 m space walled off. One of the arches contained an inscription of AD 431 mentioning a *triclinos*. A similar inscription was found at Umm Il Kutten.[35]

The housing of the Syrian villages is a very specific local form of architecture found over a very wide area, like the 'strip' housing of the north-western provinces. It is tempting to seek antecedents in local housing of the Hellenistic period, but the remains all date to late antiquity. Few sites have been excavated with modern techniques. At Dehes, in northern Syria, excavation seems to confirm the strong fifth-century AD expansion which led to the construction of many of the buildings.[36] Sondages at Umm Il Jimal, in the southern Syrian desert, provided inconclusive dating to the fifth century AD.[37] Field surveys have relied on styles of masonry and inscriptional evidence.[38]

There can be little doubt that the larger Syrian houses were apartment

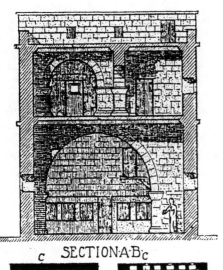

SECTION·A·B·

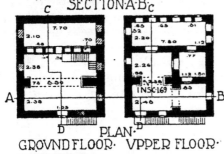

PLAN·
GROVND FLOOR· VPPER FLOOR·

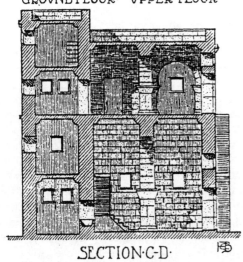

SECTION·C-D·

MEDJDEL·
HOVSE: ⌂ DATE: 431·A·D·

17. House at Il Medjdel,
Syria: plan and elevation.

blocks. This is suggested by the lack of doorways between the rooms, and the use of external rather than internal staircases. The intercommunicating rooms of the single houses at Dalloza and Il Medjdel confirm this. It is interesting to compare this with mainstream Roman traditions. The inscriptions from Umm Il Kutten and Il Medjdel mentioning triclinoi, indicate that the owners identified room functions within the classical tradition. The triclinos at Il Medjdel was on the upper floor, a piano nobile. This vertical orientation of the house was entirely the opposite to the development of apartment housing at Ostia and Rome. There were multi-storey apartments on the Italian sites, but the prime extension of Italian housing apartment or peristyle house was on the horizontal plane. The emphasis in Syria was on the vertical plane.

Having emphasised the differences between the Syrian apartment and the classical Roman house, it should however be noted that there was significant contact between the two traditions, particularly in southern Syria in the Hauran. The major cities of this area include Bosra and Umm Il Jimal.[39] Both of these sites, as indeed at Dar Kita, show evidence of peristyle houses which included the local tradition of large square rooms with a central arch. Bosra in particular was an important city and should be inscribed amongst the ranks of Mediterranean-style urban centres with full classical architecture and public buildings. The so-called 'palace' at Bosra had a ground floor of rooms reminiscent of much of the village housing described above though organised around a true peristyle.[40] On the upper floor there was a triconch reception room (Fig. 18, Plate 8): a piano nobile as at Il Medjdel, but with a fashionable Roman aristocratic form.

In northern Syria at Daphne or Apamea, on the other hand, there is no sign of this kind of 'village' housing, or a marriage of classical and rural domestic architecture.

The Syrian villages were not merely a 'rural' architecture in the sense of being limited to villages, or in the sense of being a 'peasant' vernacular. The high standard of construction, and the widespread nature of the evidence in small communities, speaks of a rural people who had a high degree of technical skill, and a considerable degree of agricultural wealth. Inscriptions from houses often mentioned architects.[41] It would seem best to accept that the buildings arose out of a ready availability of suitable stone (in contrast to a lack of wood), and an encouraging climate of local economic prosperity during late antiquity.

The Syrian apartment house emerged from a rural tradition, in contrast to the Ostian apartment which developed from the need to house a growing population in a limited urban space. Nowadays apartments are regarded as an urban phenomenon, but the Syrian evidence shows that this need not always have been the case.

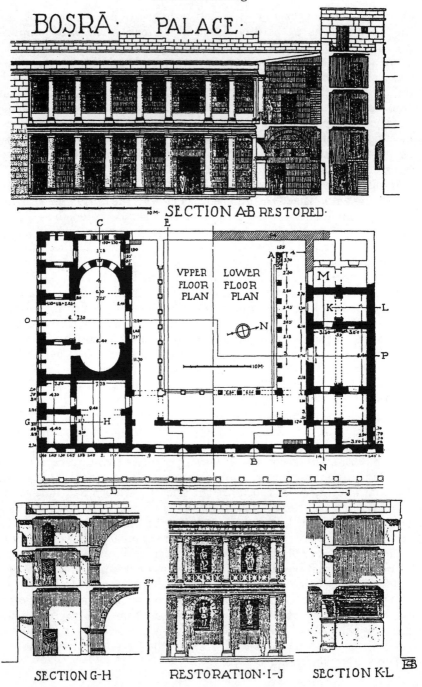

18. 'Palace' at Bosra, Syria: plan and elevation.

9. Egyptian housing

Egypt was another eastern province with a very strong local architectural tradition. It has the advantage that it preserves an extraordinary wealth of documents in the form of papyri. Unlike most of classical literature, these document everyday life at all levels of society. Even the acts of the illiterate were recorded by scribes. Amongst this huge documentation, sales, leases and conveyances of houses are commonly found.

Unfortunately whilst documentation is available in abundance, archaeological evidence is not. Early investigators were more concerned with finding papyri than buildings. The only site to produce both an extensive collection of papyri, and an extensive record of physical remains, is Karanis.

Karanis[42] was a village in the Fayum basin, some 300 km south of the Mediterranean coast. Tax registers suggest it had about 5,000 inhabitants. The streets were 3-5 m wide and formed irregular blocks. A large number of houses have been excavated; the vast majority dated from the first to the fifth century AD.

Houses (Fig. 19, Plate 9) were two or more storeys high, built of mudbrick with wooden beams for door and window frames. Stone, or fired brick, was used occasionally at the corners of buildings, or for treads of

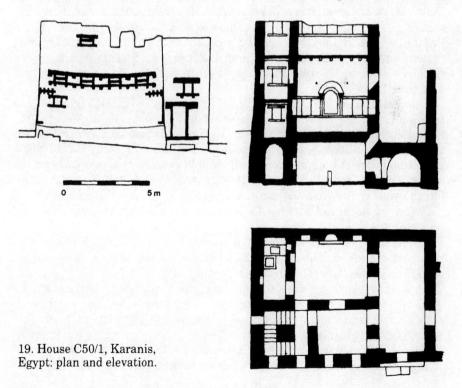

0   5 m

19. House C50/1, Karanis, Egypt: plan and elevation.

stairs to reduce wear. The main rooms were between 3 and 5 m wide.
Apartments opened off a square staircase with a central pillar, in an
arrangement similar to that found at Ostia.

The papyri provide evidence for the organisation of the apartments.[43] At
the bottom of the house there was usually a cellar (*kellios*), upper floors
commonly contained dining rooms (*triclinoi* or *symposioi*), and bedrooms
(*akkubitoi*). The papyri demonstrate that rooms of a single apartment
were commonly distributed across various floors of a building. The papyri
also mention atria (*aithria*). Though our knowledge of the architecture is
limited to a few settlements, it is highly unlikely that the term 'atrium'
refers to the Pompeian form of the room.[44] Instead it is probably applied
to a form of reception room or court.

The main living room, in common with many Syrian houses, often
contained a number of niches, some of which were highly decorated (Plate
10) in stucco, and others were plainer cupboards with shelving. There was
often a small niche near a door for a lamp or a water jug, like the Syrian
houses. Highly decorated niches in the main reception room, or the yard,
have been identified as household shrines.

It might be expected that a very different picture would emerge in the
capital at Alexandria, which was always regarded as culturally separate
from the rest of Egypt, and a major Greek city of the Mediterranean. The
archaeology of Alexandria is only recorded in a fragmentary way, including
some finds of what one would assume were fine domestic mosaics of the
Roman period. It may however be significant that the only substantial
excavation of Roman period housing has uncovered remains that were
closer in style to Karanis, or Syria, than to peristyle housing or Ostian
apartments.

A corridor, or rather a narrow yard, 18 m long by 2.5 m wide, gave access
to fifteen separate rooms, each approximately 3 x 5 m in plan.[45] At the far
end of the yard was the typical rectangular staircase with central pillar.
One of the smaller rooms on the south side of the yard may have been a
reception room. It had an irregular floor of broken marble, and a fragment
of semicircular marble dining-table (sigma table) was found in the room.
On the wall of the yard there was a fresco showing the Virgin and Child.
This might be a comparable location to the shrines in some Karanis
houses.

Parts of three other similar apartment blocks were found adjacent to
that just described. The date of the houses is uncertain, but pottery from
occupational levels was of the sixth century AD.

The excavators of Karanis also recorded a smaller settlement at
Soknopaiou Nesos[46] with a similar style of housing; otherwise our knowledge of the archaeology is confined to the re-use of courts of pharaonic
temples during late antiquity.[47]

Although there was no direct connection with the Syrian tradition of
village housing, there are a number of remarkable similarities. Egyptian

housing was in mudbrick and Syrian in stone, but both used roughly the same dimensions of room because of the scarcity of wood. Both housing traditions organised apartments vertically with a single apartment stretching over several floors, in contrast to the Ostian tradition under which apartments were organised horizontally on one or two floors. In Syria and Egypt there is little emphasis on central light wells or court-yards, in contrast to the apartments at Ostia and Utica discussed earlier in this chapter. Rooms were not organised around courts. Instead, where there was sufficient space for a yard, apartment blocks formed a uniform frontage to an external court, which consequentially had to be surrounded by an enclosure wall to ensure privacy.

There are two possible sources for this common tradition: a very old Semitic tradition, or the more recent, but still pre-Roman, Hellenistic culture. If it was the latter it would certainly be in strong contrast to the forms preserved in the main Greek settlements such as Olynthus and Delos. The full investigation of this problem is far beyond the scope of this work, and poses very important questions about early Middle Eastern history. The significance for this work is that Syrian and Egyptian houses demonstrate a strong widespread domestic culture in the eastern provinces that differed from Roman aristocratic and, perhaps, from the Hellenistic culture that preceded it.

This eastern tradition provides a good parallel to the dominant Celtic traditions in the western provinces. It serves to emphasise the limits of Romanisation. While a provincial aristocrat could easily find his way around any rich house in the Empire, further down the social scale housing traditions could be radically different. One of the most recent studies on the houses of Roman Egypt concludes that 'it seems unlikely that the poor would have been able to adopt more Romanised house-types'.[48] I do not believe that the Egyptians were unable to adopt classical-style Roman houses. Materials, techniques and skills were all available, especially in the Delta including Alexandria. The terminology used to describe houses was Graeco-Roman and the house types in both Egypt and Syria had a clear *floruit* in the Roman period. They may not have been classical Roman in form, but they were Roman in date and provincial Roman in culture.

10. Individual farms

After considering villages we now shift out attention to individual rural buildings. The 'isolated' farm often consisted of several buildings. Some of these may have been residential, housing workers or other family members, while some may have been of purely agricultural use, such as barns and byres. Often it is not possible to distinguish between agricultural and domestic use. Under these circumstances the next few sections discuss groups of associated buildings that are likely to be under the possession of a single family. Villages contain clusters of several families and often have community institutions – councils, or schools for example. Individual farms do not normally have such buildings or institutions.

Villas such as those described in Chapter 2 are of course individual farms under this definition. In some cases villas may even be held to be the same as villages, with large numbers of estate workers and communal institutions run under the patronage of the estate owner, as at Chiragan, which has already been described. Villas will indeed be referred to under this section, but the main topic is smaller settlements of a non-aristocratic character, that in early studies would have been termed 'native'.

To gain some idea of the range of farms it is convenient to take the area of south-west France, concentrating on the département of L'Hérault, but ranging somewhat wider for convenience. Near the major settlements and along the coast there could be major villas, with multiple large peristyles and extensive yards. The example of Chiragan was given in Chapter 2, and another can be found at St Juan Les Pins.[49] Such grand houses should be seen almost as towns in their own right, with an extensive personnel and equally extensive land holdings. It can be debated whether such estates were held together by tribal loyalties stemming from the Celtic past, or whether they depended on systems of tied tenancy and 'serfdom'. It seems unlikely that the evidence is sufficient to provide an answer. A good idea of the likely early plans of such villas is provided by Le Suveret, St Raphael.[50] The villa, built in the first century AD, consisted of a tetrastyle court surrounded by a single range of rooms. It was set within a long rectangular enclosure, including three or four large outbuildings.

Pre-Roman hill settlements, still occupied in Roman times, are another class of rural settlement. The development of courtyard housing at Bibracte (Mont Beuvray) was discussed in the previous chapter. An example from L'Hérault is the settlement of Villetelle (Ambrussum), where several rectangular houses with stone foundations and central courtyards have been excavated.[51] They date from the early first century AD. The site included fine carved door sills and a small altar, but no signs of mosaics or column drums.

If the reinterpretation of Glanum as a 'native' foundation is correct, it also provides good evidence for the development of housing before the early peristyle houses discussed in Chapter 2. At the centre of the site five small courtyard houses were built in the first half of the first century BC. One, House 12, had a distinctive axial arrangement with a large open-ended room, flanked by two narrower rooms. This disposition closely matches that of the typical provincial peristyle house, though there is no evidence of columns in the yard. House 11 had a square foundation in the centre of the yard, suggesting a peristyle. However, in the other three houses any central court, if such existed, would appear to have been little different in area than the adjoining rooms. This site thus had a combination of classical peristyle houses and those without a yard. The houses were independent and separated by narrow alleys, but the peristyle houses were no bigger than the others. There seems no evidence here that owning a peristyle was an indication of higher status.[52]

An interesting example of a more irregular smallholding is provided by Gouffre les Bouchers, near Nîmes.[53] Built at the end of the first century BC, it appears to have consisted of an irregular courtyard surrounded by a single range of rooms. The wall foundation around the yard could have been the base for a colonnade, except that it had a very irregular form, cutting off one corner of the yard, whilst in turn being cut by irregular divisions in the surrounding portico.

There were no doubt many small establishments like Gouffre des Bouchers throughout the area all through the Roman period, but evidence for them is difficult to find and interpret. Few major excavation campaigns concentrate on less glamorous sites without mosaics and richer finds. Where they are encountered it is during rescue excavations when it is impossible to be sure that the full extent of the building, or the settlement, has been uncovered.

11. 'Celtic' homesteads in Britain

Britain has produced more evidence of the wide range of small settlements that littered the Roman countryside than any other province. Although the balance of publication still leans towards the richer 'villa' sites, it is possible to get a full view of the range of small settlements in the countryside.

Hingley[54] provides an excellent summary of their remains as a counterweight to the study of 'villas'. He argues[55] that round houses of traditional pre-Roman design were the predominant type of house throughout the province in the first two centuries AD. Later in the third or fourth century in the southern half of the country they were often replaced by rectangular buildings. There were many simple rectangular buildings 10-20 m in length, which could be subdivided with partitions to form internal rooms.[56]

Beyond these two simple forms rural housing begins to take on more architectural aspirations. Houses become elongated suites of rooms. Sometimes, as at Frocester Court[57] they were traversed by corridors, sometimes as at Feltwell[58] they were fronted by a verandah. This is where the typology of villas begins to enter the modern archaeological vocabulary. For me the use of the word 'villa' implies the use in the house of some classical Mediterranean feature, particularly opus signinum or mosaic floors. If a verandah has a colonnade and precedes a centralised reception room, then the house may be considered to possess fundamental characteristics of a villa.[59]

There was one type of more isolated farmhouse that had some architectural elaboration and yet was not within the Roman tradition. The aisled house or barn was a large rectangular building subdivided into three

aisles. Hearths indicate that at least some of the buildings were domestic
houses, but other examples had a purely utilitarian function as agricultural storage or for industrial production.

A putative aisled barn at Thruxton was provided with a mosaic naming
several people.[60] If they were the owners of the building the inscription is
given unusual prominence, in two large panels. Each letter was as high as
the busts of seasons in the corner of the room. If the Thruxton house, which
is poorly recorded, is accepted as an aisled barn, it provides evidence for
the overlap between aristocratic and rural architectural traditions in
which particular householders could pick the tradition that suited their
personal tastes, or their purses. The aisled barn is not characteristic of the
pre-Roman Iron Age. Like the 'strip' house of Romano-British towns
discussed earlier, it can be seen as Roman by date, and vernacular to
Britain by its architectural tradition.

D.S. Neal has argued that the Roman villa at Stanwick formed around
an aisled barn to which a regular courtyard house was attached in the
fourth century AD.[61] The barn was the most important suite in the complex,
as it was on the same alignment as the main gate into the front yard. It is
notable that there were three main rooms at the rear of the hall, which
could parallel the normal Roman reception suite and flanking side rooms.
Whatever the interpretation, it provides a similar picture of coexisting
architectural traditions to the round house and villa on the site of Gorhambury, as discussed in the Chapter 2.

Small groups of houses were often gathered in enclosures.[62] The enclosures were often rectangular even though they contained three or four
round houses. There was no uniform sudden conversion from the use of
round to rectangular forms in either housing or enclosure.

In south-west Wales at the settlement of Whitton[63] people continued to
live in a small group of round houses, within an enclosure ditch, until the
second century AD. Between about AD 115 and AD 135 the round houses
were gradually replaced by rectangular buildings with stone foundations
(Fig. 20). By the middle of the third century AD two of the buildings appear
to have been provided with underfloor, hypocaust heating.

Porth Dafarch[64] and Din Lligwy[65] in Anglesey, north-west Wales (Fig.
21), were settlements of the fourth century AD consisting of substantial
stone structures, both round and rectangular. Porth Dafarch was not
surrounded by an enclosure wall, but Din Lligwy was a tightly drawn
nuclear settlement within a rectangular enclosure with a main gatehouse.
At both these North Welsh sites Samian ware pottery was repaired with
rivets, which has been taken an index of scarcity and value. The precise
socio-economic reasons for the repairs are difficult to determine.

Overall the British evidence would seem to indicate a profound symbio-
sis in which different traditions of housing were able to coexist, even
within the same settlement or estate.

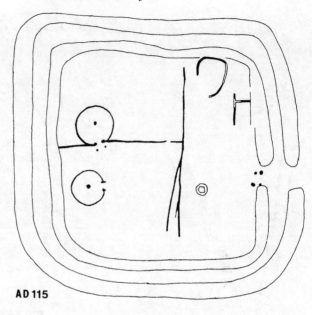

AD 115

20. Whitton farmstead, Britain: Phase 4 AD 95-115 (top); Phase 8 AD 230-280 (bottom).

0   10 m

AD 250

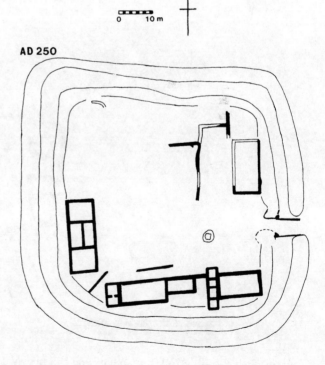

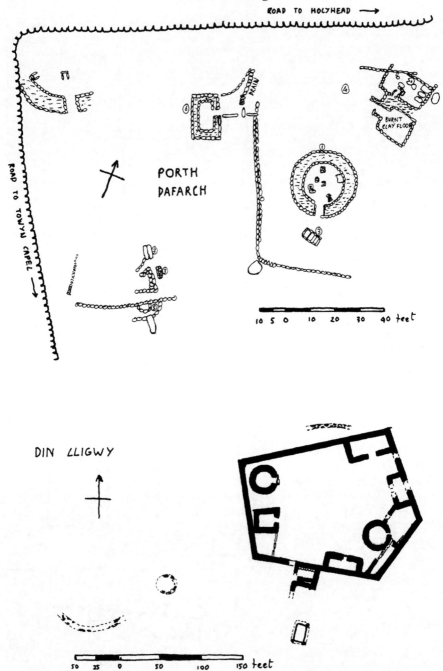

21. Farmsteads at Porth Dafarch (top), and Din Lligwy (bottom), Anglesey, Britain.

12. Fortified farms

One particular form of farm, which can loosely be described as 'fortified', was found in several different provinces and is distinctively Roman.

This type of building is best known from the 'gsur' of the Libyan Valley surveys.[66] Located on the northern fringes of the Sahara, these they were small independent units, sometimes clustered in small settlements, and sometimes consisting of more isolated buildings which exploited the seasonal waters from particular wadis.

The buildings were normally square in plan and 30 x 30 m in area. There was sometimes a small central courtyard with rooms around it, though internal arrangements were not standardised. The plans tended to be centralised rather than orientated on one axis like the housing in the Syrian villages. This more in-turned appearance was related to, or even the result of, the thick 'defensive' outside wall which probably had few windows.

Comparable though larger properties have been found in the southwest of the Iberian peninsula.[67] They share with the Libyan buildings the external 'defensive' wall, but their internal arrangements seem to have been more complex. They were generally larger buildings. This may reflect the richer agriculture of the area, or the exceptionally rich architectural tradition of Roman Spain.

These farms had nothing in common with the tradition of so-called 'fortified villas' which have been identified in African mosaics and in excavations on the Rhine frontier. These villas retain the characteristics of the classical peristyle house, and the fortification is assumed from the presence of corner towers. In many cases the corner towers on villas may have functioned as watch towers. There is virtually no evidence for their upper-storey appearance, apart from mosaic illustrations, and the rest of the villa does not seem to have been provided with any heavy defensive perimeter.

The question remains as to how much defensive capability the African and Hispanic buildings had. None of them could withstand a purposeful attack by a large army, or war band. If the defensive capability was more a functional than a decorative tradition then it must have aided in repelling small raids and bandits. In the case of the fortified villas it is possible that the corner towers served more to keep a watch on the estate than to maintain any real defence, but in Spain and Africa the ability to repel a minor raid was probably useful.

13. 'Factories'

One group of buildings in North Africa might be interpreted as 'factories'. They are isolated structures with a central courtyard and several oil presses. Like the so-called fortified farms they were surrounded by a heavily built dressed stone masonry wall.

It is possible that these buildings were olive oil collection points for the surrounding villages and farms.[68] They show several characteristics of domestic architecture; in particular, the main reception room was often in a location normally associated with houses.[69]

The only such 'factory' to have been excavated in modern times is Nador in Algeria.[70] It consists of a 50 x 50 m building with a central courtyard. A building was first erected on the site in the first century AD. It is likely that this took a similar form to the later structure which was erected on a slightly different alignment at the end of the first century AD. The main façade of this Phase 2 building was a heavy dressed stone wall furnished with a gatehouse flanked by two rectangular towers. Two large circular towers were also present at the corners of the same façade, but no towers were present on other walls. Above the main doorway was an inscription recording that the building lay on the land of M. Cincus Hilarinus, a priest of Augustus. On passing through the entrance a set of seven rooms to the left seem to have formed living quarters, while three rooms to the right were probably domestic stores adjacent to a cistern. A portico ran across the rear of the courtyard. Surrounding it were the workrooms. At the left end of the portico was a store, perhaps a *horreum*, with amphorae storage jars set into the floor. The bases of four were preserved in situ. The main store of produce was to the rear of the portico where a large store room, 12 x 30 m in area, also held storage jars. Four complete vessels were found in situ here. Behind the right-hand end of the portico was a room containing two olive presses.

A number of interpretations are possible from the architecture of this establishment. First, the presence of heavy walls and towers in this type of building has been much remarked upon as an indication of fortifications. However, it is noticeable that the towers do not project away from the main façade of the building, indicating that they would not have been useful for the tactical defence of flanking fire along the wall. Like the 'fortified farms' described earlier, the outer walls may have helped to discourage bandits rather than resist a large force. Indeed as a North African building this may relate to the 'gsur' and the pattern of cross-frontier tribal raiding that was probably common at various times in the Roman period.

Whilst the owner of the building is recorded as a priest of the imperial cult, and therefore a person of some importance, the building was not a peristyle house. It is unlikely that the owner lived in the building, and indeed attempts have been made to identify his house with a potential courtyard villa some 2.5 km to the west.[71] It is more likely that the building was occupied by a bailiff, or tenant. Given this, one might ask why Hilarinus would seek to advertise the building so much, by giving it a grand appearance and putting so much effort into its construction? It may well be that, as in the villages east of Antioch, stone working was in the local blood, and what to us appears a monumental structure, to Hilarinus was a relatively simple construction. The inscription could be taken to

suggest he took pride in the project, but could also be merely an identification of his property. In the latter case the bailiff may have been charged
with gathering in the crops from the estate.

In this second interpretation, favoured by many scholars, such buildings represent central collection and processing points for large estates.
They point out that to be successful olive crops require good networks for
marketing and transportation. Numbers of olive presses tend to be concentrated in one place where they can process the crops from a large area,
increasing income through economies of scale. This is an attractive idea
for Nador as the two store rooms with jars set in the floor could represent
the personal store of the owner/bailiff, with the larger store for the estate
as a whole. Even if this is true, however, Nador only had two presses,
suggesting that production was not on a grand scale (not grand enough to
justify the inscription?). Furthermore, while economies of scale may have
been practised in North Africa, they do not seem to have been practised
east of Antioch where presses were not concentrated at certain establishments, but widespread throughout the area.

A comparison can be made with another North African 'factory' site near
Kasserine.[72] The site is a rectangular building 37 x 53 m in area, built of
dressed stone masonry. Like the farm at Nador, it had living rooms and
commercial presses located at opposite ends of the building, immediately
to the right and left of the main entrance. The living rooms included a
large room similar to a classical-style triclinium. This room had later been
subdivided by a low wall surmounted by stone basins. Such subdivision
was common in late antiquity; both the wall with basins and its location
in the triclinium are typical (Fig. 22, Plate 11).[73] The commercial area
contained four adjacent oil presses. The press room was entered by a long
corridor from a rear entrance to the building. The corridor also ran next to
the largest room in the building which may have been a storage area as at
Nador. Opposite the entrance to the building was a long range of two
narrow rooms or galleries. These presumably also formed part of the more
commercial part of the structure.

The interest of sites such as those at Nador and Kasserine is that they
represent buildings with an avowedly commercial design. It may be
doubted whether they should truly be called 'factories', but their living
quarters did not make allowances for the expected classical villa style of
architecture. As we have seen at Nador, they most probably formed the
local 'area office' of some large villa-based estate, and represent more
'commercial' designs than regular domestic buildings, apart from shops.
For this reason a designation as 'factories' does not seem too far off the
mark.

There are other forms of building which are part industrial, part
domestic. They include potters' quarters, quarrymen's habitations and
other settlements. For quarrymen's quarters there are two principal sites
of interest, Mons Porphyritus and Chemtou.

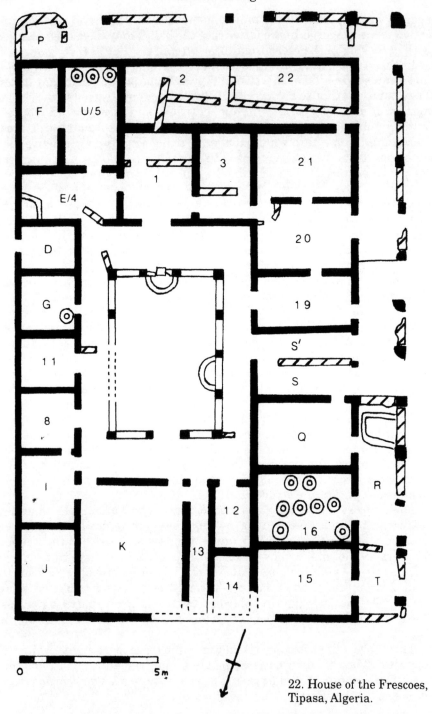

22. House of the Frescoes,
Tipasa, Algeria.

In the case of potters' quarters, there is some information available from Arezzo and La Graufesenque, both vital centres of the Empire-wide trade in red-slipped table ware. At both sites there are some rough habitations close to the kilns themselves. Potters in these leading centres did not have large houses or mosaics. Their huts, or rather perhaps those of the workers who assisted the master potters, consisted of no more than a few rooms.

Potters were not generally wealthy people, and we know that their products did not fetch high prices. Despite the location of major potters' quarters outside town, kilns have been discovered in large, rich urban houses. Their discovery has often been the occasion for the archaeologist to propose a run-down district, but there have also been finds of other unsavoury industrial pursuits in urban housing, such as fullers' establishments, which used animal dung and other strong products. The main reason groups of potters left town was to find a good supply of clay and wood for fuel, rather than any presumption against such occupations in an urban environment.

We have already had occasion to mention how often farms have been identified inside Roman towns in peristyle houses. These indicate that the Romans did not make a clear distinction between 'good' and 'bad' neighbourhoods, or between urban and rural pursuits. There are numerous complaints in Roman literature about bad neighbours, but these only demonstrate how few proscriptions there were in this domain.[74]

14. Economics and the Roman house

The previous sections have described a number of different forms of houses involved in economic activity. Traditionally peristyle houses such as those at Pompeii or rich villas were assumed to have had little or no economic function, and to have been more like 'pleasure palaces' for the rich. From the 1960s, following Columella (*On Agriculture* 1.6.1), it became customary to refer to the *pars urbana* and the *pars rustica*. The 'urban' part of the villa was the fine architecture of the aristocratic residence, while the 'rustic' was the part containing 'agricultural' or 'artisanal' rooms.[75] Such an easy distinction can no longer be upheld. Studies of the finds at Pompeii indicate that tools, such as shovels, are found through every room in the house. Many rooms were given over to economic pursuits, such as storage of commercial products. Gardens were as often for commercial, or cottage, production of vines and vegetables, as they were for flowers and statues.[76]

In modern times many people have a clear separation of home and work, but this did not exist in the ancient world. The leading citizens of the Roman state used their town houses as business venues, holding meetings and running their finances from home. Lesser aristocrats used their houses for business and for commerce, supporting commercial premises that they owned in the neighbourhood. Almost every villa formed the centre of extensive agricultural estates, giving the landowner responsibility for resolving the affairs of tenants and marketing the produce.

The distinction between the rich houses considered in the last chapter and those considered here is one of degree, rather than of kind. The lower down the social scale people were, the less money they would have to spend on luxury goods or decor, and the more they would have to run their economic activity out of a small number of rooms. It is not the devotion of space to economic activity that is a surprise, for this was a necessity in order to live. It is more remarkable that, despite their lack of cash, most inhabitants of the Roman world put so much emphasis on the provision of as rich and traditional a reception room as they could afford.

15. Romanisation outside the aristocracy

It may seem impossible, and indeed undesirable, to generalise from the wide variety of housing in the provinces of the Roman Empire. Each province had a different cultural background, different languages, and a history guided by different strong personalities. On the other hand, the whole purpose of a historian is to build a broad synthesis. Theory moves forward by producing synthesis and hypothesis which can in turn be tested by others re-examining the evidence.

Chapter 2 argued for a single empire-wide aristocratic culture. This chapter, by looking at rural housing, has emphasised the diversity of housing traditions in the Empire. How do these two approaches interact?

The first point to note is that village housing shows some signs of adopting the characteristics associated with the aristocratic peristyle tradition. In Britain an 'aisled barn' at Thruxton was given a mosaic floor, and small farm buildings at Whitton were given hypocausts. In remote Syrian villages houses had porticoes, and their main reception rooms were called triclinoi. The latter rooms may not have resembled Roman triclinia either in terms of furnishings or precise function, but the use of the term seems to indicate a desire to identify with the elite governing class, or with 'acceptable' cultural norms.

There were clear indications that the provincial elite adopted the domestic behaviour of the Roman upper class. It is perhaps possible to argue that the Gallic aristocrat whose villa had a three-couch dining room (evidenced from its mosaic settings) and a private baths was simply adopting the architecture of the Roman elite without the behaviour, but the assumption must be that the presence of such a room demonstrates use unless proven otherwise. It seems that the 'Romanisation' of the elite did indeed have its counterpart in a lesser 'Romanisation' of the lower classes. It is likely that it also involved a corresponding adoption of Roman domestic behaviour.

Archaeological scholarship in the 1970s and 1980s focused on Romanisation as imperialism and resistance. This debate has since been redefined in terms of a complex pattern of cultural interaction rather than an oversimplified confrontation between Roman and 'native'.[77] In this context it can be seen that each householder had a choice between a range of architectural styles, and between a range of behaviour patterns associated with particular domestic activities. It is certainly a more useful exercise to identify the channels whereby elements of Roman architecture and behaviour were adopted in particular localities rather than to characterise the process as one of confrontation. If an aristocrat built a private baths this was hardly a statement that he had 'sold out' to the Roman power, and if an aristocrat resisted social pressure from his peers, all of whom had baths, he was not resisting Roman control. Within their own houses everyone could create a series of spaces that met their own personal cultural needs. Social pressure and wider cultural influences would have had an effect, but in the depths of a private house their influence was, at most, muted. A private house was designed to maximise the power of the owner by drawing upon the conventions and icons of art and culture to support the status of the individual. This can be contrasted with a public building which subsumed the power of the individual to the representation of the power of society as a whole. Thus the dedicatory inscription of a Roman public building stresses the *donation* of the builder to society, whereas the dedicatory inscription of a house states *I* built it. The Roman provincial aristocrat expressed his power and status through mosaic and painting. The owners of the village houses described in this chapter expressed their status through the choices they made in architecture and decor.

A similar conclusion has been reached in a study of the re-use during the Roman period of the Bronze Age *nuraghi* of Sardinia. In an unusually relevant application of phenomenology to archaeology, Blake[78] has demonstrated how each Sard may have placed a different meaning on the act of reoccupation. For some it could have symbolised resistance to Rome, isolation from Roman culture, identification with the past, or just practical re-use of a substantial structure. Others made Roman-style additions to the nuraghi, including rectangular rooms and mosaic floors. They may have attempted to marry the traditions of power from the past and the present, by remaking earlier culture in the context of the Roman period. This negotiation of cultural mix in a very striking monument of an earlier period is a remarkable example of how provincials throughout the Roman Empire brought together local and Roman traditions. It indicates how different individuals may have placed a different meaning on their decision, and the important element of personal taste in determining domestic architecture. Whether it demonstrated resistance, or a deliberate attempt to build a 'Romano-Sard' culture, it is highly unlikely that the Romans forced the locals to reoccupy the nuraghi. Where the occupants chose to lay mosaics it was thus a deliberate choice to adopt Roman culture in a pre-Roman building.

16. Subdivision and the end of
the Roman house

In late antiquity a new style of architecture was introduced into the urban form that has great significance for housing and urban life. Its inclusion at this point can be justified in that it is a phenomenon closely related to the changes of late antiquity, and has also been associated with arguments about the ruralisation of the urban environment. The development of subdivision is also intricately bound up with the end of the peristyle house and of the Roman way of life.

Subdivision is the dividing up of older buildings and spaces to create smaller buildings, normally houses. It was driven by two related social developments: the growing obsolescence of many early imperial public buildings, and the decline of the peristyle house.

The obsolescence of public buildings was itself a product of two social forces: growing centralisation of the imperial administration and the rise of Christianity. The process of the centralisation of the imperial administration is well beyond the scope of this book. It can be said to have begun by the reign of the emperor Diocletian, who set out to increase the authority of the emperor at the end of the third century AD. It is reflected in a stream of fourth-century legislation that sought to discourage the flight of potential town councillors, who were trying to avoid the burden of paying for civic improvements and entertainment. For our purposes the key development is the abandonment of fora and council chambers as a result of the collapse of local government.

The second half of the fourth century also saw the official collapse of paganism under pressure from the Christian emperors, especially Theodosius and his sons. This led most obviously to the abandonment of pagan temples, but more indirectly to a growing dissatisfaction with public baths and amphitheatre as immoral. Without the amphitheatre, forum or baths for public assembly the church reigned supreme as the only local public building where the community met on a regular basis.

The decline of the peristyle house is a more complex development. The archaeological development is relatively clear, despite the fact that few ancient towns have been completely excavated. The early to mid-fourth century saw a flurry of house building attested by many villas in all provinces. A second flurry of activity can be detected in the early fifth century, but by the sixth century no new peristyle houses were being built anywhere in the Empire. At the beginning of the sixth century there were some new mosaics, or house extensions, but they were few and far between. By the end of the sixth century AD the housing tradition of the ancient world was effectively dead.

Subdivision is extremely difficult to date. It is probable that many examples date from the fourth century. Certainly one of its characteristic forms, the blocking in of street porticoes, is well attested at that time and other forms of subdivision surely also took place then. By the fifth century few would contest that baths, fora and other buildings were beginning to be occupied by rough habitations that subdivided the original structure into a number of housing plots. Subdivision also took over earlier peristyle houses by at least the fifth century AD. Thus a slow continuing decline in the construction of new peristyle houses was matched by an increasing tendency for them to be lost to subdivision.

I have argued strongly[79] that subdivision is not just 'squatting', but has a specific architectural form. This can be identified by the way in which walls are built in a characteristic form, and are placed in characteristic locations. The form of walls used in subdivision is often low, *c.* 75 cm in height, founded on top of (never cut through) earlier mosaic floors, and topped by large re-used dressed stones (Plate 11). Characteristic locations are blocking the intercolumniations of peristyles and palaestrae, and a transverse wall across the middle of the main reception room.[80]

Naturally, where a large baths palaestra has been subdivided, free-standing houses are usually built in the centre of the court. A good example of such subdivision is the baths at Anemurium.[81] Here there were at least two free-standing houses. The eastern house of the pair has two rear rooms fronted by a corridor. This arrangement is similar to that used in village housing in the area east of Antioch as described earlier in this chapter. The two rooms were fronted by a portico and a yard containing an oven.

A good example of a subdivided peristyle house is the House of the Frescoes at Tipasa (Fig. 22).[82] It was divided into four apartments, separated by strategically placed divisions. The north part of the house formed one apartment, with two small walls in the peristyle porticoes to mark its boundaries. A range of three street-front rooms to the north-west were joined in one apartment by a common portico. The north-west part of the house was provided with a separate entrance from the street, and the corridor through to the south-east part of the house was obscured by a circular wall, perhaps to ensure privacy in the fourth apartment in the area beyond the original triclinium, which was subdivided by the characteristic transverse wall. Pottery and coins suggest these developments took place during the fifth century AD.

The House of the Frescoes shows that subdivision was a systematic break-up of a larger building. It seems unlikely that a Roman aristocrat would deliberately build a wall across the middle of his reception room. There is no reason to suppose that receptions were for any reason falling out of fashion. Indeed it is during the fourth and fifth centuries that the leading aristocrats were adopting the more grandiose reception facilities described at the end of the last chapter. The house must have been sold or abandoned, whether because the previous rich owner had lost his wealth, given it away (as so many did to the church), or simply vanished to avoid the local tax burden. It is possible that in the future archaeologists will learn to use subdivision to estimate the extent of the 'flight of the council-lors' from tax collection duties.

Conclusions

The peristyle house spread throughout the Roman Empire, where it was adopted by all the local aristocrats. It was beyond the means of most of the Empire's inhabitants, but nevertheless they adopted some elements of aristocratic housing and behaviour. The first chapter identified areas of Greek influence and the Roman army as the instruments for the adoption of Roman domestic architecture in the west. This chapter has enlarged on issues of Romanisation by demonstrating that provincials could pick and choose which elements of Roman domestic culture they wanted to adopt. It has been shown that in Britain round houses were generally exchanged for rectangular buildings by the second century AD, whilst mosaics may have been laid in 'aisled barns'. In the east classical dining behaviour took place in non-Roman-style apartment housing. Bosra in Syria, as well as Silchester and Stanwick in Britain, had housing with a mixture of Roman aristocratic and local vernacular traditions. By showing that poorer hous-ing of the Roman period adopted elements of the aristocratic tradition, this chapter has demonstrated that it is wrong to draw too strong a distinction between the peristyle house and other forms of house.

Romanisation cannot be seen simply as becoming Roman as opposed to resisting cultural imperialism. Individual households made specific deci-sions about what elements of Roman culture they wished to adopt. All households were touched by Romanisation, even if this consisted of no more than use of pottery and coinage. Despite this, regions of the Empire, such as the north-west provinces and the east, have been shown to have maintained a vernacular tradition that can itself be associated with the Roman period.

It is sometimes said that there was no middle class in the Roman Empire. Certainly the aristocracy had a considerable degree of power concentrated in their hands. This chapter has shown that there was a wide variety of housing, including types of houses which were occupied by those who were neither aristocrats nor peasants or artisans. Several house types have been identified which cover more than one province: 'fortified' farms in Spain and Africa, 'strip' housing in Britain and Gaul, village housing in Syria and Egypt. The mixing of aristocratic and vernacular, and the ability of house types to cross many major geographic boundaries, has blurred the social distinctions which often form the basis for histories of the Roman world. It may be appropriate for historians to look at broader regional histories of Rome that are not limited to a particular province, or – more significantly – a modern nation state.

Two other preconceptions about urban and rural housing have also been dismissed. First, the distinction between urban and rural housing has been questioned. There were no functions that were purely the preserve of urban or rural housing. Some houses in Pompeii were as much engaged in agriculture as small peasant holdings. Secondly, there was no industrial function that was limited to either town or country. Urban housing could be involved in agriculture, potting, or more noxious pursuits such as fulling. In sum, Chapters 2 and 3, which have been devoted to architecture, have highlighted one fundamental difference between Roman and modern houses. The Romans saw no distinction between home and business, or between urban and rural activities in their houses.

4

Decoration

It has become customary in recent works[1] to describe the architecture of Roman houses together with their decor. This is certainly a laudable approach as it allows a full appreciation of the way in which the decor fitted with the architecture to form a conceptual whole, and the way in which the whole house created a certain 'atmosphere' for owner and visitors. It is therefore legitimate to ask why this book has not followed this admirable precedent. As has been stressed earlier in this work, the houses for which we have full detailed evidence are those of Pompeii and Herculaneum. This work attempts to set these sites within the overall framework of Roman houses in general. Huge effort has been expended on the decor of Pompeian houses and the famous four styles of wall painting. Outside the Bay of Naples evidence for wall painting is very fragmentary, but it does exist. By contrast typologies of mosaic floors, though well known at Pompeii, are usually based on major studies in a number of Roman provinces. In order to set the fragmentary evidence of wall painting from outside the Naples area in context, and to set Italian mosaics alongside those from other provinces, it is important to look at the whole realm of decor in the Roman house.

So, despite the concentration of painting at Pompeii and the wealth of provincial mosaics from aristocratic housing, it is necessary to take a broad view of the topic. This will indicate how the decor of provincial houses matches up with the decor of Pompeian and other Italian houses, which is an important consideration in discussing the balance between provincial art and Roman art as a whole.

Apart from the overall decoration of each type of room in the house, other aspects of more or less fixed decor must be considered. This includes the use of sculpture, in the form of architectural embellishments or free-standing works. Some consideration will also be given to the water supply, drainage, baths, cisterns and fountains.

1. Decorative themes

Before beginning the discussion about Roman painting, stucco and mosaic, it is important to spend a few minutes considering the range of illustrations used in aristocratic Roman decor. Many readers will be familiar with the standard depictions of Roman art, such as Neptune riding the waves, or the loves of Jupiter. Classical myth was a rich source of dramatic scenes for the artist. Nevertheless, the majority of Roman decor was more geometric and emblematic. Grand pictures of myth or everyday life leave most impression with the modern observer, but such grand scenes were the preserve of the main rooms in rich aristocratic houses. Geometric motifs could be dramatic in colour or effect, and were arguably easier to compose. The bust of a season, or a god, could be interspersed within such a geometric pattern in a decorative manner without making a complex allusion to the jealous lover, the danger of pride, or suchlike.

It will be important to keep in mind while reading this chapter that simple geometrical patterns were the most common decor in almost every house in the Empire. Myth was the most common topic for figurative scenes.

Everyday life, particularly hunting, fishing and the games, was the third major source of inspiration, especially in the later periods of the Empire. For the purposes of the present work this third theme is cited disproportionately to its presence in the monuments. This is because whilst myth presents us with many ideas of Roman emotional life and taste, its exact message is very difficult to interpret. Scenes of everyday life, on the other hand, speak more directly of the owner's lifestyle and interests.

2. The four styles of Pompeian painting

Wall painting can be considered the most important form of decoration in a house. Because of poor preservation of the upper parts of buildings outside Pompeii, the archaeologist or art historian is more used to dealing with floor mosaics. Nevertheless on entering a house it can be argued that the walls are noticed before the floor. Only those people who keep their eyes stubbornly on the ground, with the attendant risk of collision, will notice the detail of a carpet. A large complex floor mosaic can only be appreciated when seen from a particular viewpoint, and is normally observed from a rather acute angle. Floors can be covered by furniture, mats, and indeed people. The height of walls and our ability to scan them with a horizontal glance makes them a more central element of decor.

The four styles of Pompeian painting were established by Mau[2] in the nineteenth century. Whereas almost every other theory of Roman archaeology and art history has changed since that date, the painting styles have remained resistant to all attempts at revision. There are innumerable works on Pompeian wall painting. Any reader wishing to consider the subject in detail should turn to them. What follows is a brief description of each Pompeian style in order to set the scene for a broader treatment of both geographical distribution and chronological development. Pompeian painting is much too specialised for analytical comment in a work of such general treatment and broad horizon.

The First Style (Plate 12). First Style painting[3] was common in Pompeii from the second century BC. It consisted quite simply of imitation marble panels made to look as if they formed rows of plaques. The standard arrangement was to divide the height of the wall into three 'courses' of these panels. Because of their early date few assemblages have survived in any state of completeness. Most houses were repainted at a later date. Whereas in later times it is clear how painting was used to distinguish the different parts of the houses, identifying the more public from the more private suites, the lack of a complete First Style assemblage makes it impossible to provide a definitive answer for the period of its use. Two exceptions to this are the use of stucco columns to reflect the colonnades of a peristyle as a place of circulation, and the use of a separate style in bed niches. The setting for the bed couch in the cubiculum was a raised floor and a lower ceiling, creating a form of 'niche'. First Style painting emphasised these 'niches' by using different colour schemes or different sized imitation masonry blocks.[4]

The most extensive remaining First Style decor is in the Samnite House at Herculaneum where it covers the fauces and most of the atrium.

The Second Style (Plate 13). The Second Style, introduced in the first century BC, was a radical departure from First Style painting. Whereas the First Style had divided the walls into three equal horizontal zones, the Second Style gave prominence to the Middle Zone. The Upper and Lower Zones were reduced to wide borders at the top and bottom of the walls. The Middle Zone was opened up so that its panels became windows onto imaginary architectural vistas located in perspective beyond the walls.

Significantly, these vistas, or panels, were separated by painted columns posed as if they were holding up the roof of the room. Later painting style would drop all pretence that such columns served a structural role. The architectural façades seen in the panels of the walls were somewhat fanciful. Though based loosely on real elements of Roman architecture, they could not be seen as representing any particular building, except perhaps reminiscences of theatre backdrops and temple frontages.

The ultimate development of these architectural façades was perhaps the paintings in the grand oecus of the villa at Oplontis.[5] Here two-storey colonnades can be seen receding into the distance behind three registers of the foreground painting. In paintings of the later Second Style the painters stepped back from this architectural fantasy. The main panels began to have less depth, becoming panel paintings, with independent figural and landscape scenes. This later Second Style is exemplified by paintings in the House of Augustus on the Palatine hill in Rome.

At the same time similar developments were affecting ceiling design. Traditional ceilings were designed using coffers formed from wooden beams. Those few ceilings still preserved from this period[6] suggest that, during Augustan times, stucco and painting were de-emphasising the coffered form. Stucco was using delicate panelling with fine vegetal borders. Painting was using perspective and trompe l'oeil to produce more fanciful 'coffer-like' designs.

The Third Style (Plate 14). The Third Style was introduced in the last quarter of the first century BC. In some respects it would seem to have been a step back from the architectural fantasies of the previous period. The panels which had previously been windows onto a fantasy world now became flat areas of paint again. However, it is in its attention to detail that the Third Style left its mark, and it is in many ways the most attractive of the four styles to modern eyes. The columns which had framed the Second Style vistas became delicate cords and borders with beaded motifs, or slight column capitals which bore little relation to real architecture. Meanwhile in the middle of the panels were placed delicate detailed pictures of particular themes, personages, tiny landscapes or still lifes. As the artist was no longer trying to fill a complete wall with a landscape he could spend more time creating detailed true portraits in these small panels. The identification of these small panels as 'paintings' in the modern sense of works of art hanging on the walls of a gallery is strengthened by the Third Style rooms that show the paintings hanging on easels.

The introduction of the Third Style has been associated with the new moral tone introduced by Augustus.[7] The first emperor tried to impose a return to family values after the turbulence of the civil wars from which he had ironically derived his own position. It is always dubious to link art and politics, but the delicate touch of the paintings combined with the more sober background in which they are found would certainly seem to reflect the new values of the 'Silver' period of Roman culture.

The Fourth Style (Plate 15). The last style of Pompeian painting dates from the middle of the first century AD. Since it was the last style before the eruption of Vesuvius it is naturally the most common at Pompeii.

Innovative painters had begun to develop the frameworks that surrounded the Third Style panels. Instead of using slender beadings or thin columns, the borders had taken on a solid architectural forms. Borders became separate panels in their own right containing tall architectural frameworks. These constructions consisted for the most part of columns and architraves rather than the depiction of a solid masonry backcloth, but the development clearly demonstrated a wish to return to the portrayal of depth in painting.

The Fourth Style returned to the system of architectural vistas introduced by the Second Style, but with some remarkable differences. Whereas in the Second Style the frames of the panels consisted of columns which pretended to support the roof of the room, in the Fourth Style any pretence at weight bearing, or indeed reality, was lost. The Third Style had used delicate borders to frame the panels of the walls. The Fourth Style used a series of heavy receding architectural structures. In the Second Style the architectural structure had born some resemblance to buildings or pavilions. In the Fourth Style they were no more than elaborate façades with no relation to actual structures of any kind.

Floating, as it were, in the midst of these architectural vistas were the large-scale mythological paintings for which Pompeii is justifiably well known. The Second Style had used the architectural settings as a stage on which people or animals moved. The Third Style had abstracted the scenes to panels hung on a wall. The Fourth Style combined these two approaches by placing large mythological scenes on large wall panels set in architectural frames.

Scholars have identified a number of different approaches to painting in the Fourth Style, which Clarke[8] has aptly termed 'Manners', thus avoiding the difficult attempt to identify 'schools' or 'workshops'. The first of these to emerge was the Tapestry Manner. Here the major panels of the wall are perceived as hanging tapestries, with finely sewn borders and tassels. Third Style borders tend to be thin linear designs. Fourth Style Tapestry borders are wide bands decorated with complex textile designs. The flat surfaces of the main wall panels were, in a fashion, similar to the previous Third Style panels. They are offset by the intervening areas of architectural frames which provide depth and make the so-called 'tapestries' stand out from the overall composition. The panels could explicitly be given the form of tapestries or curtains by making them bow at the top, as in the House of the Vettii, or seemingly stretch tight as if tied to the corner of the frame at six points.

The Plain and Theatrical Manners may have been developed at a slightly later date than the Tapestry Manner, though to all intents and purposes all three were in vogue at the same time. The Plain Manner used flat panels like the Tapestry Manner, but instead being separated with architectural designs they were divided by depictions of fine metalwork constructions such as candelabra.[9]

In its more successful designs two particular techniques were used to create the effects the Fourth Style sought. Dark colours were used to paint the main panels of the walls, whereas light colours, particularly white, were used for the receding architectural frameworks between and above the panels. The dark colour of the panels created solidity, while the white background suggested a light external scene.

The Theatrical Manner[10] is Pompeian painting at its most over-exuberant. Endlessly receding juxtaposed constructions frame, and break the frames, for the major figural panels are left floating in the midst of a mass of dubious structures. Sometimes, especially in the uppermost register of the walls, a succession of niches containing statues or still lifes is depicted. These niches give the Manner its name, and do recall the architecture of the theatre backdrop, the *frons scenae*, but even here the niches are not solid and the juxtaposition of further architectural frames beyond them removes any sense of reality. A good example of this extravagant style is the House of the Vettii, as one might expect given previous comments in this work on the house and its owners.

While the austerity of the Third Style has been associated with the ethos of Augustus, the Theatrical Manner has been associated with the extravagance of Nero. This latter association does have some direct grounding in archaeology. Paintings in the Domus Aurea, Nero's enormous palace in central Rome (described in Chapter 2), do indeed employ the Theatrical Manner.[11] Historical sources make it clear that the palace was in large part a personal project, and imperial interest in the wall paintings is a real possibility.

In the first century AD, while the Third and Fourth Styles of wall painting were grappling with the desire to pose simultaneously receding architectural scenes and panel paintings, ceiling painting was also trying to adapt stucco frames derived from coffers with the styles of panel painting that had emerged in wall decoration. Ceiling painting had found a solution by the time the mature Fourth Style had developed. Ceilings were organised with a strong central painting framed by concentric stucco frames and coffer-style compartments. Compartments were normally 'inhabited' by vegetal or animal motifs. Whereas borders between early coffer-based compositions consisted of ribs, these later designs had vegetal borders similar to those used in Fourth Style paintings.

3. Roman painting in the second and third centuries AD

Following the destruction of Pompeii in AD 79, our evidence for wall painting diminishes to a minimal number of examples. In Italy the most important site is Ostia. The use of heavy concrete vaulting in Ostian buildings, and its inhospitable environment until the draining of the marshes at the end of the nineteenth century have ensured that some buildings preserved a considerable amount of decoration.

Clarke[12] has knit together what we know of Ostian painting with evidence from Pompeii to provide a coherent narrative from the first to the third century AD. At the House of the Muses he has identified a Hadrianic version of Second Style architectural illusionism.[13] Elsewhere in the same building a more conventional Fourth Style composition can also be found.[14]

In the first half of the second century Clarke believes that little has changed from the days of Pompeii,[15] but in the second half of the second century he finds a significant development at the House of the Yellow Walls.[16] Whilst the overall 'theatrical' framework continues to be painted with the same accuracy and delicacy as at Pompeii, the figurative motifs and landscapes are painted in a more 'impressionistic' manner. Simpler scenes with coarser brush strokes created an overall impact on the viewer without permitting specific identification of objects or personages in the landscape.

At the end of the second century and the beginning of the third century Clarke sees the 'impressionistic' approach spreading from its treatment of pictoral motifs to the architectural framework itself. In the House of the Yellow Walls this had still maintained a level of fine detail that allowed individual architectural elements and structures, such as niches, to be identified. In the House of Jupiter and Ganymede the architectural elements still have a delicacy of touch, but they are juxtaposed in a bewildering array of receding and closed scenes that are very difficult to envisage as any rational construction.[17] The Inn of the Peacock, painted in the first quarter of the third century, took this development further.[18] The walls of the rooms were painted in a series of panels containing figures in the manner of the Third Style or the Tapestry Manner, but each panel was framed by a simply outlined broad band of colour. The frames of the panels do not relate to any overall architectural design, nor are they represented in any detail. The borders simply served as frames to the figurative panels, leaving the walls as a range of isolated tableaux.

There is consistent evidence in the Severan period for a style in which a white background is divided into panels by thin lines of dark colour. Such paintings are found in several houses at Ostia,[19] as well as at catacombs and other buildings at Rome.[20]

In sum, Clarke presents the following movements in painting styles of Roman Italy during the second and third centuries AD. The Pompeian Fourth Style continued to be used until around the middle of the second century AD. At this time a new impressionistic style began to be used to create an overall emotional impact rather than relying on accuracy of depiction. Initially this style had most impact on the central motifs of the main panels, but by the early third century it had begun to affect the depiction of the architectural frame as well. Instead of a constructed series of receding pavilions, or a series of architectural constructions, there was a simple set of frames. The result was to turn the wall paintings into a set of tableaux rather than a homogeneous whole. Clarke[21] would like to identify this change with the growth of the 'late antique' mentality which placed less emphasis on accuracy of reproduction, and more on emotional content.

Clarke's schema is an attractive one. However, it must be regarded with some caution given the lack of evidence in the second to third centuries AD. The canon of the late antique has been well developed since the 1970s and Clarke's study is a bold attempt to breach the gap between it and Pompeii. There are two fundamental dangers in this approach. First, one can project backwards elements of late antique style, rather than considering second- and third-century developments in their own right. Secondly, there is a tendency to look for intervening developments that will fit the gap between the known approaches of the first and fourth century AD.

1. House of the Gilded Cupids, Pompeii, showing garden and oecus with pool.

2. House of the Gilded Cupids, Pompeii, showing garden and household shrine in portico.

3. Underground peristyle at Bulla Regia, Tunisia.

4. 'Villa of Catullus', Sirmione, Italy.

5. 'Villa of Catullus', Sirmione, Italy.

6. The 'Canopus', Hadrian's villa, Tivoli, Italy.

7. The shop of Sabbatius, Sardis, Turkey, with toilet and base for table.

8. Windows in side apse of upper floor triconch triclinium, 'Palace', Bosra, Syria.

9. House C68, Karanis, Egypt (courtesy Kelsey Museum of Archaeology, University of Michigan).

10. Niche or shrine, House C71F, Karanis, Egypt (courtesy
Kelsey Museum of Archaeology, University of Michigan).

11. Typical subdivision comprising a low wall across
middle of triclinium, Freudenhaus, Ephesus, Turkey.

12. First Style painting, Samnite House, Pompeii (courtesy R. Ling).

13. Second Style painting, Villa of Oplontis (courtesy R. Ling).

14. Third Style painting, House of G. Sulpicius Rufus, Pompeii (courtesy R. Ling).

15. Fourth Style painting, House of the Vettii, Pompeii (courtesy R. Ling).

16. Opus sectile marble floor, 'Bishop's Palace', Aphrodisias, Turkey.

17. Domestic sculpture in context, House of Cupid and Psyche, Ostia, Italy.

18. Iron window grille, Herculaneum.

19. Panelled mosaic for stibadium couch, Dewlish, Britain (courtesy of University of Bournemouth).

20. View from peristyle into triconch triclinium, 'Bishop's Palace', Aphrodisias, Turkey.

21. 'Ray tracing' reconstruction of triclinium from Miletus, Turkey, lit by artificial lighting alone.

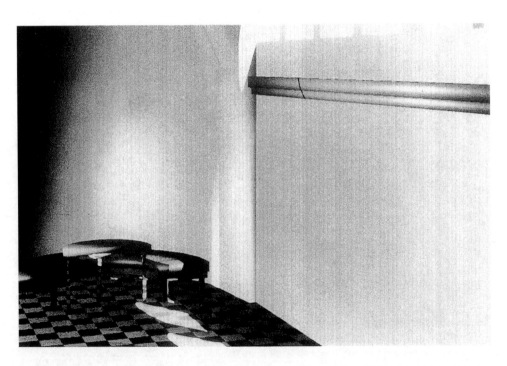

22. 'Ray tracing' reconstruction of triclinium from the Building of the Oil Press, Salamis, Cyprus, lit by daylight.

Clarke may be proved correct, especially as his study is avowedly concerned with Italian rather than provincial developments, but further work will be necessary before scholarship reaches a verdict.

4. Wall painting outside Italy

Readers may be forgiven for assuming that wall painting was the prerogative of wealthy Romans. In truth it was easy for anyone to give the wall of their house a basic colour wash, and many people did. The houses in Ostia discussed in the previous section still belonged to people who were relatively wealthy, and were examined in that context in the previous chapter.

At the lower end of the scale it is convenient to look at the houses of Karanis, also discussed in the previous chapter. Most of the houses in this small Egyptian village were painted. The colour scheme, according to the excavators, was an unappealing black wash with white paint to outline square panels in imitation of masonry (Plate 10). This somewhat dour appearance was enlivened by the presence in the main reception rooms of large semicircular niches. These were framed with stucco designs. Columns were outlined either side of the niche, the head of the niche was moulded into the conventional Greco-Roman shell design, and the arch was provided with a variety of geometric borders.

In the western half of the Empire preservation of wall decoration is extremely rare, and yet in the majority of sites from the Roman period, certainly the majority of rectangular buildings, fragments of plain coloured plaster (most often red) are found.[22] Martin Henig summarises:

> In Britain, as elsewhere in the European provinces, wall-painting in the Mediterranean tradition was practised with very few concessions being made to native artistic traditions.[23]

Likewise Alex Barbet's[24] work has enunciated the conformity of Roman Gaul to the tenets of the Four Styles. It might be argued that high society in the western provinces interpreted styles of wall painting more liberally than their Italian counterparts. A fine second-century Fourth Style painting from Leicester has a full-sized figure poised in the middle of a large panel seemingly without so much as a frame surrounding him.[25]

It has been argued that in southern France the candelabra or 'metalwork' frame was preferred over imaginative architecture, as a separator between the main panels of the design.[26] However, the candelabra is subject to 'degradation' over time as, during the second century, it turns into more of a vegetal motif. This is the case at La Croisille-sur-Briance, which has been dated to the mid-second century AD.[27] The paintings at this site are of exceptional interest in depicting a series of games provided by the villa owner. The scene, in a narrow band beneath the main panels (which were conventional images such as a bird in the centre of an overall red fill), depicted gladiators, charioteers, and *venatio* or 'mock hunt'. A badly preserved inscription provides the names of participants or donors, thus proving that it depicted a specific event. Though such scenes are found in Pompeii, they are more commonly known from somewhat later African mosaics. Like the mosaics at Rudston in Britain, discussed later in this chapter, these paintings suggest a wide distribution of motifs attributed to North African specialists, and argue for their transmission by pattern books.

In Britain, Henig[28] has tentatively suggested that the preference for vegetal borders reflects the Celtic heritage. Ling,[29] by contrast, suggests that the use of candelabra and textile borders characterises all the western provinces including Spain and the Danube region. It seems that artists in the western provinces did not indulge in the more fanciful architecture and detailed borders of the Pompeian Fourth Style.

During the mid to late Empire, from what evidence remains, ceilings were often set out in many polygonal panels formed by borders of thick painted lines. This style seems to have been common throughout the Empire. Examples can be found in Gallic houses at Aventicum[30] and La Millière.[31]

Artists working in the western provinces were able to match the quality of representation of their Italian colleagues. Experts are agreed that, while the north-western provinces of the Empire may have placed their own particular interpretation on wall painting, they generally conformed to Empire-wide traditions. Most preserved examples of Roman wall painting in the north-western provinces have been painstakingly pieced together from collapsed walls and fragments found in excavations. It is hard enough to reconstruct the main lines of provincial art without trying to place them in the particular contexts of the rooms and houses within which they stood. Nevertheless, the overall conformity with Italian traditions suggests that wall paintings in houses of the north-western provinces probably also served like their Italian counterparts, to emphasise the grandeur of reception suites and the tranquillity of the cubiculum.

5. Late antique painting

Few traces of wall paintings have been preserved from the later fourth century, but there are some suggestions that the trends observed in mosaics were also to be found in wall painting.

In Britain paintings of the fourth century AD have been preserved from the 'Deep Room' in Lullingstone Roman villa.[32] This is likely to have been a Christian chapel, and was decorated with large-scale 'orans' figures with hands raised in the characteristic early attitude of prayer. Little space is left between the figures for elaborate façades such as one might have found in any of the Pompeian styles. Indeed the figures float out in front of the frames with their hands overlapping them. These paintings have been compared with similar styles used at Dura Europos on the Eastern frontier of the Empire in the late third century. At Dura some paintings also come from a Christian chapel whilst others come from the more secular context of the local commander's house.[33]

A further comparison in the west may be made with the wall mosaics from the villa of Centcelles (Fig. 23).[34] Mosaics had always been used on walls as well as floors. During the early Empire they are best known from the backdrops to fountains. In the centre of the villa at Centcelles there was a domed room in which it is assumed the owner of the villa was buried. The dome was decorated with fine mosaics, which are comparable to the decoration in the apses of early Christian basilicas.

The mosaics consisted of three registers. In the lower register there was a typical late antique hunt, centring round a particular personality surrounded by followers. He is presumably the owner of the estate by analogy with the similar group in the mosaic of the Great Hunt at Piazza Armerina,[35] and scenes at other sites. Above this the second register contained biblical scenes, including Daniel in the lions' den and Jonah. The upper register returned to a secular theme with depictions of the four seasons.

This vault mosaic thus mixed a regular domestic theme with religious panels. The combination is certainly appropriate to a mausoleum within a domestic estate. The continuous frieze of the hunt demonstrates how the typical compartmentalised ceilings of the High Empire have broken down, in the same way that floor mosaics themselves had become less compartmentalised and more commonly based on free compositions of daily life. This might suggest that by the fourth century AD the whole system of using tableaux set in coloured panels had broken down. The paintings gave more and more weight to the figures rather than the frames and the background.

These developments can be contrasted with paintings from the Hanghauser at Ephesus,[36] which show a continuous series of redecoration from the second to the fifth century AD. The paintings are commonly set against a red or white background. Figures, both large and small, seem to float in the middle of simple panels. Some of the panels have simple ribbon or tapestry borders in the style of Pompeian walls. The use of such panels and frames recalls the similar styles used in the western provinces during the second and third centuries AD. The figures represent traditional images of high Roman culture – muses, nymphs, philosophers and theatrical scenes – in a realistic manner that accurately reproduces dress and expression. Although these figures were painted to a high standard the lack of any major mythological scenes is notable. The paintings preserved at Ephesus indicate that some elements of traditional Roman painting did continue to be used into the fifth century in the aristocratic houses of certain parts of the Empire.

It must be admitted that there are so few examples of secular wall painting from the fourth century AD that such ideas as have been pre-

0   10 m

23. Centcelles, Tarragon, Spain.

sented are highly speculative. Nevertheless, the subject matter of the Ephesus painting does find support in similar developments of mosaics, which place increasing emphasis on minor heroes or generic themes (e.g. seasons, nymphs). It is likely that such changes can be linked to a diminishing role for traditional classical religion in the face of Christianity, and an increasing concentration on the power of the individual.

I have previously suggested that the culmination of this new style is best characterised by the Byzantine descriptions of the house of the ninth-century warlord Digenis Akritas.[37] Digenis had his dining room walls decorated with scenes of his own combats. In a late antique context these would have been one-to-one combats with other heroic adversaries, perhaps shown on the wall as a series of scenes like the procession of saints along the walls of early Christian basilicas such as S. Apollinare Nuovo at Ravenna, or the one-to-one combat of huntsmen and prey in late antique floor mosaics.

Even less domestic stucco work has survived than wall painting, yet there is one particular house from the fifth century AD which has produced such a rich array of plasterwork that it must be mentioned; indeed it helps to illuminate some aspects of the present discussion. The Building of the Oil Press at Salamis in Cyprus (Figs. 24-5)[38] was a regular late antique peristyle house with an apsidal reception chamber. Stucco is preserved from the reception room and from an upstairs room. Stucco was naturally suited to decorative frames raised above the background wall. It is no surprise to find that the decoration of the Salamis house is formed by colonnades half emerging from the wall surface. The three levels included in Pompeian painting are still maintained, a dado, the main register of the wall, and then a short upper register. The upper register contains a running stucco scene of hunting, whilst many of the capitals that separate the panels of this register are 'inhabited' by cherubs.

The Building of the Oil Press demonstrates that in the fifth century AD there was still a considerable appreciation of the broad framework of Roman painting as witnessed at Pompeii. Architectural frames were still used for paintings, and the hunt was still a regular motif.

6. Mosaics: origins and compositions

Whereas wall painting is dominated by the Pompeian evidence, mosaics have been found in every Roman province and from every period of Roman history. The vast majority are floor mosaics, but it is important to remember that there were also many wall mosaics, such as those from Centcelles discussed in the previous section. There are very many works on mosaics from every province of the Empire, and there is no point in duplicating the massive amount of work by generations of specialists. Instead this section seeks to draw out a few general trends of mosaic development in the Roman period.

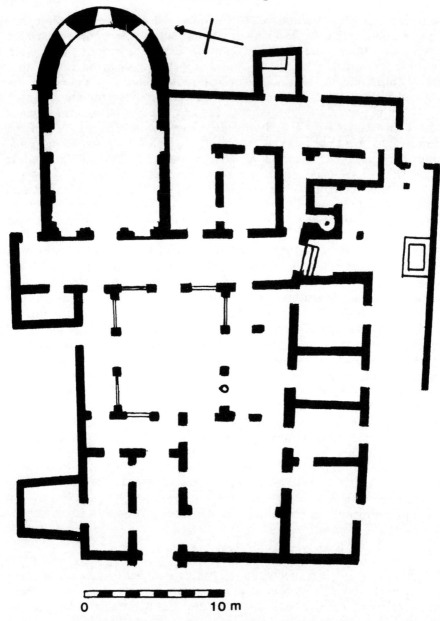

24. Building of the Oil Press, Salamis, Cyprus.

Mosaics are so dominant in considerations of Roman art that it is useful
to set out some of their limitations as an art form. Mosaic design is a very
different art to painting. The use of a coloured cube instead of a deft brush-

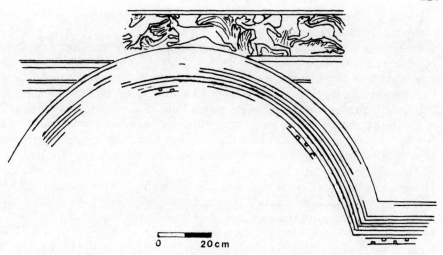

0   20cm

25. Stucco arch, fifth century AD; Building of the Oil Press, Salamis, Cyprus.

stroke renders any mosaic impressionistic, but at the same time mosaic cannot use such subtle changes in pigment to render emotion.

At the beginning of the chapter it was claimed that floor mosaics had a less immediate impact on visitors than paintings. Their position on the floor certainly affected the designs that could be used. There was a top and bottom to a wall painting, but a floor mosaic would be examined from many different directions. The question of viewpoint for a mosaic presented some problems for the Romans, and they tried various means to resolve them.[39]

The earliest Roman mosaics, following the Greek, and perhaps Carthaginian precedents, adopted the approach of the emblema. The emblema, a small high quality tableau set in a broader composition, has already been described during discussion of the development of wall painting, where it begins to be used in the development of the Second Style. Early emblemata were created with many very small cubes of glass to give the picture a very bright intense colour. At Zliten, mosaic emblemata set in tile boxes were found set into a floor of coloured marble, an *opus sectile* floor.[40] It is often thought that fine mosaic emblemata were transported in similar boxes.

As in the development of the Third Style of wall painting, mosaic images became larger. The emblema became a larger element in the composition. Where there was a large uncluttered space, especially in public buildings, the opportunity arose for a figural composition of larger than life proportions. Most characteristic of such compositions are the mosaics from public baths depicting Neptune. Large-scale compositions would of course look overblown and out of proportion in most houses, other than in large reception rooms. For secondary rooms the Romans developed a series of tableaux, of somewhat coarser composition than the original emblema, set within complex geometric or vegetal borders. Sometimes the geometric or vegetal composition took up the majority of the floor's surface; at other times it was limited to strictly narrow rectangular frames for the tableaux. A common composition of the latter type in Roman houses was the Season mosaic.[41] A season mosaic was often divided into nine square panels. In each corner of the room was a bust of the appropriate season, while in the central panel was a suitable deity representing the year as a whole. The square panels in between could be filled with 'mats' composed of interlaced vegetal or geometric motifs.

These 'mat' designs could be used to solve the problem of the point of view of the observer. In the House of the Triumph of Neptune at Acholla,[42] there were three large reception rooms, one of which had the telltale plain mosaic panel marking the location of triclinium couches. The mosaics in each room were composed of many small panels containing figures. The figures were all orientated to be seen from the nearest side of the room. It should be mentioned in passing that this house had several important retiring suites, consisting of a cubiculum and a vestibule, which were positioned in the corners of the building away from any activity that might have disturbed their occupants.

Such mosaics were the commonplace floorings of Roman provincial houses in the first and second centuries AD. Even when myths, or seasonal motifs, were interpreted somewhat clumsily, the floors made an impact by their use of bright colours, or the depiction of an unusual scene. In aristocratic houses throughout the Empire mosaics must have left a deep impression on those poorer citizens who were allowed to set foot on their shining stones, which told such dramatic stories. Geometric mosaics without figurative motifs could be quite engaging by creating three-dimensional effects, with coloured boxes or fences that seem to stand out from the floor, and mazes that enticed the viewer into trying to solve them.

The use of several figural tableaux in the early imperial mosaics allowed them to be viewed from several angles. This avoided the problem of having one central emblema, which had to be viewed either from the entrance or from the interior of a room. The use of a central emblema did however persist in the triclinium and other major reception rooms. First, large-scale compositions were of course appropriate to the grandeur of the main reception room. Secondly, much of the sides and rear wall of the triclinium was occupied by dining couches. It was thus common to put bland geometric panels in areas where the floor would be hidden by the couches, while an emblema would be placed in between them, in the centre of the room, where any guest looking down would be close enough, and stationary long enough, to take in every detail of a complex mythical scene.

The problem with placing an emblema at the centre of the reception room was its orientation, which could either be towards the diners with the aforementioned benefits, or at 180° where it would create an impression on first entering the room. The normal orientation of such mosaics is towards the guests, indicating that it was more important to have an interesting topic for dinner conversations, to demonstrate the depth of the owner's culture and learning.

Nevertheless, the threshold of the dining room was still important, and a first impression could be created for those entering in two ways. In a small dining room a threshold mosaic could be placed in the doorway. This could be of quite a fine composition, and could represent still life, food, or a laudatory inscription.[43] If the dining room was large there would be a sizeable area in front of the couches. This area was used for display, and for entertainers. On the floor there was often a second figural scene – one that could be seen from the entrance, or perhaps from both sides.

7. Mosaic schools in Africa and Britain

Particular schools of mosaicists have been identified throughout the Empire. They used characteristic designs, interpreted myths in particular ways, or had a preference for particular kinds of geometric or vegetal border. Generally speaking, it would seem that such schools operated across groups of three or four major towns in each province.

The most famous school of mosaicists known from Britain was based at Corinium (Cirencester), in the fourth century AD.[44] They produced a series of mosaics showing the magic musician Orpheus. He is shown in the centre of the mosaic, whilst the animals that he charmed are depicted in panels, circling around him. A mosaic with close similarities has been found at the late Roman imperial capital of Trier in the Rhineland.[45] The original idea for using such an unusual design in Britain might have come from a particular patron, perhaps the owner of the most splendid such pavement at Woodchester in Gloucestershire. This villa was described in Chapter 2. In the early fourth century there were two mosaic schools working in the Corinium area, the 'Orpheus' school, and the 'Saltire' school.[46] While the Orpheus school favoured large figural depictions of the musician and his animals, the Saltire school preferred geometric designs of cable (known as guilloche), meanders, and the saltire (St Andrew's) cross.

The contemporaneous existence in one area of two markedly different forms of mosaic composition demonstrates the degree of choice available to the house owner. It is easy to assume that an early Roman tradition of geometric designs was replaced by the grander figurative scenes. This is not the case. Large-scale figured scenes may have become more common, especially in areas such as North Africa, and have attracted more attention from modern scholars because of their dramatic imagery, but they were always used alongside an extensive repertoire of geometric designs.

A different mosaic workshop has been identified at Corinium in the second century, but during the third century Britain went through a 'Dark

Age' when seemingly no mosaics were laid. Archaeologists dispute how much this was a real socio-economic crisis, matching those elsewhere in the Empire, and how far the dearth of dated sites reflects lack of dating evidence resulting in some sites being mistakenly assigned to the second or fourth centuries. It is possible to interpret the revival of mosaics and rich villas in south-west England during the fourth century as the result of Gauls fleeing barbarians and disturbances on the Continent.[47] However, the idea of foreigners being necessary to revive villa life and decorative arts seems unnecessary. Architecturally the villas of south-west England were as splendid as any late antique residences in the Empire. They had several peristyles, polygonal rooms, and huge reception rooms, many of which had apsed dining suites. This movement is better seen as part of a growing solidarity in aristocratic culture across the Empire. Fluctuations in the fortunes of the mosaic schools are best seen as reflecting changing demand for their products.

By contrast one can examine the fortunes of mosaic schools in North Africa.[48] The British schools are identified on the basis of broad stylistic traditions, including major themes such as Orpheus, preferences for particular geometric designs, and idiosyncrasies in their figural scenes. In North Africa schools can be distinguished on the basis of the use of particular mosaic borders, and the use of particular 'badges' – items such as flowers or symbols, which are given prominence in the design. At Carthage acanthus borders were favoured; at nearby Thuburbo Maius laurel borders were preferred. Choice of myth can be the basis for distinguishing schools, but there is much more consensus on overall theme in the African provincial repertoire than in Britain. Schools are thus distinguished more by decorative detail rather than by the major themes illustrated on the pavements. It might be possible to interpret these differences as the result of more unified aristocratic culture in Africa, or a more independent/idiosyncratic aristocratic culture in Britain.

One potential set of third-century mosaics from Rudston[49] in Britain incorporates extraordinarily strong North African influence. One mosaic shows a charioteer, a theme otherwise unknown in Britain where there were no circuses for chariot races. Another mosaic from the building shows the badge of a North African amphitheatre 'club' and two named animals. These clubs were groups of aristocrats who worked together to provide animals for the games. A bull on the Rudston mosaic is named Omicida. Such clubs are unlikely to have existed in Britain, certainly not using the same badges as their African counterparts. The figures used in the mosaic are very crude and were clearly not produced by African mosaicists. The motifs must, under these circumstances, derive from pattern books or the patron's personal knowledge. The wall paintings from La Croisille-sur-Briance mentioned in earlier discussions also demonstrate an early interest in the north-western provinces in the 'African' theme of villa owners boasting about their provision of games, but they do not use the specific club badges found at Rudston.

The contrast between Africa and Britain is very informative for the way in which themes of domestic mosaics were transmitted. In the third century a single patron at Rudston attempted to introduce something of an African mosaic style into far-flung Britain. He was unsuccessful. The African style of rural scenes never flowered in Britain, but in the fourth century AD it did flourish all around the coastal lands of the Mediterranean. An African fashion that did not fit in Britain in the third century became the height of imperial culture a century later. Such are the vagaries of fashion and the taste of house owners.

In Africa the various amphitheatre clubs, and the supporters clubs for the four chariot race factions – Blues, Greens, Whites, and Reds, after the colours they used in the circus – were a major source of patronage for mosaicists. The interest in the amphitheatre and the circus can be identified as one reason for the richness of African mosaics, and perhaps helped to inspire the free-flowing style of composition which dominated Roman art from the fourth century AD.

8. Italian black and white mosaics

It is curious that in the first century AD, while most of the Roman world was rapidly developing complex coloured, figural mosaics, many Italian mosaicists returned to using monochrome. It is easy to describe this change, which resulted in the loss of tonal variation and moulding in the depiction, and the production of more of a silhouette style. It is more difficult to see why mosaicists should choose to abandon moulding, or realistic depiction of a three-dimensional form, to choose a more abstract style. Clarke's book[50] discusses the advantages of black and white mosaics in this regard without actually offering an explanation for the use of the style in the first place.

One reason for the change to black and white may have been the difficulty in viewing the mosaic from several different angles. One example will suffice to make the point. It is perhaps stretching the concept of the house to include the Caupona of Alexander Helix at Ostia – a public bar –[51] in this study. Nevertheless, it is instructive to note that such bars had a reception area fronting on the street in which there could be a small fountain recalling the domestic atrium. This particular establishment was located to one side of one of the main entrances to the city, the Porta Marina. The main scene in the mosaic, which dates to between AD 210 and 235, depicted two boxers, named Alexander and Helix, and was positioned so as to be seen on entering the bar, in front of the cistern and fountain or impluvium. Between the figures is a fan, while to the right is a large cup, which presumably refers to the function of the establishment. There was a narrow free space between the fountain and the bar itself. At the end of

this space, which was orientated to be seen by someone standing at the bar
and looking away from it, was a figure of Venus with a cupid in attendance.
At the far end of the bar near a secondary entrance, but again orientated
to be seen by someone standing at the bar, was a humorous scene of two
gymnasts holding spears or arrows. One of them is attempting to remove
two short spears that have been stuck in his behind! The subjects chosen
for the mosaics demonstrate that the topics of bar room conversation have
not changed in almost two thousand years.

All the figures have the same proportions. Their muscles are outlined
with lines of white against the overall black outline of their bodies. It is
noticeable however that, compared to polychrome provincial mosaics of a
similar date, the border of the Ostia mosaic is a plain black band, and that
there is no attempt whatsoever to set the figures within any panels or
frames, geometric or vegetal. The advantage for the mosaicist in using this
style is that figures can be inserted into the pavement at any angle or in
any position without needing to follow any strict overall pattern. The plain
white background has no other decorative elements which the viewer
might use to set a viewpoint for the composition. The placing of the figures
relates more to the general plan, furniture, and pattern of circulation in
the room. By using this style the mosaicist could resolve the problem of
having a single viewpoint for an emblema. Instead of trying to integrate
the figures into a single composition they were simply placed against the
white background as isolated elements.

The fundamental advantage of the black and white style is thus the
abstraction obtained by losing a realistic coloured portrait. This allowed a
freer overall composition against a monochrome backdrop. The polychrome mosaics of the Roman provinces rarely resolved this problem
before the fourth century AD. It was indeed during the fourth century that
the black and white Italian style finally gave way to polychrome mosaics.

9. Late antique mosaics

In the third century AD a very influential style of mosaic began to emerge
in North Africa. In a single field covering the whole mosaic it depicted the
local countryside.[52] The most common theme was hunting, showing dramatic captures of wild beasts such as stags, boars and lions. Sometimes
these scenes reflected the venatio, or simulated hunt in the amphitheatre.
Africa provided many of the beasts for the games at Rome, and estate
owners could boast in mosaic how they had provided large numbers of
animals and made a great profit.

The ideal of the Roman aristocrat, as expressed in literature from at
least the Augustan period, was to live on his country estate and go out
hunting in a very similar way to the 'hunting, shooting, fishing' mentality
still found today. The African mosaics, which have mostly been found in
town houses, reflect the townsman's wish to escape to the countryside for

these pursuits. Some mosaics boasted about beasts provided for the amphitheatre, others about the particular estates of their owners. These boasts were made by depicting the rich nature of the countryside and the wide variety of game to be found on the estate.

In some mosaics this interpretation can be demonstrated conclusively by the depiction of the owner, and even the villa, within the scene. In the House of Bacchus at Djemila (Fig. 29),[53] the main body of the mosaic is a conventional depiction of huntsmen confronting a variety of game, but at the head of the mosaic one particular rider rides rampant across the scene, raising one arm in a grand gesture. Behind him, at the apex of the mosaic, is a villa. There can be little doubt that this is the owner demonstrating the rich game to be found on his estate. Most famous of all such mosaics is the Lord Julius mosaic of the late third century AD from Carthage in which the owner and his wife are seated in front of their villa. The surroundings again illustrate the agricultural wealth of the estate. The owner and his wife are shown receiving produce brought to them by estate workers.

This style of mosaic spread across the whole Empire during the late antique period. It probably attained its highest artistic quality in Antioch, the capital of the eastern provinces.[54] Here a mosaic such as that which gave the House of the Buffet Supper its name uses an extraordinary richness of detail to show the liberality of the house owner in a sumptuous feast. The mosaic also demonstrates a masterly overall composition. The supper itself is shown on a semicircular panel which was probably the setting for the main dining couch when the room was in use.[55] The semicircular panel is also set within a scene of large mythical figures, and yet there is no clash between the two elements. This composition was the polychrome answer to the earlier monochrome mosaics of Italy. Within the semicircular panel the buffet supper can be viewed from the couch. The composition outside the panel can be viewed from the entrance to the room. Many viewpoints can be adopted without disturbing the composition of the whole. The depiction of food had a long tradition in mosaic art, stretching back to a characteristic Hellenistic depiction of the dining room floor with the discarded remains of a dinner.

Domestic decor had thus moved from Republican times when a tableau was suspended on a wall, or set in a floor, to where there was enough confidence to use large life-size figures without losing the proportion of the room in which they were set. Pompeian artists were very conscious of the single point from which their compositions could be viewed to best effect. By the fourth century AD figures had escaped the frame, and compositions could be viewed from several angles at once.

Depictions of the villa owner can also be linked to another major development in late antique art: the revival of interest in the hero.[56] Many of the minor heroes of myth – Bellerophon, Meleager, Ganymede and Orpheus – seem to be common motifs in late antique domestic mosaics.[57] There are reasons to associate such heroes closely with the villa owners.

Late antiquity was a time when power became more nakedly associated with individuals as much as with the holding of official office. The breakdown of local government made it more effective to solve problems through a man of power with influence at court than through legitimate bureaucratic routes. The emperors since Diocletian had consciously adopted more ceremonial, making themselves seem remote, untouchable and impassive. Local magnates naturally followed the role model of the emperor.

Minor heroes appealed as an identification because they were not gods themselves. They were normally men who had strayed into the path of a divinity, or who had been elevated to divine status because of their achievements. Many mosaics reduced these heroes to the status of human beings. Meleager in particular, as a hunter, could be indistinguishable in appearance from a local huntsman.[58] This reduced stature can also be noted in sculpture. A series of small-sized sculpture of heroes and animals made its appearance right across the Empire.[59] The confrontation of hero and animal – Ganymede and the Eagle, Meleager and the Boar, Bellerophon and the Chimera – made it easy to identify with the conventional one-to-one combat of huntsman and prey.

There may also have been a sense of movement involved. In the British Corinium mosaic school the beasts circle around Orpheus in procession. In the same way I have noted how in the Palace of Lausus, the chamberlain of Theodosius II, in Constantinople a major statue collection was governed by Kairos, a personification of movement and opportunity. Kairos and Orpheus may symbolise both the magnate and his ability to control his subjects.[60]

10. Opus sectile

Increasingly in later Roman times wall and floor could be covered with marble. During the expansion of the Roman Empire many local marble quarries had been exploited, and the great variety of available stones had been noted. Marble wall plaques were commonly used for grand public buildings, and so inevitably were introduced into houses (Plate 17). The wall design tended to consist of large veneer panels, usually in white or grey stone. Floors, on the other hand (Plate 16), took on a wide range of colours. They used small pieces, and so could easily be sourced from broken elements of other buildings. By the fourth and fifth centuries, when opus sectile was particularly common in the reception rooms of large houses, it is probable that the majority of floors were built out of re-used stones.

11. Sculptural decor

This chapter has devoted an extensive discussion to walls and floors, but there are other elements of the fixed decor of a Roman house that should be taken into account before reaching any kind of overall conclusion about how such ensembles functioned.

The most important of these secondary elements is sculpture. Aristocrats might have whole galleries of sculpture, often copies of Greek
originals. Many houses at Pompeii had large sculptures placed in gardens
and rooms where they complemented elements of the wall or floor decoration.[61]

It is normally accepted by art historians that the Romans did not collect
sculptures on particular themes. Thus while all the paintings in a room,
or in several rooms, could be linked by particular themes such as heroic
conflicts, or the loves of the gods, sculpture does not seem to have been
grouped in quite the same way. This was perhaps because of the rarity of
good quality sculpture. It may be that the Romans were more concerned
with the quality of the sculpture than its subject.

There are I believe two exceptions to this rule, at least where domestic
collections are concerned – portraits of emperors and philosophers. It is
clear, as a starting point, that very few people would keep busts of such
'bad' emperors as Nero or Commodus, unless constrained for political
reasons during their rule. Portraits of good emperors were, on the other
hand, common in domestic contexts. Portraits of particular emperors may
have been chosen simply because they were in stock when the purchase
was made, but I believe some selection must have been involved in what
by the third century AD was a substantial catalogue. Augustus, Caesar,
Hadrian and Marcus Aurelius dominate, but more unusual choices such
as Pertinax, Gordian III, and Constantius Chlorus may indicate a
particular benefaction to the family, or a particular appreciation of
character and achievements. These are among the choices for a collection from Daphne in Antioch; a similar collection from Chiragan was
discussed in Chapter 2.[62]

In the case of philosophers, portraits of Socrates, Plato, Seneca, Aris-
totle and others were probably readily available for those who could afford
them. The distinctions between the various philosophical schools were
well appreciated in ancient times, and one would assume that a particular
bust would have been chosen either to identify with the school, or to
provide a discussion point at table. Having the bust of a particular
philosopher, such as a Stoic, might, under certain emperors, be politically
sensitive and could be seen as a personal statement as much as a literary
bent.

Sculpture seems to have been generally employed, like mosaics and
wall painting, to provide a certain context for the room or setting in which
it was placed. It was for example common to use pendants – paired
sculptures that shared a common theme. Sometimes these were images of
companion gods such as Diana and Venus, sometimes identical copies of
the same statue. Such paired statues could be used to frame doorways and
corridors or to suggest particular motifs in the decoration. Bartmann[63] has
signalled this use for a second-century house in Rome where they framed
the passageway to the main reception room.

In late antiquity a similar collection of pendant statues is mentioned in the Palace of Theodosius II's chamberlain Lausus.[64] The collection was dominated by a statue of Bonus Eventus, or Kairos in Greek, and may be an allusion to the chamberlain's role in organising the imperial court. Lausus' collection also shows signs of being organised in pairs, which probably lined the multi-apsed dining room in which it was kept. Statues of Fortune and Bonus Eventus which flanked the main reception room of a British villa at Llantwit Major in South Wales indicate that even on the far west frontier of the Empire sculpture was arranged meaningfully as pendants.[65]

The ways that sculpture could be used in an architectural context is best appreciated at Pompeii. In the first chapter of this work the use of images of Priapus was noted in the House of the Vettii (Fig. 1). One, a wall painting, was located at the main entrance from the street to indicate that luxury and wealth were, as it were, the guardians of the house. This image foreshadows a statue of the god which would have been visible backlit, in silhouette at the entrance to the peristyle. Significantly the Priapi can be seen as pendants juxtaposed along the main axis of the house, but one is a wall painting and the other a statue.

Another unforgettable sculptural setting was in the House of Cupid and Psyche at Ostia, where the modern visitor turns the corner into a small intimate court at the centre of which is a statue of the two lovers. Both the statue and the wall decoration are of white marble. The small size of the room, hidden away from the rest of the house, and the silence add to the atmosphere (Plate 16).

There is thus much reason to argue that whilst sculpture in Roman houses was undoubtedly seen in its own right as a work of art, its primary role lay in complementing the other decor of the building, in framing views and creating those foci of a room that, in a dramatic fashion, draw the attention and still the visitor's speech.

12. The use of water

The use of water was of central importance to Roman houses. At a functional level aristocratic houses required wells and cisterns for drinking and washing facilities. Water was also important on a symbolic level. In the Mediterranean climate a good, if not continuous, water supply is an indicator of status. The 'wanton' use of water for fountains and private use demonstrated that an aristocrat could afford to let it flow from source to drain without re-use.

Like sculpture, with which water display is closely associated, the use of water could lend a particular atmosphere to a room, whether by a pool in the atrium, or a fountain in the peristyle. From Republican times fish ponds were held to be a particular sign of luxury.[66] Fish ponds add tranquillity and create a visual impact of colour and movement. Fountains create an impression of movement and sound. They were often played over mosaic to enhance the vivid colours.[67]

Fountains, even more than sculpture, formed focal points within houses. Common locations were the centre of a court, as a backdrop opposite a dining room, or within the dining room itself.[68] In late antiquity public fountains took on a more monumental appearance. They were sometimes several storeys high and consisted of ranges of niches, like the stage front of an ancient theatre. This monumentality also caught on in houses, where the whole of one side of a peristyle might be given over to a large niched nymphaeum.[69] A magnificent late antique fountain in a house in Apamea was discussed at the end of Chapter 2.

Many peristyle houses in the Mediterranean area had their own private cisterns. They were normally located in the atrium or peristyle, where they could collect water from the roof through a series of gutters and downpipes. In some cities, such as Pompeii, water was directly piped into the houses from a public supply. This, with its continuous flow, was more suitable for fountains, and one presumes also for drinking. Water was normally available in Roman towns through wells (public or private), and public fountains or nearby springs. Cistern water may have been used for washing people, clothes and floors, as well as being a supplement to the public supply if it ran dry in the heat of summer. It may be presumed that attention was given to ensure that figured mosaics were cleaned, and suitably exposed, before important guests arrived. In truth, however, there has been little or no research into how water was used in the domestic context.

13. Domestic cults

The richness of mythological allusion in domestic decor has often led authors to suppose that the room in question housed a domestic cult. Prime examples are the room with paintings of scenes from the Mysteries at the Villa of the Mysteries in Pompeii, or the 'Deep Room' with paintings of water nymphs, and later with Christians in prayer, at Lullingstone in Britain.[70]

The majority of such interpretations rest solely on the basis of the decor, rather than the architecture. Whilst many houses, such as examples from Pompeii discussed above, have confirmed examples of household lararia to the household gods (Plate 1), few other proposed 'cult' rooms have produced any religious objects of note, other than the decor. It is always possible to claim that any mobile elements of furniture had been moved prior to deposition, exacerbating the problem of interpretation. Moreover many everyday objects, such as pottery lamps, have religious motifs – Chi-rhos, heads of gods and such like – this occurs so often that if they were used for cults, every room in the house would be a cult centre! As a consequence mobile objects can rarely be used to prove a cult association.

The architectural setting might be expected to help. An unequivocal private chapel existed in the Palace of the Dux at Apollonia in Cyrenaica.[71] It is instantly recognisable because of its cruciform plan, and the identification was confirmed by the discovery of a stone reliquary within the room. For most putative identifications, however, the context is much more ambiguous. It is possible, for example, to note that the room with the Mystery paintings at the Villa of the Mysteries is not located on the main axis of the house, and would thus preserve the privacy of the supposed cult, but there is nothing that singles out the architecture of the room as particularly appropriate for a cult.

All that is left is the decor itself. Art historians have been heavily divided between those who would see, for example, the confrontation between beast and man as symbolising the conflict between good and evil,[72] and those who would see such illustrations as a straight representation of a hunting scene.[73] Most mosaics with a potentially deep symbolic significance are found in the largest room of the house that would normally be regarded as a reception room. Certainly, where the room is located in the traditional place for a reception room, on the opposite side of the peristyle to the main entrance, the identification as a cult room looks dubious. Such a room is most likely to be a regular reception room, and the symbolism more of a talking point for dinner parties than the basis for religious ceremonial. It would seem unlikely that a room could double up as dining room and reception room, as well as being a sanctified space for devotional purposes.

I have argued strongly that the triconch 'Orphic chamber' at the villa at Littlecote in Britain (Fig. 11) is little more than a formal dining room.[74] Several other houses have similar multi-apsed suites in the same position relative to the rest of the house (Fig. 29), and there are texts which describe dining in such rooms.

This is not to say that private cult rooms did not exist; only that strong contextual evidence must be available. The 'Deep Room' at Lullingstone in Britain is a case in point. The paintings of water nymphs in what must have been a damp cellar are strongly suggestive, and the fact that they were later replaced by figures in prayer (orantes) suggests a continuity of religious function.

All figural, or even geometric, designs can be given a symbolic interpretation, but this may not have been the intention of artist or patron. The extent to which this happened depended on the degree of education and the inclination of those using the room. To interpret a room as housing a cult, it is necessary to be certain that religious observance took place there, and that the owner not only interpreted the decor in a symbolic manner, but actually used the decor as the backdrop for ceremonial. The latter is extremely difficult to establish.

14. Houses in the context of their decor

It is difficult to overemphasise the influence that the decor of a house could have on inhabitants and visitors, when Roman decor was so rich. Several recent texts have presented sensitive, extremely eloquent, accounts of such matters based upon particular approaches to the subject. All that remains for this book is to summarise these accounts.

The simplest way to achieve impact was with colour. In the modern age of synthetics it is easy to achieve any shade or colour. In Roman times some colours had to be produced from very rare natural products, such as yellow cinnabar. Using Pompeian housing, Wallace-Hadrill[75] has ranked the colours used in Roman painting in order of expense and rarity. Anyone entering a yellow room would immediately be in awe at the expense involved in painting a complete room with such a colour. The simple colour of a room could thus impart to a visitor, or servant, that here was an important reception room which should not be entered without the owner's permission.

A step up from the use of colour was the use of an unusual scene. The charioteer on the mosaic at Rudston in Britain no doubt occasioned much comment. Another example from Britain is the depiction of Marsyas at Keynsham.[76] An unusual mythological scene served to demonstrate the high education of the owner, and the ignorance of his guests if they did not recognise the derivation. Another way of achieving the same result was to include a direct literary allusion in a scene, or an inscription.

Alternatively the decor could be used to evoke a certain image. Bergmann[77] has documented how paintings in Neapolitan houses of the Roman period show scenes of bays, pavilions and islands. They evoked an atmosphere of idle luxury, rich gardens and tranquil harbours. It has been suggested in this work that hunting mosaics evoke the estates which the town dweller had not the time to visit, and coastal scenes may suggest a similar idyll. Another popular theme in Roman times was the Nile, depicted with pygmies and hippopotami. The most famous of such mosaics is that from Palestrina in Italy. This 'pseudo-Egyptian' style evokes the exotic environment of far-off lands, and no doubt led the owner to tell of many fabulous places he had supposedly visited.

Finally, a number of owners, especially in North Africa, chose a more blatant approach. Easiest was a short inscription at the threshold to a room, 'I built this' (*sic*). The next step was for the owner to depict his villa, or himself on the estate. Even more preposterous was to state brazenly how many beasts had been provided for the amphitheatre, and at what high cost, as at Smirat in North Africa.[78] Mosaic depictions of hunts usually showed a non-specific illustration of what could be found on the owner's estate, but this last class of mosaics showed a specific event. One imagines they could have become very embarrassing if the family later fell on hard times!

When all these different interpretations are set together it is clear that Roman decor was not just meant to impress. Sometimes it was intended to astonish, through its richness, or through the evocation of a particular scene. It was meant to be bright and colourful, to show fierce beasts and heroes. It was meant to provide a measure of the owner, his courage, his status, and sometimes blatantly his bank balance. By balancing these rationales and the depictions in each room, an owner could indicate appropriate behaviour for the guests. A high-class dining room, or retiring room, might have tranquil scenes of the Bay of Naples. A reception room might have large-scale dramatic scenes from mythology to draw a gasp and provide a talking point. A hunting scene might evoke a few stories about the last trip to the country.

There is, for example, one famous mosaic[79] from North Africa in which the diners are having a riotous meal, and the words of each are recorded in the floor. One says 'Let's sing, let's dance', while another notes the night's supposed entertainment: 'Shh! The bulls are sleeping!' Roman decor could even evoke a sense of humour!

15. The use of decor to distinguish room functions

The various room functions in aristocratic Roman houses were described in Chapter 2 from the point of view of an architectural historian, but it is often said that decor can be used to distinguish room functions. As we have seen, Wallace-Hadrill points out that rarer, more expensive colours such as cinnabar were used to mark out the richest reception rooms.[80] Themes of paintings are also said to mark out room function.[81] Reception rooms had heroic or major mythological scenes, bedrooms had more intimate scenes, and baths were decorated with waterside scenes or myths.

However, many rooms had several functions and precise messages could not be conveyed by decor. In bedroom 11 of the grand Neronian villa of Oplontis, the alcoves for the beds had lower ceilings, were framed by stucco mouldings and preceded by separate mosaic panels in a typical Second Style design. This creates a functional distinction within part of one room.

Ling[82] notes that, under the Third Style, the distinction between bed niches and the front part of the room breaks down, and he suggests that the positioning of the bed may have been up to the individual, or rooms may have had a wider function. Pliny the Younger (*Letters* 2.17.7-10) says that some suites in his villa could be used for guests, or as servants' quarters. One would normally imagine that guests were housed in the richest rooms that emphasised the owner's status, while servants were lodged in poorly decorated, remote rooms.

The implication of this discussion is that while room decor can provide some indications of room function and status, such indications can be misleading. Decor often did mark out the status and function of a room, but only through creating an atmosphere for what might be appropriate behaviour in that room. Such signals might be misleading, even to the ancient visitor, and could be changed or ignored by the owner of the house.

16. Themes in decor and their significance for the conception of housing

It has been suggested that it is inappropriate to place great emphasis on the symbolic interpretation of Roman decor. Scenes such as those illustrating hunting can be seen as reflecting the preferred past times of the Roman aristocrat, and heroic scenes may have been intended to identify the power of the hero with that of the house owner. A major reception room at the Villa of the Mysteries at Pompeii was decorated with a life-size scene of some form of ritual that probably derives from the 'Mystery' religions, but this is not sufficient to prove that rituals took place in the room. Mythological scenes could be interpreted in a variety of ways, from the everyday to the ritual and symbolic. We should not assume that every visitor understood all of the associations, and indeed it is quite possible that the modern observer can see more symbolic associations in the decor than either the artist or the patron originally intended. It is often inappropriate to criticise a particularly complex symbolic interpretation of Roman art on the basis that the association claimed by a modern author does not exist. The association often does exist; but more importantly we cannot tell whether an ancient observer would have seen it.

An alternative approach to the art is to consider what it tells us about the Romans' conception of their domestic life. It is clear, for example, that the many hunting scenes in Roman art reflect the aristocrats' interest in country pursuits on their estates. As previously suggested, aristocrats were often town-bound and did not have many opportunities to indulge in hunting, but hunting was still one of the ideals of the owner. The hunting scenes expressed the idea that a Roman should live on a large estate with a wide variety of game.

Similarly landscape scenes can sometimes be taken as an expression of the ideal setting in which a house should be located.[83] Such scenes in mosaic and painting often emphasised a grand view over hill and stream. These views are also extolled extensively in texts.[84] Portico villas were clearly built to take advantage of the view over seas and bays (Fig. 2). This demonstrates that the Romans believed that a country house should be positioned with a landscape setting that overlooked part of the surrounding area. They clearly appreciated the view from the window and the countryside round about. Even urban houses developed a 'rural' view, by setting out gardens and fountains in the peristyle.

There was an element of the 'exotic' in many landscapes, most obviously in the fashion for depicting 'Nilotic' scenes with pygmies and hippos. Obviously this did not reflect the landscape of real life, but the taste for the exotic shows the interest in finding a real villa setting that was perhaps out of the ordinary. In the case of portico villas, this exotic element could be provided by the use of cryptoportici and caves for outside entertainment. In Hadrian's villa at Tivoli the emperor took considerable trouble to make the exotic reality, in fanciful architecture such as the Egyptian-style Canopus. In a more remote province like Britain the use of polygonal rooms and domes may have been an 'exotic' element, even if local artists did not depict hippos or elephants.

Pictures relate directly to the conception of the house and its surroundings when the buildings themselves are represented. Considerable attention[85] has been paid to the extent to which such images reflected real architecture. The conventions by which different architectural forms were illustrated have been explained, but less attention has focused on what such illustrations signify for the Roman's conception of the ideal house.

For the early Empire attention has mostly concentrated on paintings in the villas at Stabiae. Good examples in a similar style can be found in the House of Lucretius Fronto, the House of the Ephebe, and the House of the Little Fountain at Pompeii.[86] For the later period a group of mosaics showing villas from the region of Carthage and Tabarka in northern Tunisia has been studied. In the Italian examples the extensive porticoes fronting the buildings are the chief feature of the illustrations. In both the early paintings and the later African mosaics, domed rooms (probably private baths), and elevated tower-like structures are given prominence. In architectural terms this suggests that the elevation of the structures was particularly significant for the owners. The emphasis on tall columns at Stabiae, and domes or towers in Africa, also indicates the importance of the more exotic or ornate elements of villa architecture, as was suggested by 'Nilotic' mosaics.

Villa depictions, especially in North Africa, are also associated with hunting or rural scenery. For example, the seven-apsed reception room in House of Bacchus at Djemila (Fig. 29) has a mosaic showing the owner riding triumphantly in front of his villa, and a regular hunt scene with duels between men and wild animals below him. This might either allude to his provision of games in the local arena, or it could indicate the rich fauna on his estate. Similarly the Mosaic of Lord Julius from Carthage[87] has been held to represent the master and lady of the estate receiving the fruits of the season from their tenants or workers. They each sit in majesty at the bottom corners of the mosaic while tenants offer them gifts. Around them a regular rural scene depicts the activity of the estate.

These rural villa scenes show that, to the Roman aristocrat, a villa was the high 'palatial' centre of an active estate, rich in agricultural produce and wild animals. The African villa scenes were found in urban houses, so if they did represent a specific house, it was not the house in which they were located.[88] Representation of the villa and the owner was a way of personalising a mosaic, in the same way as other house owners might have chosen a particular mythical scene to reflect their tastes. The difference was that some owners chose myths to idealise their cultural aspirations, while others chose houses to idealise their wealth and property. The latter seem, to modern eyes at least, to have been more materialistic in their interests.

17. Decor and ambience in smaller houses

It is legitimate to ask what evidence there is that smaller houses used similar methods to demonstrate the wealth of their more modest owners.

In the Syrian villages we have noted how houses of very un-classical room arrangement, like that at Il Medjdel (Fig. 17), had inscriptions that commemorated the construction of triclinia. These have close parallels to the threshold inscriptions at the entrances to the triclinia of peristyle houses.

It has also been noted how villages or farms in Egypt and Britain used simple painting on their walls. In Egypt a black wash was used alongside rich stucco (Plate 10). In Britain poorer houses used simplified painting schemes. In Syrian villages many houses had sculptural decor on door and window frames. In the last chapter mosaics were noted in houses without peristyles such as the putative 'aisled barn' at Thruxton in Britain, and the House of the Brick Walls at Djemila in Algeria. It would thus seem that all classes of Roman society tried to decorate their houses within the means at their disposal. Many of those who could not afford stone walls or cement floors, would have used decoration in wood or plaster that has not been preserved.

Many types of poorer houses used decorative traits which were within the tenets of mainstream Roman provincial art. It is common for the middle classes to copy the habits of richer classes. It is another indication, to be set alongside similar architectural trends, that Romanisation was not limited to the aristocracy.

Conclusions

This chapter has concentrated primarily on paintings and mosaics. Study of painting is dominated by the wealth of evidence from Pompeii and Herculaneum, whereas mosaic studies are dominated by evidence from outside Italy. The traditional picture of a growing trend away from naturalism during the imperial period has been accepted with reservation. The growth of mosaics illustrating the countryside, beginning in North Africa during the third century, has been noted, as well as the interest in minor heroes in late antiquity.

Sculpture and water features functioned primarily to enhance the domestic decor. It has been accepted that domestic collections of sculpture did not have unitary themes, but it has been suggested that choices of particular emperors or philosophers could have helped to establish an owner's political and intellectual credentials. Liberal use of water was a sign of wealth and status.

Substantial doubt has been cast on the degree of symbolic interpretation of mythological scenes in a domestic context, especially where attempts have been made to associate depictions with 'cult' rooms. Nevertheless, it has been suggested that certain themes in the decor reflect the domestic interests of Roman aristocrats. Hunting scenes reflect the desire for rural pursuits, landscapes emphasise the Romans' wish to have interesting views from their houses, and depictions of houses, farm produce, or the owner himself imply the desire for self-promotion. Domestic decor is on safer ground in identifying broader domestic themes than room functions. Decor created a certain atmosphere in a room, but architectural context and the owner's whim had the main role in determining how a room was used.

Smaller houses also had wall paintings and mosaics. The lower classes of society adopted the ideals and practices of the aristocracy, when they had the means. Each province had its particular domestic themes and schools of decor. Some ideas spread from one province to another, others did not. African countryside scenes spread across the whole Empire during the fourth century AD, but isolated examples of 'games' mosaics from Rudston in Britain illustrate one African theme that did not catch on in all provinces.

5

Furniture

This chapter is the last to cover a particular aspect of the material evidence for Roman houses. It is largely concerned with the mobile part of the house – its furnishings – though other aspects which have not been included in earlier chapters – gardens and baths – will also be discussed.

Furniture is one of the least studied aspects of Roman domestic life. Of that which survives, much is in fragmentary condition. Whereas the architecture and decor of the house were only subject to very occasional change, furniture was easily moved and could be changed quite cheaply. As well as being subject to a considerable degree of movement in antiquity, furniture was also moved after burial. Moreover, most aristocratic houses would have been kept neat and tidy, especially if there were fine mosaics to be seen. The majority of objects found by archaeologists in layers above such fine floors are dumped debris brought from other buildings in antiquity, but after the abandonment of the rich house. It might be assumed, for instance, that a collection of broken statues found in the cistern below a dining room was exhibited within that room, but short of a statue plinth cemented into the floor there can be no certain proof of this assertion. Even at Pompeii, where objects such as bronze candlesticks are found where they fell after the eruption of Vesuvius, it is sometimes hard to be sure whether this location represented their permanent setting within the house. It is always possible that lights and other furniture were moved between rooms as occasion demanded. Many houses at Pompeii were also disturbed when owners dug into the remains shortly after the eruption to retrieve prized possessions.

Only couches show some sign of permanence. Often mosaics of reception rooms and bedrooms have a number of plain panels (Fig. 27, Plate 19), which did not require decorating because they were positioned under couches. Such plain panels would have looked strange if they were seen uncovered in a room, and thus indicate that many dining suites and beds were given relatively permanent locations.

Many modern ideas on ancient furniture are derived from depictions in ancient art. Art will not feature greatly in our discussions here, for two reasons. First, the difficulty of understanding the artistic context – funerary couches, for example, may not be the same as those used in houses. Second and most pertinently, this chapter attempts to examine the way that furniture related to activity and the spatial arrangements of the room and the house as a whole. Whilst many artistic representations show objects as they may have been used in a domestic context, very few actually represent the domestic context by showing an identifiable house interior.

1. The atrium and tablinum

The atrium is the best starting point for our discussion, since it is one of the most distinctive rooms of early Roman housing. The atrium and tablinum suite is important because it is one of the few suites in the Roman house for which we have clear evidence for a range of different functions. Originally the tablinum functioned as the main bedroom, and the atrium had an early role as a kitchen.[1] The atrium was also the location of the household shrine, and thus had a role in the domestic cult. The tablinum came to be the room in which the master received clients for the morning greeting, or salutatio. Later in the day the mistress of the house controlled the housekeeping from the room.[2] The atrium also had a role as the archive room housing the chests with all the family records.

Only two of these functions influenced the architecture and decor of the room. It is the reception function that had most impact, because a reception room needed to be richly decorated to impress visitors. The domestic cult is represented by the preservation of an occasional shrine, as a niche or painting. Religious decorum also required a certain level of decor; other activities did not.

In Chapter 2 reference was made to the family records stored in the arcae, or chests, located on each side of the atrium. Chests have been found in the atria of more than ten Pompeian houses.[3] In Egypt such 'archives', consisting for the most part of wills, letters, house purchases and legal disputes, are occasional finds. Most are found in secondary locations, redeposited as rubbish or re-used as mummy wrappings. It is extremely difficult to know, even if found in a domestic context, whether they can be associated with the owner of the house concerned.[4]

When the master of the house received guests in the atrium and tablinum, he seems to have made use of chair and table. Certainly it was common for a marble table, the *cartibulum*,[5] to be located against the far side of the impluvium in the Pompeian atrium.[6] It seems more likely that the table held the papers for the day's affairs, rather than being used to display prized possessions as McKay suggests.[7]

As the main open space in the front of the house it was natural for the atrium to become a space for storing many objects required in this part of the house. This might include items required in the adjacent shops as well as those being transported in or out of the house. One Pompeian house is recorded as having a 'cart' in the atrium, while in another house the atrium and impluvium were full of amphorae.[8] Such finds could of course represent a 'degrading' of a fine atrium from a reception room to artisanal use.

but this is an unnecessary reinterpretation unless it is backed up by further evidence from other parts of the house. Allison[9] has concluded, from the frequency of domestic finds in the atrium, that it normally served as a 'service court' with a 'fairly utilitarian function'. The atrium was undoubtedly the main service area for the house, and no doubt often cluttered with the remains of the daily household chores, but this does not rule out its role as a reception room, which is demonstrated by its rich decor and close association with the tablinum. In modern houses the dining room is often cluttered with everyday objects, rather than being a neat and tidy reception room, but its primary function is still dining and reception. The distinction here is between everyday use of a room, and its place in the overall design or conception of a house.

In the early atrium house the tablinum was completely open onto the court, but in houses with a peristyle it developed a second open frontage facing backwards onto the peristyle. It is not clear whether this double frontage was more important in creating a grand entrance to the peristyle, or in allowing the reception room to face both ways. I believe the latter is more likely.[10] The tablinum continued to play a role in the morning salutatio throughout Republican times, and it would have been inconvenient to have the main entrance to the peristyle, which led to further reception suites, running through a room that was in active use. That the tablinum continued to have an active function in reception is indicated by the use of wooden partitions, valvae, to close off one end of the room. Examples at Pompeii seem to indicate that these were normally placed at the end of the room closest to the peristyle, allowing continued use of the tablinum.

Such partitions seem to have become an integral part of the reception facilities in later houses. From being a way of creating a closed reception room they became valued for their use in altering the aspect of the reception room. Pliny the Younger[11] prides himself on the best reception room in his villa, where such partitions were located on every side of the room. They could then be opened up to disclose a variety of views across the countryside depending, presumably, on the time of day and the weather.

Views from the house were always valued by their owners. Several times in this book we have alluded to the importance of the view from the dining rooms into the peristyle to disclose a garden or fountain. Shutters were also put on bedroom windows to create intimate views or let in shafts of daylight. They are preserved, for example, in the possible imperial villa of Nero's reign, at Oplontis.[12] Oplontis also offers good examples of square 1 m openings in small retiring rooms which served to frame views through other rooms or into the garden. These openings mimic the receding frames of wall paintings which also demonstrate the Roman appreciation of a picturesque view.

Other forms of window could involve metal grilles (Plate 18), or window glass, which was very common in the western provinces. Thin veneers of marble, presenting a decorative though obscured view, could also be used, as in the preserved panes of the fifth-century AD Mausoleum of Gallia Placida at Ravenna.

2. Reception or dining rooms

Dining rooms give most scope for discussion of furniture. They preserve couch settings, they often had particular features associated with receptions, and it can be assumed that the richest dinner services of the house were deployed there during dinners, if not stored or displayed there in cupboards.[13]

In Chapter 2 it was mentioned that the dining suites of Greek houses also had preserved couch settings in the form of slightly raised platforms on which the couch stood, or as plain cement areas around a mosaic. Greek couches appear to have extended around all four sides of the dining room, in a single line, end to end.

In early Roman times three couches were placed in a U setting, called a triclinium after the Greek for couch, *klinê*. However, it is noticeable that the Roman couch was somewhat wider than the normal Greek equivalent. The Romans did not eat with diners lying head to toe on the couches, instead they lay at an angle, each with head to the table and feet to the wall. Each guest thus lay almost in the lap of his neighbour, and three couches would take up to seven diners.

A second form of dining couch, the semicircular stibadium, had been introduced by the first century AD. Here five to seven diners could lie radially about the central table (Figs 26-7). This arrangement reduced the space between the diners, allowing a very small table about 1 m wide to be used. Originally the stibadium was used for open-air dining, but by the end of the third century AD it had begun to be used for dining indoors.[14]

It was natural to take three semicircular couches and place them at right angles like the three couches of the rectangular triclinium. The result was a triple apsed room, each apse according the space for a stibadium. This was a common arrangement in houses of the early fourth century AD (Fig. 29).

The Romans never used a large dining table such as we use today. They preferred small tables. When rectangular couches were used the tables were set up for one or two guests each. When the stibadium was used all the guests shared the one semicircular table, the *sigma*,[15] no more than 50 cm in radius and nestling between the couches (Fig. 26). Both kinds of table were more the height of modern coffee tables, say 75 cm above the floor, than the high dining table required for sitting meals.

The supports for both couches and table were normally built from a slender bronze or wooden frame. Couches such as this have been found at Pompeii, and are shown in late antique manuscript illuminations.[16] Whilst

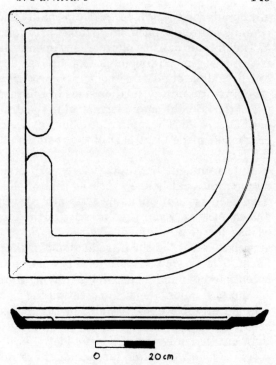

26. Example of a sigma table,
for use with the stibadium
semicircular dining couch.

O   20 cm

a few masonry settings for tables are known,[17] the majority seem to have
used a bronze frame.

Masonry foundations for the rectangular arrangement of couches are
known, but these are more common in garden contexts, as at Pompeii.[18]
Masonry foundations for stibadia are found inside houses.[19] Their existence may indicate that these later dining rooms were becoming dedicated
suites with immovable furniture. Rectangular couch arrangements are
usually identified in archaeology by the plain mosaic panels that lay below
them. These would also suggest some permanence in the furniture locations, but not as much as the heavy masonry stibadia. Moreover, it is not
uncommon for some presumed couch panels to be quite richly decorated,
indicating that the furniture was movable and the panels were definitely
intended to be seen. The case of the House of the Buffet Supper at Antioch
was remarked upon in the previous chapter.

This relative permanence of the furniture in the reception room or
triclinium is in contrast to the furniture settings in the atrium and
tablinum, where as we have seen there were several very different activities, which probably necessitated storage space and a more mobile
furnishing.

The sigma table itself was made of marble and semicircular, or occasionally circular in shape (Fig. 26). It normally had a raised lip, with a channel running out of the back of the table, presumably to catch the drips.[20]

The greater density of diners grouped radially around the sigma table meant that the arrangement took up less floor space. The distribution of couches all around the room in Greek times had been followed by a grouping around the further sides of the rooms in Roman times, but the use of the stibadium and sigma led to the dining area retreating to the far end of the room. The main reason for this seems to have been an increasing emphasis on the front part of the room as an area for display and entertainment.

Entertainment had always been expected at aristocratic dinners. At more traditional homes, such as that of the Younger Pliny, there might have been a reading of a new literary work. Otherwise there were dancers and musicians. Even the entrance of the food itself could be used as an excuse for entertainment. Petronius' *Satyricon* makes good use of the surprise element in the introduction of dishes to the feasts in Trimalchio's house. The previous chapter of this work emphasised the rich decor of the reception room and its use in magnifying the achievements of the owner.[21]

Another major element in creating the right atmosphere for the dinner was lighting. If we are to judge by the rooms at Pompeii, many triclinia, especially in the early Imperial period, had few or no windows; exterior light entered only through the wide main doorway. Late Antique dining rooms, which were often larger, may have relied on clerestory lighting. It was traditional nonetheless for dinners to continue through the afternoon and into the night. At the House of Bronzes in Sardis a large *polycandelon* (a chandelier holding many oil lamps) was found where it had fallen on the chord of the apse just over the position of the dining table. One lamp was located in a small niche near the entrance to the room, to be used in lighting the main lamp, like an ancient light switch.[22] It is most likely that the majority of Roman dining rooms had such a feature.

Throughout Roman times oil lamps were also set on tall stands that could be placed in the corners of the room. Smaller lamp stands or candles could be placed in the dinner area, on small side tables of marble or bronze. Pottery lamps on stands were preferred in most of the Roman period, but during late antiquity glass lamps set in a polycandelon became more common. One must therefore imagine the diners at the back of the room looking down the room and through the door towards the peristyle garden or fountain. Within the room flickering oil lamps illuminated displays of food, reflected mosaics, and created a theatrical backdrop for entertainment.

Using computerised 'ray tracing' it is possible to create an impression of the lighting in such rooms (Plates 21-2). Ray tracing allows the precise elevation and intensity of the light to be calculated, as well as the degree of reflectivity from plaster or mosaic. It would even be possible to position the daylight for the late afternoon meal, based on astronomical calculation for that particular era, given knowledge of the particular geographical position and elevation of the remains. It would be dangerous to rely too much on this technique as an accurate reconstruction, nonetheless enough has been said here to indicate that the results are carefully calculated.

We are used to lighting which provides blanket coverage of a room. Reconstructions of Roman lighting indicate that rooms had many dark corners. Shadow could be easily taken into account when decorating the walls of a room, when positioning the entertainers or servants, or when bringing forth new dishes.

The House of Bronzes at Sardis provides a well preserved example of a late antique dining room. The floor was laid with opus sectile, a floor made of many varieties of brightly coloured marble (by this late date probably re-used), and the floor of the apse where the dining couch was located was slightly raised. The aforementioned six-lamp polycandelon lit the diners. Part of a marble semicircular dining table was found. A sword, perhaps a souvenir of military service, probably decorated one wall. A bronze censer – a small hexagonal 'bucket' hanging from a chain – may have provided secondary lighting or a pleasant perfume. A bronze lock decorated with a pair of doors may have come from the family strongbox. This could have been a feature of the triclinium, as its earlier setting, the atrium, had been obsolete since the first century AD. Two thin rectangular iron frames represented a folding stool, which provided supplementary seating. In the main body of the room there were three iron tools – a small trowel, a shovel and a narrow bladed 'chisel' – which were clearly not related to the dining/reception function of the room.[23]

In a small chamber just outside the dining room were two fine bronze *authespae*,[24] jugs for warming the wine, as well as a small shovel for stoking the fire. The room, which one assumes was a store cupboard for the 'silverware', also contained two other bronze jugs and two spare censers.[25]

E. Salza Prina Ricotti has published a most evocative book[26] examining Roman arrangements for dinners and setting recipes alongside this analysis. The traditional Roman supper during the late Republican period began with a boiled egg, a symbol of renewal. It was followed by a main course of fowl.

Wine would be brought into the triclinium in amphorae. There it would be mixed with vinegar and warmed in a special flask: the authespa which was found at Sardis. A scene from the sixth-century Vienna Genesis (fol 17v) shows Joseph and Potiphar at dinner. They are entertained by flautists, and a servant passes behind the dining couch with the wine.

There might have been a fountain in the central area of the room. Noises of water falling in the room, or outside in the courtyard, can only have added to the impression made on guests. The use of fish pools was closely associated with undue luxury in the late Republic and early Empire. In theory they were used for fish breeding, but in fact for the majority of aristocrats they provided more of a talking point, and the bright colours of the fish no doubt added to the entertainment value.

The tableware used at dinners ranged from pottery to silver. From the fourth to the sixth century AD silverware carried a particular status. Large silver dining sets were often presented to aristocrats if they won the favour of the leading imperial officials or the emperor himself. The set might be stamped with the imperial standard or the donation might be recorded in a more informal inscription.[27]

The most valuable possessions of the Roman house were stored in the arcae, heavy chests, kept in the atrium of the house.[28] However, it is noticeable that cupboards were common in the triclinia (Fig. 10). Sometimes these took the form of free-standing wooden cabinets; sometimes they were shelved recesses in the walls of the room.[29] Given that the overall decor of the reception room placed so much emphasis on impressing guests, it hard not to believe that these cupboards held valuable possessions such as silverware. Such cupboards, as at the House of the Hunt at Carthage[30] were normally small, between 50 and 100 cm wide or high by 30-50 cm deep, and this space was subdivided with a shelf, so there was little room for larger dishes. The cupboard was located in the wall of the reception room just in front of the masonry stibadium dining couch. A freestanding cupboard in the House of Opus Craticum at Herculaneum is discussed later in this chapter.

The dishes were brought into the dining room one by one, paraded round the room and apportioned to each guest. They were not left in the room for any length of time, but removed before the next major course was brought in.[31] In late antiquity the small size of the sigma table, only 1 m across, left little space for dining. Manuscript illuminations and mosaics, most commonly scenes of the Last Supper, show one large central bowl and loaves of bread around the sides.[32] Each diner is sometimes shown with a knife or a goblet. This would have left little space for the largest silver plates which were over one metre in diameter.

Other items of dining room furniture existed. In the previous chapter mention was made of small statues, about 1 m high, that might have been set in reception rooms. Statues, smaller lamp stands, and indeed displays of food might all have been arranged on a variety of side tables that have been found in houses of all periods and are recorded in the literature. These were usually about 50 cm wide, could be semicircular or rectangular, and commonly had bronze frames.

3. Reception furniture in smaller houses

The previous two sections have concentrated on the classical peristyle house, but it is important to ask to what extent such furniture and associated domestic behaviour existed in the poorer kinds of houses examined in Chapter 3. For the Greek east, evidence has been presented that the term triclinium continued to be used throughout the Roman period to describe the reception room, and that it was used in village housing that bore no relation to aristocratic peristyle houses. However, unequivocal examples of furniture in its original setting are rare.

The most significant example of classical reception facilities in a non-peristyle house is in the so-called 'Bishops Palace' at Histria.[33] Histria was a frontier town on an island in the Danube. The house consisted of eight rooms, four either side of a central space that was more of a corridor than a courtyard. The rooms were stone flagged, and there was no sign of stucco or mosaic. However, the room nearest the main entrance to the house was apsed and had a stone foundation for a stibadium and sigma table.

The House of the Ass at Djemila[34] also has an apsidal reception room in a house with no central courtyard. However, the reception room does contain a large nymphaeum along one wall. The House of the Ass is still a relatively rich house architecturally, in a city where mosaic and large reception rooms were common. The Bishop's Palace at Histria is in a comparatively much more marginal context, at least as far as classical culture is concerned. It was the richest house in the city, and thus probably belonged to an official (the presence of the bishop in the house is unproven).

Another illuminating example of the furnishings of a non-peristyle house is afforded by shop E19 at Sardis (Fig. 14).[35] The finds of the shop date to some time in the seventh century AD, and indicate that this was an office or house rather than a commercial premises.[36] The nature of the destruction deposit at the site suggests that the furniture was left in its original position. In the debris of the upper floor, which would have formed the living quarters, were found the remains of a fine marble table and a bronze candelabrum. The table had two legs, one with a claw foot and a lion's head, the other with a small statue of Dionysus in front of a plain column. Since the legs did not match it must be assumed that the table was composed out of remnants. The two legs were found along one side of the room suggesting a lean-to table some 1 m wide. The candlestick, or lamp stand, was 40 cm high. It had three claw feet, a slender contoured shaft, and a leafy 'capital' supporting a plate and a single spike.

The table and candlestick seem a motley assortment of objects, but they were found in a modest two-room house. They indicate that its owner, or tenant, could aspire to pieces of furniture that, when in good condition, would not have been out of place in a richer abode.

4. Furniture in a 'provincial' context – Britain

The previous section has established some indications of the extent to which furniture was used in smaller houses, but the provincial context should also be taken into account.

There are very few provincial studies of furniture in the domestic

context. Most publications consist of a particular industry, or of a distribution of products, rather than the context in which the objects were used.
In order to examine context it is necessary to trawl through detailed
excavation reports, which in any case are not available in significant
numbers for many provinces. Such detailed analysis, though perhaps the
most significant work that still requires to be undertaken on Roman
housing, is beyond the scope of a general work such as this.

Instead we must be contented with an examination of Britain. Britain
has the advantage of being a province in which many of the aspects of rich
Roman culture were not paralleled in the pre-Roman period. It also has
the advantage of a seminal study of Roman furniture by Liversidge, which
unfortunately has not been revised some forty years after its publication.[37]

The best known furniture industry in Britain is that of Kimmeridge
shale.[38] As in the case of most provincial industries, many sites have
produced fragmentary objects, but rarely has a complete item of furniture
been recovered. Liversidge estimates that one group of circular Kimmeridge tables was about 40-50 cm in diameter.

The Kimmeridge industry is best known for its decorative table legs.
They copied many of the types known from Pompeii with griffin heads and
claw feet. They would appear to have come from so-called side tables, the
tops of which were 1-1.5 m by 1 m in area. Similar tables were also carved
from other stones in south-west Britain, such as Purbeck marble. Kimmeridge shale was very soft with a tendency to flake, allowing some fine
carving if carefully worked. The other stone tables were carved using a
'chipping' technique that led to deep geometric patterns along the edge of
the table top.[39] These tables can be definitely identified as side tables since
one side remained uncarved, where it stood against the wall of the room.
Side tables were used in both cubicula (see next section), and triclinia at
Pompeii. I assume that they were often used to hold short candlesticks
which were not tall enough to stand direct on the floor.[40] In triclinia they
could have been used for the display of food before or during a feast.

It may be no coincidence that such tables have been most closely
associated with south-west Britain. Villas in this area were the richest in
the province during the fourth century AD, to which most of the tables are
dated. In view of the use of Roman-style side tables, it is however surprising that there is little evidence for Roman dining tables from Britain.
British villas have reception rooms that match the architectural pattern
of a triclinium centralised on the main axis of the house, and yet there are
no mosaic panels suggestive of U shaped dining couches. There are some
fourth-century mosaic panels for semicircular couches, but no fragments
of sigma tables have been recognised (Fig. 27, Plate 19).[41]

The folding iron stool appears to have been a common item of British
furniture, though many examples are from funerary contexts and it may
be hard to recognise examples based on small fragments of iron recovered
from excavation.[42]

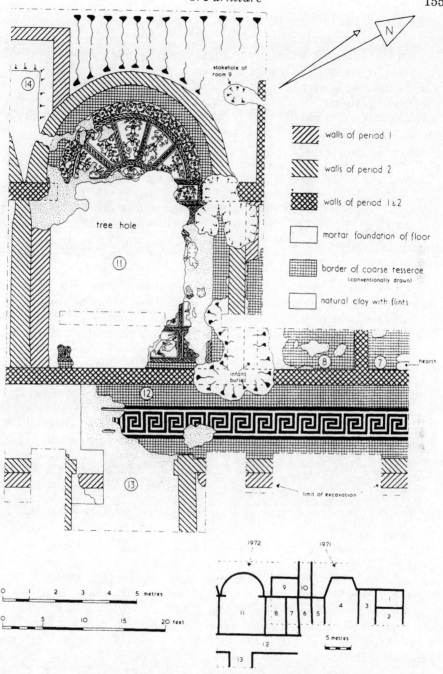

walls of period 1

walls of period 2

walls of period 1 & 2

mortar foundation of floor

border of coarse tesserae
(conventionally drawn)

natural clay with flints

stokehole of
room 9

tree hole

infant
burial

hearth

limit of excavation

1972

1971

27. Dewlish, Britain (courtesy of University of Bournemouth).

5. Cubicula

The standard Roman bedroom was a small room wide enough for one bed
and perhaps one third as long in the other dimension. The bed was placed
against the rear wall, as is demonstrated by numerous mosaics with the
ubiquitous plain panel where the couch stood. A good example of such a
bedroom with a fine bed has been found in Boscoreale.[43] The bed was finely
carved with 45° head and foot boards contoured for head and feet. The
bases of the boards were marked by small busts, which were duplicated
just below on the bed frame itself. In front of the bed was a matching
footstool, as the bed was just under one metre from the floor.

Occasionally, as at Boscoreale, there was a window in the back wall, but
normally bedrooms were dark with a narrow doorway.[44] The lack of
windows and the small size of many cubicula suggests that they were
indeed used for sleeping. It can be objected that it is wrong to translate
cubicula as bedrooms, since they could be used by anyone who wanted
some time in a more secluded place, but this is more of a question of
semantics. In the modern house many bedrooms, especially those of
teenagers, serve a much wider range of functions than just sleeping. A
cubiculum was, after all, a room containing one, or perhaps two, beds. The
fundamental role of the room was to hold these beds, and activities that
took place in the room were all most probably related to the use of this
furniture. The main distinction is that the Romans also used 'beds', or
couches, for dining and other activities.

The distinction between dining rooms and cubicula as 'couch-holding'
rooms can be seen from their aspect. Triclinia or oeci were usually sited to
look out on the peristyle and garden. Cubicula were often located at one
step removed from the peristyle. Thus in the House of the Vettii (Fig. 1)
they were placed with a small side court tucked in beside the dining room.
At Dehesa de Soria (Fig. 5) the central apsidal dining room has a wide
entrance onto the peristyle, but the adjacent apsidal cubicula open onto
side corridors rather than directly onto the portico. This locational aspect
is one reason why cubicula have often been described in this work as
'retiring' rooms.

It can be claimed that the plain mosaic panels in cubicula do not
guarantee that such rooms always held a couch (and certainly not always
on top of the mosaic panel). Nevertheless, in interpreting Roman houses
as architectural structures we should be examining the role that they were
designed to fulfil. If the designer went so far as to put in a mosaic setting
for a couch or bed we can assume that the house was designed with that
function in mind, and that the wall decor probably reflected both the
function of the room and the viewpoint of someone on the couch. The fact
that at some other time the purpose of the room was changed is of
secondary importance unless we can identify the nature of that change and
assess its significance through architecture, decor or finds. The use of

plain mosaic panels in cubicula and triclinia does indicate specialisation in room function. If there were secondary uses of such rooms, they were just that.

Furthermore, given the specialisation of functions in the aristocratic house, we should not automatically rule out specialisation in other types of house during the Roman period. The Egyptian papyri, describing some relatively modest houses, still identify dining rooms and cubicula. Inscriptions from the Syrian villages discussed earlier also mention such rooms. In the western provinces there is little direct evidence for such specialisation, but houses there may have had particular room functions that related to local traditions.[45]

The stools that were often placed before high couches are found in an variety of forms. The most common were so-called folding 'camp stools'. Though used in the army, they were also widespread in civilian life and are one type of furniture discovered in almost every Roman province, and in a wide variety of houses. Sometimes they were made of wood; if it has since decayed, they are recognised from the bronze ferrules or decorated rings that circled their legs. Sometimes their frames were entirely of iron.

Another remarkable bedroom is that in the House of Opus Craticum at Herculaneum.[46] Here an upper-storey room, opening onto a balcony, was inhabited by an adult and a child. The adult's bed was in the traditional location, in a slight alcove or bed-niche, across the far end of the room. It had deeply carved, finely turned wooden legs and was only some 30 cm off the ground. The child slept at one end of the presumed parent in its own smaller bed.

At the other end of the upper floor was another apartment with well-preserved furniture. This was a small room at the top of a staircase leading up from the ground floor. It had a somewhat smaller bed than that in the room on the balcony, also some 30 cm above the floor. There was also an adjacent side table. A small side window, facing south, brought in a modicum of light. An adjacent room was a triclinium, which may have doubled up as extra sleeping space. It had beds around two sides of the room. There was a tall wooden cupboard, similar to a small modern wardrobe, containing glassware, lamps, a necklace and eight statuettes.

The latter group of finds suggests the storage of a dinner service, as well as some personal effects. The statuettes might have been extracted for a short prayer, or might have been ornaments with little active religious connotation. A bronze table leg, suggestive of a dinner table or side table, was also found in the room.

It is interesting that the parent and child chose the largest well-aired room as their bedroom, rather than as a reception suite. Its larger doorway and view of the exterior fulfil two of the requirements for a reception room, so much so that one wonders if that had been the intention of the architect, or the first owner. A small side table on a single leg in the adjacent room

of the apartment seems to indicate that it was the reception room, although there are no signs of couches.

This is in contrast to the rear apartment where the dining room, with a
window on the court of the house below, was the best lit and largest room.
The bedroom was a smaller badly lit room, as it normally is in other
houses.

The better preservation of wooden objects at Herculaneum provides
much material for a study of furniture. Apart from the previous house,
attention must be given to the House of the Carbonised Furniture.[47] Here
a cubiculum preserves a fine couch, close to the ground yet again but with
high sides. These sides appear to have been of studded leather, giving the
whole the appearance of a somewhat lightly padded modern sofa. A small
circular bronze side table, some 50 cm in diameter, stood nearby. It had
three legs, with the characteristic elbow bend and claw feet.

In an examination of thirty Pompeian houses containing some 129
rooms that might be identified as cubicula, only six contained evidence of
beds and bedding, though four other rooms had bed niches. From this it
has been concluded that such rooms were not always bedrooms.[48] Undoubtedly the small closed rooms usually identified as cubicula had many
uses, but the presence of a bed niche, or a plain mosaic panel, implies that
a bedroom or retiring room was the intention of the architect, decorator or
owner.

6. Kitchens

One might think that the kitchen would be one of the easiest rooms to
identify in the Roman house, but this is far from the case. Aristocratic
houses sometimes had separate kitchens, identifiable from large ovens
built of brick and stone. Such ovens often had a domed appearance, like
that of the industrial kilns which are a common archaeological feature.

In Pompeii, identifiable separate kitchens are relatively common. Their
location was governed by two factors – proximity to the dining room, and
fire risk. Both these factors meant that they were usually located to the
rear of the house, near the garden or peristyle. They were normally
furnished with the aforementioned oven, a masonry bed platform and the
household shrine. Foss[49] has shown that it was more important to have the
shrine close to the cooking area, to watch over food preparation, than near
the dining room to watch over food consumption, though shrines were
often located in the peristyle as well.

The presence of a bed platform in the kitchen is of interest. It is
normally interpreted, as in the case of the House of the Vettii described at
the beginning of this book, as the cook's bed. It is, however, unusual to find
a servant provided with such a solid piece of furniture, and further
consideration should be given to this feature. It is possible, for example,
that it also had a role in food preparation. It may be that the cook was the

only slave who required a permanent bed, as the other slaves slept around the house as dictated by their duties.[50]

When houses outside Pompeii, and certainly outside Italy, are examined for kitchens they are few and far between. The Palace of the Dux,[51] a splendid late antique house with an audience chamber and private chapel from Apollonia in Cyrenaica, has one, but it is an exception. The kitchen is located between the audience chamber and the main reception room, a suitable location for rushing food to either. The room is marked by the ubiquitous brick oven, as well as four wall cupboards which might have been used as larders.

Apart from the later destruction of such cooking facilities, several explanations have been advanced for the absence of identifiable kitchens, and all these have some merit. It has been suggested that the Romans rarely ate hot food – a conclusion which would seem to be born out by ancient recipes, both as regards lack of mention of dishes being 'piping hot', and by the elaborate preparations involved which were not conducive to keeping the food hot.[52]

It has also been suggested that the Romans often bought 'take aways' from nearby bars or cafés. This is implied by the large number of such establishments in Roman towns, especially Pompeii and Ostia. Fire regulations in apartment blocks, such as those at Rome and Ostia, also suggest that cooking within the flats was regarded as dangerous.[53]

Finally, it is often assumed that cooking took place on small portable braziers of bronze or pottery. These were no bigger than a camp stove, suggesting that large dishes must have been eaten cold or lukewarm.

In poorer houses, such as at Karanis in Egypt, or in many rural settlements of the north-west provinces, ovens are found outside the house in the adjoining yard. In Egyptian contracts they were the common property of the apartment owners. It is significant that in late antiquity, saints, who were portrayed as the very image of poverty as a sign of their Christian morals, usually ate soup with bread and cheese. The more common incidence of hot food and ovens at the homes of the poor may indicate that they ate hot food while their betters did not.[54]

7. Furniture – conclusions

The study of furniture from Roman housing is still in its infancy, but several important conclusions can still be drawn. Pompeian specialists[55] are still grappling with interpretations of the data, but excavators on many other sites have been well aware of the difficulties of interpreting the distribution of artefacts.

The distribution of finds can represent storage rather than use, but there are severe difficulties in using them as evidence for room function at any site. Artefacts are not reliable in determining room function because of their mobility. Architecture and decor is more reliable because of its relative permanence. It is possible to use a reception room for storage, but it still remains by design a reception room, and if the family needs to receive important visitors it will be the best decorated room in which they will receive them.

In considering the Roman house, we should begin with the function of the rooms as envisaged by their designers, rather than the uses to which the rooms were later put. The design of the house expresses the broader cultural and societal traditions, and artefacts are more likely to represent passing preferences. For the majority of houses artefact distributions are meaningless, as no intact deposits of furnishings will be preserved.

Instead of trying to identify the particular range of furniture associated with a particular room, it is perhaps more appropriate to ask to what extent a wide range of furniture suggests a wide range of different functions, or a degree of variability in function. It has, for example, been suggested that the furniture of the reception facilities became progressively more permanent as the central role moved from tablinum, to triclinium, to stibadium. Evidence of locks and storage facilities at Sardis, Egypt and Herculaneum has been used to suggest that the family treasures were placed in the triclinium after the atrium fell out of use in the first century AD.

It has always been assumed that Roman houses were sparsely furnished. This is now proved not to be the case. It is apparent from studies of Pompeii[56] that there was some storage facility in every room, either a chest, or a cupboard. The preservation of bronze locks also suggests that such storage chests were common in many other types of Roman house. In Middle Eastern houses with few rooms it is common for bedding to be placed in a chest during the day, and this is likely to have been the case in much housing during antiquity. Evidence from papyri provides some support for this view in the case of Roman Egypt.[57]

The presence of tools has usually been associated with agriculture or artisan activity, but evidence suggests they were to be found throughout the house.[58] This may as much reflect the common need to clean rooms or make fires, as any concentration of non-domestic functions, and should not unduly surprise us.

8. Private baths

Baths are a definite indicator of Romanisation. The habit of bathing, especially socially or when conducting business, was quintessentially Roman. It may seem odd to include bathing in a chapter about furnishings, but it was a very important aspect of Roman private life, which required a particular kind of room, organised on particular lines. A holistic treatment of the subject is necessary before considering Roman social life in the next chapter.

The structure of a Roman baths was standardised, whether it was a public building or a private house. First there was a changing area. From there the bathers entered the *tepidarium*, or warm room. They would then pass to a hot room, the *caldarium*. The floor, normally of mosaic, lay on a thick cement bed above small piles of tiles, between which hot air flowed, driven by the fire in a stoke hole on the edge of the room. Around the edge of the floor clay pipes conducted this hot air up the walls. Similar forms of heating were often employed beneath the reception rooms of large houses in the northern provinces and are known as hypocausts.

On the edge of the caldarium there were often hot and cold plunge baths. They frequently took the form of semicircular niches off the main room. The bathers were rubbed with oil before entering the baths. Their sweat and grease was scraped off after bathing with a bronze scraper known as a strigil.

The most significant fact about Roman bathing is that it was a social process, commonly associated with business negotiations, and as a preparation for visiting friends for the main afternoon meal. This explains why in many houses, especially villas, private bath houses were located at the front of the house. A good example is at the famous fourth-century AD villa of Piazza Armerina (Fig. 28).[59] Here there was a monumental entrance in the form of a semicircular portico, like that noted earlier at Montmaurin. The baths lay right behind this entrance, where they could be entered by the weary traveller newly arrived at the villa. They were public rooms, to be used for significant groups of associates. Given this location of many baths, and their size, they probably had more of a public aspect than many reception rooms. Although reception rooms, as at Piazza Armerina, could be considerably larger, they are normally located much further back in the villa structure. Baths were less likely to be large rooms as they were more complicated to build with their heating systems and domed roofs. A large bath would also be difficult to keep hot.

Apart from their social role, the other factor governing the location of baths was the presence of fire. For reasons of economy in the provision of fuel, and the danger of combustion, baths were often placed away from the main building or in the 'service area' of the house. In a large villa such as Piazza Armerina the entrance was sufficiently remote from the main living quarters to make them safe. In urban houses this was more difficult. There safety could override social propriety and the baths were placed near the kitchen in order to concentrate all risk of combustion in the same area. A good example is the House of the Menander at Pompeii.[60]

The provision of a private bath suite was always exceptional even amongst those who owned peristyle houses in Italy and the provinces. The first baths would appear to have been built into houses at the end of the Republican period. One might expect that they were first added in villas, where a rural location would preclude easy access to urban facilities. By the mid-first century BC they were available in many rich urban houses as well. Petronius' *Satyricon* has the diners going to a public baths, where

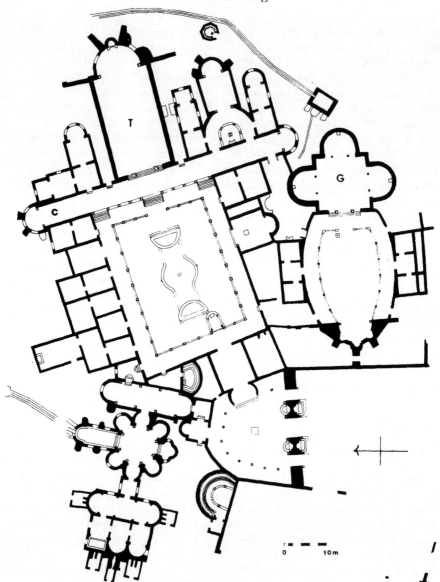

28. Piazza Armerina, Italy.

they first meet Trimalchio, their host for dinner. They go straight to his house from the baths. After dinner, and therefore late at night, they then join him in his private bath suite. This is a good illustration of bathing to remove the sweat of the day's work, and then to alleviate the stomach-ache or further reduce inhibitions after an over-hearty meal!

The construction of baths in a more distant province such as Britain clearly indicates that aristocrats expected to receive visitors in a like manner. Whereas it is possible to build a magnificent reception room and use it just for show, it was hard, even for a Trimalchio, to be pompous in the baths. To take a bath in the north-west provinces was to act as a Roman, unless one is to claim that the many private bath suites in Romano-British villas never had their heating stoked. In the latter case it would simply demonstrate the lengths to which an aristocrat would go to 'appear' Roman.

9. Gardens

The study of Roman gardens has been re-established by one remarkable personality, Wilhemina Jashemski.[61] Her work in identifying and studying the root patterns of plants at Pompeii has opened up a completely new perspective on the Roman house.

The gardens of Pompeii can be clearly classified into a number of characteristic designs. Domestic peristyles were often, as in the House of the Vettii with which this book began, set out with a formal arrangement of flowers, shrubs, a few trees and low box hedges (Fig. 1). Here the garden space formed an area in which to walk, with sculptures sited to create points of attention (Plates 1-2). People in the adjoining rooms, or colonnades, could catch glimpses of art works or a fountain. Such formality strikes the same 'cultured' tone as Pompeian wall paintings, which themselves often represented such garden scenes. Peristyles could also be used as orchards or contain vegetables:

Peristyle gardens were often planted to produce food; and finally informal plantings were not unusual even in ornamental gardens.[62]

The orchard in the peristyle of the House of Polybius seems to have produced figs, olives, lemons, and cherry or pears. At Pompeii most peristyles, however ornate, produced some food.

In other provinces the formal decorative gardens have drawn most attention.[63] This is because the setting-out trenches for the box hedges, sculptures and ornamental fountains are most likely to be preserved in the archaeology. All these features do indeed indicate formal gardens, but it is well to be aware that they do not indicate an exclusively decorative use for the garden space. This interpretation is very much in agreement with the discussion in Chapter 2. There the decorative mosaics of many Greek peristyles were contrasted with the development of the Roman peristyle from the garden or hortus. Furthermore, it was emphasised that in Roman housing it is impossible to separate the residential and domestic, from agriculture and industry.

However, many houses at Pompeii had larger rear yards. These spaces may have been fronted by a portico on one side, nearest the house, but otherwise were more like a walled garden. Jashemski found that many of these urban plots were engaged in commercial production. Vegetable plots, orchards and vineyards with over 100 stalks were all common.[64] In the midst of them could be found the stone foundation for outdoor triclinia, which were sometimes sheltered beneath a pergola. Shops or bars might also have their own vineyards. These plots seem to indicate that the house owners were deliberately setting out to make some money from their gardens. It may be that the householders also owned true farms near to the city, to which their town plots contributed. Nevertheless, the common provision of garden triclinia indicates that these plots also had a definite role for entertainment of friends and family. Just as ornamental gardens produced food, seemingly commercial gardens also had their domestic side.

The evidence from Pompeii is unparalleled, yet there is good reason to suggest that a similar picture would emerge from towns across the Empire. Evidence of sculptures and fountains has already been cited to indicate that ornamental gardens existed in every province. In Chapter 3 attention was drawn to the empty areas in some British towns which are commonly assumed to have been farmed. Wall paintings and mosaics in all provinces depict garden scenes and rural life, which suggest an interest in gardens like those of Pompeii.

Conclusions

The subjects discussed in this chapter cover some of the most exciting new areas for study in Roman housing. As a result much remains uncertain, including how to interpret the evidence. The rare discovery of intact furniture raises as many questions as it answers. Was the room designed for this function? Does the furniture represent the normal use of the room? Lighting is a completely new area of study which has only become possible in the last few years following the development of appropriate computer systems. There has been much progress in the study of gardens, but the composition of provincial gardens still remains largely unknown.

The domestic facilities outlined in this chapter have begun to move discussion away from mere structure to examine in more detail the breadth of the behaviour within houses. The use of partitions in the tablinum and triclinium shows how space within the Roman house was flexible and responded to different functional requirements. The ability to segregate activities within a room is one factor that deserves more consideration when examining the archaeology. Discussion has demonstrated that spaces could have simultaneous commercial and domestic uses. Furniture in the atrium and tablinum show that these rooms were used for social receptions and for business activity. Study of peristyle gardens suggests that they contained ornamental plants and some plants for commercial production. It has been shown that domestic baths were important for both social and business meetings.

The importance of lighting in the Roman house has been emphasised. The effects of light and shadow, natural and artificial light, on Roman art and domestic behaviour have never been studied. Furniture has provided evidence to support the conclusions of previous chapters that behaviour associated with aristocratic housing also took place in smaller, non-peristyle houses. This includes the use of side tables, dining tables and couches.

6

The House and the Family

This chapter will examine the house within the growing body of literature concerned with the social history of the Roman family, and the importance of the house in Roman society as a whole. Discussion will deliberately take on a more theoretical approach, covering ideas that go well beyond the scope of the material evidence.

1. Circulation patterns

It will be useful to begin with patterns of circulation around the house. This has the advantage that discussion is still close to the physical remains and will introduce some of the arguments to be rehearsed later in the chapter.

Circulation is at the heart of the debate on the Roman house. It is the dynamic by which the building was used. It is also an area of study in which a number of theories have been put forward, but the assumptions these theories embody have not been recognised.

One of the most explicit and simplistic theories derives from the statement of Columella (*De Agricultura* 1.6.1) that Roman villas were divided into 'urban' and 'rural' sections. From this archaeologists have concluded that the part of the villa containing rich mosaics, the reception rooms and baths, was the domain of the aristocrat and the high class visitor; the 'urban' area. Agricultural, industrial and poorer rooms were the 'rural' area, the domain of servants.

The most concrete expression of this theory is the publication of the villa at Sette Finestre by Andrea Carrandini.[1] In interpreting the remains he produced a plan, on which the rooms of the urban part are marked with lines in one colour to demonstrate circulation by the owner and his family, while lines in another colour mark the circulation of estate workers.

The limits of this theory in explaining circulation patterns are simple to state. Servants would be needed in every part of the house, to clear the dinner table, rearrange furniture, run errands etc. Equally one would expect the owner to visit the 'rural' section from time to time to check on production (assuming he did not want to 'get his hands dirty' on a more regular basis). The strict division between owner and servants, living rooms and production rooms, cannot hold. People living in the Roman house had individual patterns of access to particular ranges of rooms to perform the activities expected of them. There was no hard and fast divide between rich and poor, owner and servants, or rooms for living and production. The indivisibility of urban and rural functions in both rural and urban houses has often been mentioned in this book.

Wallace-Hadrill[2] presents a two-dimensional model for circulation in which 'grand' is opposed to 'humble', and 'public' to 'private'. He sees access to particular rooms being governed in part by the quality of their decor, and in part by servants who acted as gatekeepers. In assessing the decor he takes into account the use of expensive pigments or other materials, and the qualities of original imagery or high artistic merit. This model is more subtle than that of Carrandini. It allows a finer gradation of access rights, which is not limited to particular classes of inhabitants, but is determined more by their perceptions of the room they are about to enter. It also allows for other members of the household to guide progress and put the inquisitive back on track. A further important advantage is that in basing the theory on the decor of particular rooms it allows it to be used to interpret the physical remains of houses.[3]

There are, however, weaknesses in Wallace-Hadrill's theory. There is a fundamental assumption that a 'humble' visitor about to enter a richly decorated room would indeed feel that he was going somewhere he shouldn't. The attested use of servants as gatekeepers demonstrates that decor was not always enough.

A second weakness is more in the application of the theory than in the theory itself. Those who base circulation on decor tend to group parts of the house as being 'servants' quarters', or 'family rooms'. This is a return to the 'urban' and 'rural' house in a different guise. A learned Greek tutor might live in a room adjacent to the owner's children. It is known that slaves often slept at the door of their master's room. Such sleeping arrangements would have entailed circulation right across the house. Pliny the Younger (*Letters* 2.17.7-10) says that some suites in his villa could be used for guests, or as servants' quarters. Moreover, these rooms were located next to Pliny's personal library, which we may assume was one of the most intimate rooms of the house. This demonstrates, in the villa of a leading senator, that no attempt was made to create a major division of space between the various 'opposing' groups in Wallace-Hadrill's model. The distinction between guests, owner and servants are well drawn. The model is more one about the place of houses in Roman society rather than an explanation of the function of and access to the various rooms in the house.

A third theory that has found favour with archaeologists since the 1980s is that of Hillier and Hanson.[4] This is based on a mathematical analysis of the number of spaces within a house and their articulation with each other. It can be applied to houses of all ages, allowing the comparison of different cultures and periods.

Hillier and Hanson examine the distance of a room from the street. They calculate 'depth' on the basis of the minimum number of turns that need to be taken to reach the room after entering the building. In a further refinement, termed 'relative asymmetry', they express this distance as a fraction of the total number of rooms in the house, and in relation to average 'depth' of the house. This allows one to compare a room that is at the far end of a very large house with a room at the far end of a small house.[5]

They also assess 'relative ringiness' by calculating the number of rooms opening off any space in the house.[6] This expresses the degree to which the house is open or closed to circulation, and the extent to which particular rooms can be entered from other parts of the house. A house in which each room has but one entrance and exit would be one that is closed and restricted. Access could be totally blocked at one point. Chains of rooms develop in which the room at the end of the chain is a long distance from the start.

More open houses have central spaces from which many rooms or suites open. Access is determined by these courts, but on entering a court a number of rooms lie immediately within reach. The peristyle house was essentially an open house, whereas some of the houses examined in Chapter 3, such as Lot 11 at Utica, were more closed houses based on corridors.

Hillier and Hanson's analysis is attractive in that its very mechanistic nature tells us much about the organisation of physical space within the house, but in contrast to Wallace-Hadrill it takes no account of the decor and meaning present in the atmosphere and design of particular rooms. Hillier and Hanson's theories are somewhat mechanistic, and most historians would rightly wish to include more substantive discussion of the social context for the aristocratic house and its art. Nevertheless, they serve a useful purpose in demonstrating the importance of architectural design and layout in determining accessibility.

Calculations of relative asymmetry of several large late antique houses by the present author suggest that, in the largest houses, the main reception room was very isolated at the back of the house.[7] The construction of complex reception facilities, such as audience chambers near the main street entrance, had the effect of increasing the relative distance of the reception room from the outside world.

These results can be compared with the published relative asymmetry figures of one of the largest Pompeian houses, the House of the Faun.[8] It is interesting to note that while the House of the Faun has a larger number of rooms, its reception facilities are more accessible than those of the late antique houses. This is because many of the spaces in the House of the Faun lay immediately adjacent to an atrium or peristyle, whereas in the late antique houses one passed through a more complex series of reception rooms before reaching the central peristyle.

If an alternative view of circulation is to be suggested to these earlier proposals it is that the nature of the routes through the house itself should be examined. Whilst we should consider that some rooms are more appropriate for master than for servant, and for inhabitant rather than visitor, a more dynamic model needs to be developed.

An important way of separating different systems of circulation in the Roman house is by time of day. First thing in the morning circulation was dominated by the needs of the salutatio, when the owner received his clients. The aristocrat then left for the forum and the baths, when the house was left to the domestic personnel under the control of the owner's wife. In mid-afternoon the owner returned, often with dinner guests, resulting in a pattern of circulation that was once again dominated by the needs of visitors and business associates.

Wherever possible owners and architects tried to introduce a central court into a house. Although some houses had corridors, in the majority of cases rooms are grouped around the central court, and do not communicate directly with each other. The Roman house was essentially an open house. To pass from one room to another, it was most probable that one would have to cross the court, making it very likely that one would encounter another member of the household. Under these circumstances it was very difficult to segregate visitors, family and servants. While particular visitors and servants may have been expected to only visit particular rooms, it would have been very difficult to limit social encounters or to prevent inquisitive visitors from wandering when unattended.

Different circulation routes through a house could still be made available to different groups of people. For example a number of houses have doors leading into the apex of the dining room. They include several houses at Volubilis whose dining arrangements were described in Chapter 2. Pliny the Younger (*Letters* 5.6.30) mentions a secret entrance to one of his rooms for use during dinners. From all that has been said in Chapters 2, 4 and 5 it is certain that an aristocrat would want to introduce guests to the dining room through the main entrance to the room, from the peristyle, where its rich decor could be properly appreciated. Rich displays of food, such as those at Trimalchio's banquet in the *Satyricon*, would also have been brought through the main doors in order to impress the guests. The rear door must have had another purpose. Space around the rear of the dining couches was limited, but servants did pass behind the diners, as can be seen from the scene in the Vienna Genesis (fol 17v) showing Joseph and Potiphar at dinner. It is likely that this rear door into the dining room was for servants to approach the diners, especially the host, directly at dinner. The approach to the rear door would thus have been explicitly for servants. Another 'service corridor' can be identified in the House of the Menander at Pompeii. It snakes round the back of the main reception rooms to a group of smaller ill-lit, poorly decorated rooms that are identified as servants' quarters.

Aristocratic Roman houses were essentially 'open' in terms of circulation. Design might suggest suitable routes for visitors by using grandiose architecture, by framing vistas into further rooms, or by hiding secluded doorways. It will also be suggested, in the next section, that the use of audience chambers in late antiquity was a way of preventing lower-status clients from entering the rest of the house. Overall, though, Roman houses were dominated by the peristyle. The need to cross the peristyle to reach other parts of the house made it inevitable that guests, servants, and members of the household would meet in relatively unplanned encounters.

This brief review of circulation patterns in Roman houses has demonstrated that, while certain rooms had specific functions, and while specific measures were taken to control access to aristocratic houses, they were remarkably open to different members of the household and their guests. The implications for the interpretation of the physical remains are that great care should be taken before assigning a room or suite to a particular person or group within the household. In particular, servants may have been rare in so-called servants' quarters, which could also represent the rooms of guests or lodgers.

2. Salutatio, dining and other formalities

The previous section covered movement around the house and the roles of different inhabitants. In this section consideration is given to particular patterns of behaviour within the house. Some of this behaviour can be regarded as 'ritual', but this may only mean that it was regular domestic activity as opposed to particular formal or ceremonial actions. Certain aspects of Roman behaviour appear from the written texts to be very formal, when they may have simply been regular habits (a modern example might be walking to pick up the daily newspaper). Equally it is possible that some behaviour which appears from the texts to be very informal, such as dining, was a very structured social interaction.

An example of domestic behaviour which would appear to have been very formalised was the morning salutatio.[9] One of the first duties of the day for the humbler inhabitant of Rome was to go and greet his patron. Traditionally the patron would be seated in the tablinum of his house, though important clients, or associates, might be brought into the cubiculum for a levée. The meeting between client and patron would be the occasion for the client to ask the patron's help in activities such as obtaining a job, resolving legal disputes, or resolving problems with other men of influence. In return the client would be expected to vote for the patron, or his candidate, at elections and support him in other dealings as requested. As a token of the patron-client relationship the client would be given a small 'fee', the *sportulae*.

The patronal relationship took on an increasing importance in Roman society. The advent of the Empire meant that anyone who could find the ear of the emperor might circumvent official procedure in achieving their objectives, whether it be denouncing an enemy as a traitor, or obtaining a position. By the late antique period local civic government was collapsing under the weight of central administration and the need for town councillors to guarantee tax payments with their personal savings. The centralised late antique state meant that anyone local resident with influence at court was more powerful than a local official. Such patrons with rank at the imperial court relied on their houses as centres of influence.[10] Several late antique houses with audience chambers have been associated with these men. The use of an audience chamber suggests a need for a large gathering of clients, and its location near to main entrance from the street suggests a desire not to let the humbler clients disturb the main house. This last interpretation is supported by the analysis of patterns of circulation developed by Hillier and Hanson, and described in the last section.

The development of audience chambers in late antique houses is a clear sign of developments of Roman society affecting domestic architecture. The increasingly formal nature of patronage required a suitable space in which to hold meetings of clients. An apsidal room, recalling the contemporary basilican structures used for civil assemblies and churches, allowed the aristocrat to appear in some ceremony in the apse surrounded by his closest associates. It was a continuation of a traditional behaviour going back to Republican Rome, but it reflected the increasingly autocratic nature of Roman society.

A similar change may be observed in dining practice. The modern image of aristocratic Roman dinners is that they were easy going affairs at which wine, women and song flowed freely. However, all may not have been as it appeared. By the early Empire some people were already paid sportulae to attend dinners at their patron's house. The poorest clients who had to live from sportulae were abusively called 'parasites', after a stock theatrical character.

Dinner parties could be the occasions at which business deals were finalised and political plots hatched. It has often been remarked in this book how the decoration of dining rooms served as a means for the houseowner to demonstrate his education and cultured nature. Dinners were therefore occasions when aristocrats vied with each other over their degree of learning, and where poorer clients were invited because of their wit, or simply to act as the butt of jokes. In the fifth century AD Sidonius Apollinaris recalled (*Letters* 1.11) how he was invited to dinner with the emperor as the 'parasite', in order to entertain several important imperial dignitaries. He was charged with issuing a slanderous poem and had to compose a poetical recantation.

Many dinners could have been intimate family occasions, or relaxed encounters between close friends, but such occasions are rarely mentioned in our sources. The widespread use in every Roman province of complex artistic imagery and allusion (as argued in Chapter 4 in all media, but especially mosaic), suggests that most wealthier citizens of the Empire felt the need to indulge in intellectual or political sparring matches with their friends or rivals.

Furthermore, as in the case of the salutatio, there is evidence to suggest that such exchanges became more formalised, or gained status, in the late antique period. The spaces devoted to dining in the richest houses became even more grand and ornate. It was common to have several large reception rooms. Main reception rooms, still located on the main axis of the house opposite the main entrance, became enormous halls and some of them were given triconch apses in order to accommodate three stibadia (Plate 20). In addition there existed what I have termed 'grand dining halls' (Figs. 11 and 29). These were located to one side of the aforementioned main reception suite, but normally had a very direct entranceway from the street. Since the rooms were at the far end of the house this could necessitate a long corridor. Three apses were the norm for these rooms, but they might have five or seven. A hall of the latter type, such as the House of Bacchus at Djemila, would have seven stibadia hosting up to 49 diners: a sizeable part of the aristocracy of any provincial town.[11]

At the same time mosaic art, as discussed in Chapter 4, demonstrates an increased interest in representing the power of the owner in a direct fashion through depictions of the house, inscriptions recalling the construction of the house, and scenes of minor heroes who could be associated with the house owner.

The changes in the development of patronage and dining behaviour illustrate how trends in Roman social history impacted on the development of domestic architecture, or rather how Romans adapted their houses to reflect their changing role in society. Other changes have not left such an obvious mark in archaeology.

The degree to which such social changes penetrated the lower ranks of society should be considered. Apsidal reception rooms can be found in Britain by the end of the third century (Figs. 11-12), indicating that changes in dining practice reached the province soon after they became fashionable in the Mediterranean region. At the villas of Littlecote and Keynsham there were triapsidal grand dining halls located in the expected position off one corner of the peristyle on the same side as the main reception room.[12] It is thus clear that in Britain the aristocracy copied Empire-wide trends, and a visiting aristocrat from Antioch or Carthage would not have felt out of place. If provincial aristocrats followed social trends at the centre of the Empire so closely it is reasonable to suggest the possibility that lower classes of provincial society continued to follow the behaviour of local magnates. Evidence in support of this hypothesis has been discussed in Chapters 3, 4 and 5.

This study of the dinner and salutation, two of the few aspects of regular Roman domestic activity about which we have detailed knowledge, has

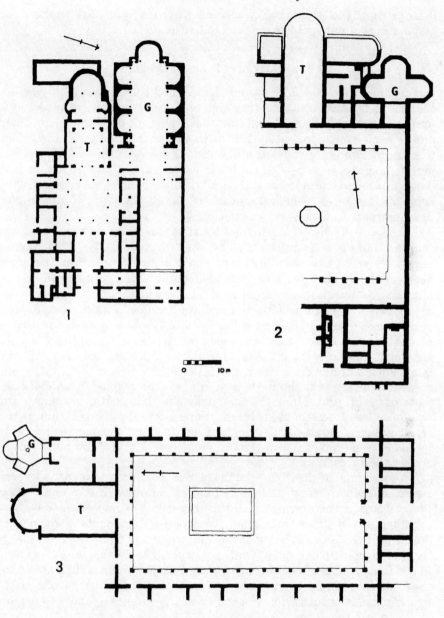

29. Plans of late antique houses with 'grand dining rooms':
    1. House of Bacchus, Djemila, Algeria;
    2. 'Palace of Theodoric', Ravenna, Italy;
    3. Villa at Mediana, Niš, Serbia.

demonstrated the impact behaviour and attitudes could have on the decor and settings of particular rooms in the house.

3. Family and household size

During the 1970s social historians determined that it was highly exceptional for a house to contain a true 'extended' family which included aunts, uncles, or grandparents. At that time it seemed that the Roman household might be an exception, but by 1995 it was clear that the social historians were right. Roman historians still question the definition of the nuclear family, and the degree to which other forms of family relationship may have resulted in extended households, but there is no doubt that following demographic and sociological models the family unit that occupied most Roman aristocratic housing was nuclear.[13]

In the case of aristocratic Roman housing the strong authority in law of the *paterfamilias* suggested that he was responsible for the extended family. However, two major arguments have demonstrated that this would not necessarily lead to a true 'extended' family. First, Saller and Shaw[14] have shown that the great majority of funerary inscriptions in the Empire are between members of the immediate 'nuclear' family, composed of parents and children. Secondly, the work of Hopkins[15] on survival rates has shown the extent to which early death was a feature of even the senatorial class. Saller and Shaw's work, though open to many explanations, such as funerary custom and bias in the epigraphic record, would seem to indicate that the nuclear family was, as throughout history, the most powerful unit. Hopkins' work indicates that death, in infancy and childhood, reduced seemingly large numbers of children in one family to a small group of adults. This group of adults often did not include both immediate parents, resulting in frequent remarriages and adoptions to ensure the succession.

The problem of death in childhood was common amongst all social strata and provinces of the Roman Empire. Similarly inscriptions reflect the customs of the literate in all provinces, so it would seem that these arguments hold water throughout the Empire. Arguments might be produced for the Celtic societies of the Empire to say that, since they were tribal, they had an extended family structure. Their tribal nature, at least in pre-Roman times, is not in doubt, but given the evidence cited above and the conclusions of the French school of family history, which have stood the test of time, it is surely for proponents of the extended family to demonstrate its existence.

Sociologists and anthropologists rightly associate adoption and remarriage as 'inheritance strategies'. In the ancient world land was the source of power and wealth. It was vital, therefore, if a family was to maintain its power, that land was not divided between many children. In tribal societies it was possible to avoid this dilemma by investing title to all lands in the tribe as a whole or in the person of the chief.

In traditional Roman society the law was the major instrument in ensuring the succession, and is consequently an important source of information on the Roman household. Roman inheritance was 'partible'.[16] Instead of transferring all property automatically to a single, usually the oldest, child a Roman could divide his property between all his children, including daughters. In principle, therefore, a Roman's estate would be dispersed when he died. However, it has been shown that survival to adulthood was not a certainty, and families sometimes had to rely on adoption (as Caesar adopted Octavian) in order to pass an inheritance to the next generation. Although in theory the Romans divided their property among their heirs, in practice a single person inherited.

It is interesting to contrast this situation with that in Egypt during the Ptolemaic and Roman periods. In Egypt partible inheritance was also practised, but tended to be enshrined in law in a rather different way. Many Egyptian house sale documents divide ownership of the house between all members of the family, including members of the extended family. The largest number of owners recorded for a single property is 20 living in one tenth of a building![17] This is exceptional. Normally (presumably again because of high mortality rates) the nuclear family are the owners, but cases of four or five owners are relatively frequent.[18] The case of the 20 owners cited above makes it clear that not all of them could have inhabited the house, and scholars consider that the sales documents represent rights of ownership, or more precisely rights to title, rather than right of abode. The most significant point is that while Roman law emphasised the role of the paterfamilias, Egyptian law emphasised more communal rights to the house. In sum, Egyptian law gave more of a role to the extended family but even there it would seem that the nuclear family was the prime occupant of the house.

Egypt is the one area of the Empire where true demographic study is possible, thanks to papyri recording house sales and leases, but especially because of several census returns which are preserved. The censuses are recorded by 'household' but the extent to which one household represented the inhabitants of a single house is unclear. The sales documents may, as we have seen, reflect ownership rather than occupancy, and this may also be the case with census returns. Furthermore, as will shortly be demonstrated, it is very hard to distinguish how many households lived in one building.

With these limitations, the household structure of Roman Egypt would seem to have been similar to many other pre-modern societies.[19] There were some one-person households, and some households whose members while related (usually siblings) did not contain any married couples. The nuclear family of husband, wife and children (if any) formed the largest proportion of the population. Nevertheless, there was a large proportion of extended and multiple family households, forming some 36% of the total. Most significantly, when Bagnall and Frier compared the proportion of larger households in towns and villages, they found that such households formed 26.4% of towns and 43.2% of villages.[20] In fact nuclear families formed a small proportion of village households: 36.8%.

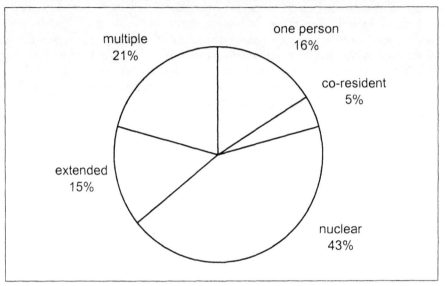

30. The population of Roman Egypt (source: Bagnall and Frier (1994), Table 3.1).

Bagnall and Frier's sample was a very small number of households (167), but still sufficient to put in question the accepted view that the Roman family was always a nuclear institution. Even in the towns nuclear families may not have formed the majority of households, and in villages larger families were the majority. Town-based households were, as might be expected, more likely to include lodgers or servants.[21]

Previous work on household size, which has been cited below, has been based on inscriptional evidence. This probably biases the record towards cities, and certainly towards the literate upper and middle classes of society.

Another important point raised by Bagnall and Frier[22] is the way in which a family changes its composition throughout its life. They cite changes in structure undergone by several families traced across several censuses. A partner dies, children die or leave home, parents die, marriages take place, and children are born. It must be appreciated that houses often held family structures for which they were not designed.

There is growing evidence that there were regional differences between the sizes of families. Preliminary results from a wide-ranging study of family relationships recorded in epigraphy and literature suggest variations even within Italy. However, the mass of the evidence is from epigraphy which has severe limitations as it is based on traditions of commemoration rather than actual family composition. The study records family structures rather than household structures which are more impor tant for this book. There is much further work to be done, but it seems certain that wide regional variation will emerge.[23]

Social historians also distinguish between households and housefuls. The former represent kin, whereas the latter include servants, tutors, lodgers (where they do not have self-contained accommodation) and other dependants. There can be little doubt that aristocratic houses always had a number of inhabitants who were not kin. In Rome they would have been slaves and tutors. In the western provinces they might have been clan retainers of Celtic society. Historians have given little consideration to the latter.

The definition of separate households within one building has not yet been fully developed by historians. It is normal for those studying Pompeii to separate out households/housefuls on the basis of a separate entry from the street.[24] However, instances of separate facilities within the house might indicate separate households. It could be argued, for instance, that the second, 'servants", kitchen in the House of Menander indicates a separate household. This separate household could represent servants who fulfilled duties for the main house, but it is also worth considering whether they might have been lodgers who were, or were not, related to those in the main house. Such a suggestion might have important impli- cations for patterns of circulation within the building, which might have been determined by household structure.

Indications of a locked door can identify a bedsit. At Ostia, for example, the provision of locked doors has been used to identify property divisions.[25] A single locked room within a larger house could have housed a lodger though there might be little physical evidence for separate facilities. It would be interesting to know whether there was any relationship between the two families identified in the House of Opus Craticum at Herculaneum (see Chapter 5). It is useful in this regard to consider the identification of households by modern censuses, such as the 1991 British census. The modern census has had to develop elaborate rules to distinguish between communal, shared and separate households. These depend on whether there are separate entrances, locked doors, and shared kitchens or bath- rooms.

The houses of all nobles and officials were subject to continuous visits from friends, clients seeking favours, traders and business associates. Their role and behaviour, in the baths, at dinner, and in moving around the building, has emerged at various stages of this work. It is likely that as one moved down the social scale such visitors became less frequent, and the house owners themselves more likely to be visiting others; but even in modest houses visitors must have been frequent. The Romans did not have offices from which they worked. Their home was explicitly their place of business as well as their residence. There has been very little research on the status of visitors to different classes of household.

Two groups of family members who have received much attention in the 1990s are women and children.

It is conventionally accepted that in Greek housing and society the movements of women were restricted. In Chapter 2 the identification of the reception room for men within Greek houses, the andron, was discussed. The room is usually identified with a room near the house entrance so that visitors would not disturb the main area of the house, the women's domain. However, the material evidence supporting the existence of the andron does not provide many arguments for identifying where in the Greek house the women's apartments lay.

In Roman houses the distinction between the man and the woman's place in the house depended on the time of day.[26] The paterfamilias ran the house first thing in the morning, and from the late afternoon. In the early morning he received visitors and clients, before setting out for the forum, baths or market. From the late afternoon it was time for the main dinner, which was also a time for business and entertaining friends. In between these times the materfamilias ran the house, managing the household and housework, or receiving visitors and traders.

Apart from this distinction of roles, Roman law gave women a certain amount of equality with men, at least on paper and for those who could afford it. Women could initiate divorce, they were present at the dinner table during major receptions, and they could inherit property. It was thus quite possible, if rare in practice, for a woman to own a major house.

In 1960 Phillipe Ariès published an enormously influential study of the growth of the concept of childhood, in which he argued that until the nineteenth century children were ignored as part of the household, and were depicted in art as tiny adults. From this he deduced that in the pre-modern era there was no real concept of childhood, or understanding of children's behaviour.[27]

His arguments are still very pertinent for the Roman household, though modern historians have been slow to accept them in their entirety. Roman authors wrote, occasionally, about children. Epigraphic studies demonstrate that a large number of funerary dedications concern children. Nevertheless most literary evidence concentrates on children's display of adult-like behaviour. Aristocrats expended much money on providing tutors for their children, or spent time teaching them to hunt, but there was little concern for the virtues of playful behaviour, bringing children together to play with each other, or parental bonding with children younger than teenagers.[28]

Most depictions of children are as little adults, or at least teenagers about to become adults. Significantly, the epigraphic evidence has been associated with the sentiment of lost opportunity for continuation of the family. All this supports Ariès' notion that there was no real understanding of what childhood meant.

The significance for Roman housing is that there was no space in the house allocated for children. Like that other at times invisible group, the servants, they probably stood or played in corners of rooms or gardens, and they probably slept at the foot of their parents'/masters' beds, as was demonstrably the case in the House of Opus Craticum discussed in Chapter 5.

The question of 'visibility' within the Roman house holds much of interest. In a physical sense the lack of blanket artificial light left many shadows. Rooms could be effectively closed off, or corners of rooms with their paintings could be hidden by positioning the lamps some distance away. Servants, in particular, may have deliberately stood in the shadows until asked to come forward. Though a house may have been inhabited by many people, a large proportion of them may have remained invisible, especially at a given time of day.

In conclusion, while in theory and in law the Roman house was inhabited by a large number of people, in practice it probably appeared to the visitor as very much the preserve of the paterfamilias and his wife: a nuclear, domestic unit.

The great increase in studies of the Roman family since the 1980s has demonstrated the wide range of occupants in Roman houses. There were many different types of occupants and families, nuclear and extended, lodgers and kin. A single household went through many generational changes, and indeed during a single day the role of different members of the household changed. By examining the social history of the Roman family we see the house as a very dynamic place rather than a static collection of rooms labelled as reception, retiring or cooking spaces.

This section has reviewed the evidence for Roman family structures. A comparison of Roman and Egyptian evidence has demonstrated something of the range in Roman family structure. It is likely that the nuclear family remained at the heart of Roman society, but that, in other provincial contexts such as Egypt, a variety of different household forms may well have existed. The range of people to be found living and visiting the aristocratic Roman house illustrates the range of functions that it served. The difficulty in locating, through analysis of the buildings, such central members of the family as the children of the owner, indicates the limitations in our ability to interpret the physical remains.

4. Ownership

The principles of ownership and land holding are fundamental to the understanding of the way in which Romans regarded their houses. In the preceding section it was shown how land holding was the basis of wealth in the ancient world, and in order to maintain this wealth a family had to pass on its estates intact to the next generation. The house therefore became the fundamental legacy. It follows from this that those who rented, instead of owning their own house, were at a severe disadvantage both in terms of maintaining their status and indeed of keeping hold of their wealth.

A considerable amount is known about rented housing thanks to the common use of apartment blocks in Rome, and the well preserved examples of such housing at Ostia. The latter were discussed in Chapter 2. As Roman law was concerned with land, only the ground floor of an apartment block was actually owned.[29] The upper floors were all rented from those who owned the ground floor and the land on which it stood. Apartment blocks were often built by property speculators, out to make money by charging high rents and hoping to see an increase in property values. Such speculators were the butt of early imperial satirists, and were also blamed for profiting from the great fire in Rome during Nero's reign.[30]

There was thus no penthouse in Roman housing, but rather a superior ground floor flat, in terms of decor and facilities. Cooking facilities and water were in short supply on the upper floors.

Another important feature of ownership was the strong rights of the owner compared with those of the tenant.[31] The landlord had the right of entry to a tenant's flat at any time, and practically unlimited powers of eviction. Much law was concerned with preserving the rights of the house-owner against a variety of robbers and attempts by others to usurp properties from the rightful heirs.

This is a striking contrast to the situation in Egypt, where, as pointed out in the previous section, large numbers of people could share ownership of a single property.

In France and Britain archaeologists have long looked for evidence of a communal tradition of ownership based on the tribe or extended clan. The most cogent assertion of this idea was by J.T. Smith[32] who, in identifying British villas with a central court, believes that they were occupied by two or more households living in apartments either side of the court. His ideas are not convincing. Some of the villas cited match traditional Roman types, in which the supposed 'central court' is actually the traditional large covered central reception room. Others of his examples belong more to the 'aisled barn' tradition, in which a large room is subdivided into a number of aisles by lines of posts. One might expect that more Celtic traditions could be associated with the 'aisled barn' type, but the case is very difficult to prove. Smith does not compare villas in the north-western provinces with those outside the Celtic world, neither does he consider whether the same patterns of rooms existed in urban housing.

The Egyptian evidence, although coming from a province deliberately run under a unique administration, does suggest that the Romans could accept other patterns of ownership, landholding and inheritance. The case has yet to be proved for many other provinces.

The fact that, as identified in Chapter 2, there was such a strong common style to aristocratic Roman houses, suggests that in the upper classes of provincial society the legal principles of personal property also held true across the Empire. The application of strong legal support to individual property owners is one reason why J.T. Smith's arguments about British villas must fail. The British villas clearly express the personal wealth and interests of individual aristocrats, whose private, personal, legally protected homes they were.

If aspects of Celtic and other traditional patterns of landholding did persist under the Roman Empire it might be possible to claim that in many provinces it was the Romans who introduced the concept of personal land holding, in which a paterfamilias or other title holder maintained a tight hold on a particular parcel of land or property. Trespass, itself clearly expressed in Roman law which is the foundation of modern European law, may have been introduced into the provinces with Roman housing.

The strength of the Roman legal concept of property ownership also supports the development of the Roman house as a personal display of wealth and luxury. Since Roman wealth was in land and property, a house should clearly demonstrate the status and income of its owner.[33]

Late Republican senators complained about the undue luxury that leading aristocrats were lavishing on their houses.[34] They did not like columns, rich paintings, or too many other works of art. Traditional ancient historians have had a tendency tacitly to uphold these complaints. Many of the aristocrats thus accused, such as Lucullus the conqueror of Asia Minor, had enormously inflated incomes. These riches may have been acquired by somewhat dubious means, such as pillaging cities. However they acquired their money, they suddenly had considerably greater wealth than earlier generations of their families, or even than those traditional senators who had not had the good fortune to be involved in wars of conquest. Since the Roman house was the expression of wealth and land holding, it was natural for these 'nouveaux riches' to express their wealth in domestic architecture.

Indeed, in the early Empire such displays of wealth were less a direct reference to wealth and power than in late antiquity. At the end of Roman history, as was shown in Chapter 4, aristocrats began to adopt more blatant expressions of wealth by commemorating their achievements in domestic mosaics, and associating themselves with the imagery of minor mythical heroes.

Sarah Scott has drawn on the ideology of 'conspicuous consumption'[35] to bring out the extremes of architectural splendour and the glittering imagery of mosaics in late antiquity, but it is worth re-emphasising the significance of wealth and land holding. In late antiquity social changes had placed more absolute power in the hands of leading imperial aristocrats. The great patron was more effective in resolving problems than local officials. The demise of civic government and civic buildings meant that the patron had to hold court for his clients in his own house.[36]

In late antiquity expressions of wealth were not just 'conspicuous consumption'. They were statements about the extent of the great man's influence. If such statements helped to increase his following they increased the political power on which his very position depended. The patron's great rival, the local holy man, maintained power in the same way, by attracting clients with a display of miracles. The miracles brought more clients who donated to the church, allowing the building of fine basilicas. The fight for influence over the people was thus between the house and the basilica. It is no coincidence that these two buildings had the richest decor in the fourth and fifth centuries AD. Ideally the aristocrat could draw in clerical as well as secular power. The Palace of the Dux at Apollonia in Cyrenaica had a private chapel containing a reliquary, which might link loyalty to the saint with loyalty to the house owner.[37] The mausoleum of the villa owner in his house at Centcelles in Spain (Fig. 23) also points to an attempt to maintain aristocratic power after death.[38]

It is important to consider how the coded messages of wealth and power were transmitted. If we consider architecture, the houses of the Syrian villages were indeed fine examples. As a modern archaeologist used to examining fine Roman buildings, it is sometimes hard to believe that these houses were built by villagers rather than townspeople. The masonry was well crafted, there were many inscriptions, and decorative carving was common. Yet to a contemporary Roman aristocrat the proportions of the building would probably have seemed ill-conceived, and above all the lack of mosaic decor and, one presumes, fine wall painting would have marked out the householders as outside the realm of classical culture.

The Roman aristocracy created a Mediterranean-wide culture, not just by obtaining a certain degree of wealth, but by creating a very definite cultural standard. The remarkable aspect of this achievement is that over several hundred years they managed to impose this over a wide range of cultures with a wide variety of traditions. Indeed imposition is not the right word, since it would seem that the majority of these cultures adopted Roman ideals willingly and with enthusiasm.

5. The development of reception facilities in aristocratic Roman houses

The previous section examined various ways in which the Roman citizen identified with his house as a means of expression, identity and power. The rooms which most epitomised this identification were the reception suite of the house. It is now possible to describe more completely how Roman reception facilities changed from the fifth century BC to the fifth century AD.

In Chapter 2 the abandonment of the tablinum in favour of the oecus was identified as a move to a 'more private' reception room. The oecus gave more control over visitors, and at the same time stressed more intimacy by taking guests to the far end of the house. The move to a single reception room (instead of atrium and triclinium or oecus) in most provincial peristyle houses suggested that the salutatio and the formal dinner were now held in a single space, though the two functions were differentiated by the time of day at which they took place – the salutatio in the early morning, and the dinner in the late afternoon. The increasing use of permanent or semi-permanent couch settings (see Chapters 4 and 5) suggests that dining was becoming the pre-eminent function. This pre-eminence is also reflected in the adoption of such dining behaviour in provincial houses of lower status than the peristyle type, as identified in Chapters 3 and 5.

The development, at the end of the third century, of the audience hall and the grand dining hall would then seem to be a reversal of this process. The audience hall's location next to the street was close to the location of the tablinum in the Pompeian house, and it has been suggested that in both rooms the aristocrat presented himself in a rather formal way. The development of the grand dining hall, alongside the oecus/triclinium at the far end of the house, suggests that receptions for more intimate clients were also becoming more formal. In late antiquity there was thus both a return to a 'less private' (more public) reception of poorer clients in the audience hall, and an increased formality in the reception of both poorer clients and the more favoured guests who continued to be received in the audience hall and grand dining hall.

Conclusions: housing and society

It is still extremely difficult to build a complete picture of housing across the Empire during the Roman period. Besides the difficulty of covering a huge geographic area which contained many different cultural groups, there are a number of more obvious gaps in our knowledge. Despite the large amount of urban housing from North Africa, our knowledge of the attendant rural housing is restricted to a few areas with survey evidence. In the Balkans, from Bulgaria in the east to Croatia in the west, the same can be said to be true. There are a few key sites and a smaller number of surveys, but the extent to which they represent the wider landscape is uncertain. In Asia Minor the picture is also incomplete. There is enough evidence to make some statements about rural housing along the southern coast from Lycia to Rough Cilicia, but not for the rest of the country. In Spain the evidence is not complete, but survey work is rapidly increasing.[39]

There are two larger areas for which we have sufficient evidence to develop a relatively complete profile in Chapter 3 – the north-western provinces and the Middle East from Northern Syria to Egypt.

The area of the Middle East may hold the fewest problems. In the highlands east of Antioch, in the basalt deserts of southern Syria and Jordan, and in Egypt, there was, as we saw in Chapter 3, a common style of rural housing. It had two key elements. The first was an architecture linked by the use of ranges of rooms, each some 5 x 5 m in plan. These ranges of rooms can be fronted by porticoes, especially outside Egypt, and beyond the porticoes there was a large yard surrounded by an enclosure wall. The yards were not peristyle courts, but open areas for storage or animals. Yards, with some exceptions in southern Syria, were not surrounded by rooms on more than one or two sides. The Egyptian houses were built in mudbrick with barrel vaults. The Syrian houses were built of dressed stone with flat wooden roofs supported by one arch across the centre of the room. Yet despite the difference in material they shared the common architectural traits described.

The second common characteristic of Syrian and Egyptian rural housing was the vertical orientation of the apartments. Each apartment was distributed across several storeys, as evidenced by Egyptian papyri and some Syrian inscriptions. This contrasted with Roman Italian apartments, which tended to have all their rooms on one floor. The contrast also existed in law. Roman law stressed single-person ownership under the paterfamilias, whereas Egyptian law stressed ownership by all the members of the extended family.

The Egyptian house type can certainly be traced back to Ptolemaic times. The Syrian house, though it may also have a Hellenistic origin, definitively found its *floruit* in the Roman period. In the case of this Eastern type of housing we are therefore considering a rural housing that emerged from pre-Roman traditions (whether Greek or Semitic), but which developed a strong identity that can be closely associated with the period of Roman rule. In Syria, if not in Egypt, it may be further suggested that this *floruit* was a product of the pax Romana – a period in which rural incomes could build savings without being hampered too much by civil disturbance or war.

In Middle Eastern cities Hellenistic architecture had resulted in the use of the peristyle house before the Roman conquest, yet the strength of Hellenistic tradition meant that Roman styles of reception room and domestic life do not appear to have taken hold until the second century AD.

In the north-western provinces there was a tradition of wooden-built settlements of round or rectangular houses in small villages. This kind of rural housing is relatively securely attested in modern Britain, France, Northern Italy and the Rhineland. The peoples of these lands had had a degree of contact with Classical culture before the formal Roman conquest. This culture had spread north from the French Mediterranean, resulting in peristyle housing in southern and central France, before the first century AD. Rectangular buildings and urbanisation had seen considerable progress before the Roman invasions.

After the Roman conquest the elites throughout the north-west quickly took up the peristyle tradition. At the same time 'urban' settlements of 'strip' housing became common. The development of peristyle housing in the west was very different from that in the east. Elite housing in the Middle East already had many 'classical' attributes in the pre-Roman period. In pre-Roman Celtic society 'classical' style architecture was still a rarity. Despite this, by the end of the first century AD peristyle housing had reached all the upper classes of Celtic society, and may be said to have included many middle-class artisans. Changes in culture associated with these developments are harder to identify.

The result was that increasingly from the second to the fourth centuries it is possible to speak of a single Empire-wide elite culture. Members of this class travelling from one end of the Empire to the other would have been able to appreciate the domestic decor, and architectural design of almost any elite house in the Empire. It is this aristocratic culture which is normally described as 'Roman'. However, housing in the north-west provinces and Egypt/Syria demonstrates that there were alternative cultural groups, spanning several provinces, which could also be described as Roman. They may have called their dining rooms 'triclinia' and used some classical imagery in their decor, but they did not adopt the peristyle and the colonnade. The aristocracy of the Empire assimilated a particular way of life, but other social groups adopted an alternative form of 'Romanitas' that reflected their cultural traditions. In Egypt in particular it has been shown that housing reflected both a different family structure and a different inheritance system.

During the third to fourth centuries AD Roman culture entered the transition period of late antiquity. The period is transitional in the sense that it preceded the Middle Ages, but it should be seen as a period of history in its own right. While some features of late antique culture became important for mediaeval life, it would be wrong to say that the adoption of such cultural elements created a mediaeval society. The latter only emerged between 500 and 1,000 years later. People in late antiquity were conscious of social change but still considered themselves part of the continuous tradition of Roman rule.

Archaeologists always have difficulty dating events within the third century AD. There was such military and economic disturbance that it is extremely hard to reconstruct the cultural sequences on which dating depends.[40] Within these limits it would appear that from the last quarter of the third century AD a number of notable changes appear in elite housing. They can, as described in Chapter 2, be associated with the introduction of the sigma semicircular dining couch into regular use indoors (it had been a garden feature since the first century AD).

At around the same time, or soon afterwards in the early fourth century, the largest houses built triconch or tri-apsidal reception rooms, which could reach huge proportions. Sometimes large apsidal chambers were also placed next to the entrance to the house, where they formed audience chambers.

It is likely that all these developments are associated with a more despotic form of government,[41] introduced by Diocletian to reinforce the authority of the Emperor following the troubles of the third century. The system inaugurated by Diocletian resulted in more authority being given to imperial officials and a reduced role for the oligarchic local government of the cities. Many local aristocrats who had formed the town councils, the curial class, lost influence and their money during this period of heavy central taxation following on from economic depression.

Those individuals with imperial rank found themselves in a privileged position. With the ear of the imperial court they could solve local problems by direct intervention in a more effective way than the local council, to whose members they were often superior in rank. As explained earlier in this chapter, it was natural for them to build rich reception suites and audience chambers at their residences, which were their power base.

The fourth century was also a time of prosperity for much of the Empire, so while aristocratic housing was becoming richer in architecture and decor, many rural residences were also expanding. Syrian villages reached their most extensive with many solid houses fronted by colonnades. In Britain there were a large number of substantial villas (Figs. 11-12). In fourth-century Sicily a number of very important villas such as Piazza Armerina (Fig. 28) and Patti Maritima were built.[42] In North Africa many town houses were extended or refurbished (Fig. 29). The most elaborate Spanish villas also date to this century (Figs. 5-7).

As far as housing is concerned this period of rebuilding and redecorating lasted until the mid-fifth century, when political problems began to affect domestic life again. By this date much of the western Empire had suffered the great barbarian invasions. The Vandals controlled North Africa, the Goths much of France and Spain, as well as Italy including Rome. Dating, as during the similar disturbances of the third century, is difficult. Some of the Middle Eastern villages may have continued to expand, but more archaeological evidence is required to be sure.

It is more certain that urban housing began to decline by the mid-fifth century. Towns throughout the Empire and its former dominions in the west experienced a decline in the number of large houses under occupation. Many peristyle houses were abandoned, or subdivided into several smaller apartments.[43] Some new peristyle houses were being built, and some existing ones were altered, but many more peristyle houses were no longer in use.

This abandonment would seem to be associated with continuing trend to concentrate power into the hands of a relatively small group of citizens with imperial rank, and the flight of many town councillors who would have owned such houses, under an increasing burden of taxation.

From the middle of the fifth century until the middle of the sixth century, we enter the period during which the Roman way of life disappeared for ever. In North Africa extensive work on Roman towns makes it fairly certain that no new peristyle housing was built after AD 450. The same is true of the other provinces lost to the Germanic tribes – Gaul, Spain and Britain.

In the mid-sixth century under the Byzantine emperor Justinian (AD 527-565) there was a brief revival in some areas. The emperor managed to 'reconquer' North Africa, Italy and a small part of southern Spain. In the eastern provinces there was a revival of house building, with some evidence of extensive additions, and, possibly, some new peristyle houses. However, the revival, at least in terms of housing and the Roman way of domestic life, was ephemeral. It resulted in no new 'rich' housing in the reconquered provinces, even though some of the leading citizens of the Empire resided there.

In the east the end of the sixth century saw the absolute end of the Roman house. Ironically the last echoes of Roman housing are probably to be found in the palaces of the first Arab dynasty, the Ummayads, who used Byzantine or local Palestinian mosaicists and painters to decorate them.

If out of all late antique housing we should be looking for an origin of the mediaeval house, it is probably to be found in the vertical-style apartments of Syria and Egypt. It is possible that such vertical apartment housing came to be the main house type of the Byzantine Empire, and from there had a heavy influence of western house types such as the Venetian palazzo. This development, however, is the subject of another book.

7

Conclusions

The overall objective of this book has been to present a summary of Roman housing. It has brought together a number of diverse areas of study. Many studies of Roman housing have concentrated on the peristyle house, its decor of paintings and mosaics. Studies of Pompeii continue to dominate this literature because of its exceptional preservation. This study has compared Pompeian houses with others found throughout the Roman Empire, both provincial houses of the elite and houses of lower social classes. There are many studies of housing in particular provinces. This study has compared houses across all provinces. Finally, this book has attempted to integrate into this picture several subjects for which there are no recent overall studies, such as furniture and lighting.

In reflecting upon this work it is worth beginning by comparing Roman domestic life with that of contemporary western society. Many aspects of Roman domestic life seem deceptively familiar. The design of all housing, ancient and modern, depends on the personal choice of the owner. Roman housing like modern western housing shows a strong measure of personal choice, especially with regard to the decor. Three other social factors encourage comparisons with modern society. Aristocratic Roman households consisted primarily of nuclear families, because, in spite of having many children, they suffered from high mortality. The head of these Roman households had strong control over his property; as we might say, 'his home was his castle'. Lastly, the Romans could, and did, divide their property amongst their heirs. High mortality often meant that there was but one heir, but this principle did allow for occasional wider opportunity. It resulted, in particular, in some wealthy women house owners.

These strong areas of commonality between Roman and modern western domestic life often blind us to major differences, or characteristics specific to Roman housing. The most important difference, which has been stressed several times in this book, was that all housing of the Roman period had a business function. Even the richest aristocratic houses functioned as offices and political bases for their owners. Further down the social scale, urban houses could be involved in agriculture or 'antisocial' industries such as pottery making or fulling, which created noxious smells, smoke and risk of fire.

Many aspects of family life were very different to modern western society, in particular the status of women and children. Theoretically women could inherit property and, under certain circumstances, could initiate divorce proceedings, but in practice their rights were heavily circumscribed compared to those of men.[1] In the case of children this work has upheld the views of Ariès[2] that children were 'invisible' unless they appeared in their role as 'small adults'. Servants, and indeed slaves, were also 'invisible'. Some have identified 'servants' quarters' in Roman houses, but it has been suggested here that servants (like children) often shared space with the adults of the owner's family, sleeping near them and inhabiting the same space during the day.

A review of theories of circulation has suggested that the most appropriate classification might be one based on time of day. The house owner controlled circulation at the beginning of the day when poorer clients would come to greet him at the salutatio. Later, when he left for the town centre, the owner's wife would be in overall charge of the house, which would largely be given over to domestic activity. The owner would return in the late afternoon, when visitors might once again be expected in many parts of the house, such as the baths and dining room.

The two key events that brought visitors to the aristocratic house, the salutatio and the main meal in late afternoon, provide some indicators of differences between social life in a Roman and a modern western house. The salutatio was a very Roman institution. The vast majority of Romans were under an obligation to a patron of higher social rank, to whom they owed advancement in their career, business or political opportunities. To modern eyes this 'corruption' or 'nepotism' seems to verge on the immoral, but to the Romans it was, unless taken to extremes (e.g. vote rigging, murder), a normal part of life. The poorest 'clients' of a patron in the city of Rome would live off the payments they received for attending the salutatio or the receptions of great men.

It might be assumed that, since Roman houses normally had specific dining rooms, Roman dinners would be similar to modern dinners with friends or business associates. Of course, as is well known, the Romans ate lying down, and our vision of Roman dinners has been clouded by the supposed 'orgies' of early emperors. However, the use of fixed dining furniture, seating by order of rank, the specific allocation of space for entertainers, the presence of paid diners or clients, and literary records of highly charged discussion, all suggest that dinners were much more formal than in the modern west.[3]

Architecture, furniture, and especially art have been used to elucidate a number of areas in which domestic life and housing held meaning for the Roman aristocrat. Literature, and countryside scenes in Roman urban mosaics, demonstrate that Roman aristocrats yearned for their country villas and took great pride in their estate produce. Literature, urban garden arrangements and landscape paintings also demonstrate that Roman aristocrats placed great emphasis on the settings of their houses and the views from reception rooms. Many mosaics stressed the exotic, most notably through Nilotic scenes, suggesting a taste for the unusual, which was also expressed through imaginative villa designs like those in Spain. All literary and artistic themes have a tendency to include elements of personal display, including blatant records of particular achievements or events, which were designed to make an impression on influential guests. This blatant self-promotion is alien to modern western society, but it must be remembered that land and property was the main basis for social status in Roman society. It was therefore natural for Romans to express this in their houses.

Some of the artistic motifs of Roman decor, such as the use of country-side scenes, were diffused throughout the Roman Empire. Others were limited to particular regions. The example has been cited of the North African circus charioteer, and amphitheatre scenes at Rudston in Britain, which were not otherwise attested in the province.

While certain artistic themes may not have caught on in other provinces, elements of Roman dining behaviour, as practised in peristyle houses, were adopted in other types of provincial house, as evidenced by inscriptions, mosaics and furniture. The Roman army and early Greek influence in the west have been identified as channels by which Roman housing spread to the western provinces.

By the second century AD a single elite domestic architecture had spread across the Empire. Minor provincial variations, such as African fondness for two reception rooms, and Italian villas' use of extensive garden terraces, are of less importance than the strong unifying elements of peristyle, triclinium and decor. Alongside the aristocratic tradition this work has identified provincial vernacular styles; vernacular in the sense that they were limited to a range of provinces, did not relate strongly to elite culture, but were largely confined to the Roman period. These styles include 'aisled barns' and 'strip housing' in Britain and the north-west provinces, as well as village apartment houses in Syria and Egypt. However, since these vernacular styles adopted elements derived from the peristyle housing 'canon', it would seem that many of the lower classes of Roman society did indeed aspire to a rich villa.

In late antique times a more centralised, autocratic society led to the used of audience halls and grand dining halls to receive poorer clients and social equals respectively. This movement towards more formality and privacy has been identified as a reversal of the movement which saw the abandonment of the atrium and tablinum in the first century AD. These new great houses were owned by those with imperial rank who could call on influence at court to help their clients. Town councillors lost influence and wealth as they had to guarantee taxes with their personal incomes. This led to an increasing polarisation of society. As a result, by the mid-fifth century, many peristyle houses became subdivided as their own-ers fled, or had no money to maintain them. Some rich villas continued in use under barbarian rule during the fifth century, but the Roman way of life had begun to disappear. The brief Justinianic revival did little to change this, and no new peristyle houses were built after the middle of the sixth century.

Throughout the fifth and sixth centuries it is possible to detect another social change which had an impact on housing. Practices of inheritance had also changed. Increasing sums of money were given to the Church, and entrance into the ranks of the clergy was often seen as one way of keeping private fortunes from the tax collector. The increasing dearth of rich houses at a time when rich churches were still being erected and imperial aristocrats could still travel at ease throughout the Mediterranean, suggests that the leaders of the Empire still had private fortunes but were less inclined to invest in houses. Thus excavators at Arles, Carthage and Marseilles have all remarked on the lack of rich houses in the fifth and sixth centuries AD, when the cities were prosperous with trade and inhabited by people renowned throughout the Mediterranean.[4]

The degree to which Roman behaviour, and an ideal of a Roman way of life, spread throughout the lands under Rome's control demonstrates its effectiveness at influencing those it governed. The Roman house is a definitive reflection of the state of Romanisation. This book has demonstrated that Romanisation was not imposed by force. It was a result of many individuals seeing something desirable about the Roman way of life. That something may have been the political and monetary rewards that rapprochement with Roman society could bring. In many cases, though, such a reward is by no means clear. It is hard to see a direct political reward for someone who built a private bath, or chose to have a stibadium dining suite in a town at the mouth of the Danube. Many aspects of the Roman way of life were simply attractive to a wide range of people. At the end of the Empire, it may not have been the barbarian invasions, political, or economic factors that destroyed the Roman way of life. It was perhaps just that Roman behaviour was no longer of interest to those of substance.

Map of principal sites discussed. Numbered sites in Britain:
1 Woodchester, 2 Chedworth, 3 Great Witcombe, 4 Frocester
Court, 5 Lullingstone, 6 Silchester, 7 Fishbourne, 8 Littlecote.

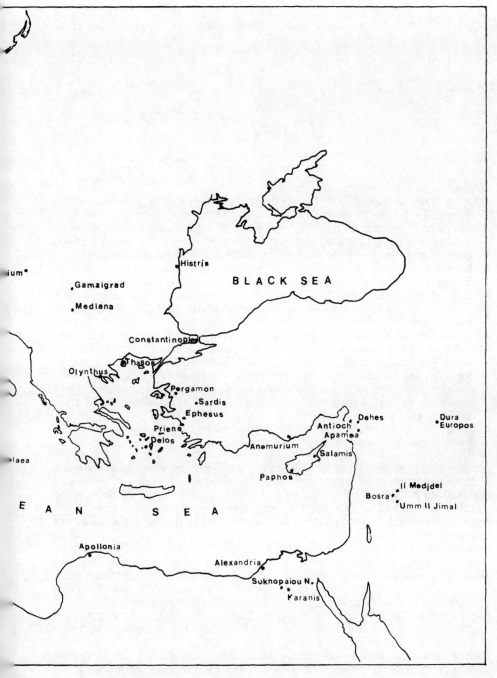

BLACK SEA

ium

Gamzigrad

Mediana

Histris

Constantinople

Thasos

Olynthus

Pergamon

Sardis

Ephesus

Priene

Delos

Dehes

Antioch

Apamea

Anemurium

Salamis

Paphos

Dura
Europos

Il Medjdel

Bosra

Umm Il Jimal

laea

E A N   S E A

Apollonia

Alexandria

Soknopaiou N.

Karanis

Glossary

abacus a side table, commonly of stone.

alae two rooms in **atrium**-style houses, located at either side of the far end of the **atrium**. Each room was completely open to the **atrium**.

amphora large ceramic jar for carrying wine or olive oil, with a distinctive shape relating to the region of manufacture. Amphorae had round or pointed bases, which meant they had to be supported or sunk in a floor to remain upright.

andron the men's reception room in the classical Greek house. Usually located near to the front door in order to prevent visitors entering the main house.

arca chest containing family valuables and documents. Traditionally, a pair (arcae) placed one on either side of the **atrium**. Later stored in the **oecus** or **triclinium**.

atrium a covered court in the traditional late Republican aristocratic house. The central area of the court was uncovered to allow rain to fall into the **impluvium**. The atrium might be **compluviate**: roof tilted down towards the centre, **displuviate**: roof tilted away from the centre, or **testudinate**: court completely roofed with no central hole. A **tetrastyle atrium** was one in which the central opening in the roof was supported by four columns, resembling a small **peristyle**.

authespa a jug, or flask, in which wine was warmed and mixed before being served. Probably stored in the **triclinium**.

basilica a room with internal colonnades. A civil basilica was a large hall used for a meeting of all the citizens in a Roman town. Early churches are often called basilica, since they took the same architectural form.

cartibulum a table, usually of marble or bronze, found at the entrance to the **tablinum** in the atrium house. Used in the **salutatio**.

cenaculum a form of apartment house, characterised by the use of a **medianum** instead of a court.

cryptoporticus an underground corridor, usually built into the side of sloping ground, or a cliff. Lighting was by shafts or arches out to the sloping ground.

cubiculum bedroom. A room with a single couch used for sleeping, or for privacy, hence termed a 'retiring room' in this work. Often identified by a plain mosaic panel, a raised section of flooring, or an arched 'niche' within the room.

dominus 'lord' or 'master'. Normally used under the Empire to describe an aristocratic estate owner, or patron. In late antiquity associated with the autocratic control of a client's rights and property.

domus the normal Roman word for an independent house. It can also be applied to a family, and hence an organisation – **domus publicus** the offices of the public officials at Rome.

emblema a fine mosaic, or painted, panel which was usually inserted into a background design. An emblema was often manufactured off site or cut out of an older work.

exedra an ill-defined term that is usually applied to a large recess opening off a **portico**. It is assumed that such features provided sitting areas on the edge of courts and gardens, similar to modern 'summer houses'.

fauces the entrance corridor to the traditional atrium house, running to the **atrium** between two flanking rooms.

frons scenae term used to describe the backdrop of an ancient theatre stage. Consisted of alternating semicircular and rectangular niches framed by columns. The niches would have contained statues. The whole would be several storeys high.

Hippodamian grid. The system of laying out a town as two sets of parallel streets intersecting each other at right angles, to create a series of rectangular blocks. Said to have been invented by the Greek Hippodamus.

horreum a granary or store room.

hortus the traditional garden 'patch' of a Roman house. Usually located to the rear of the house, in the area which was sometimes incorporated into the **peristyle**.

hypocaust Roman underfloor heating system. The floor was supported by blocks of brick or masonry. A stokehole on the exterior wall of the building was used to send hot air under the floor.

impluvium the central pool of the **atrium**. Often had a cistern beneath it.

lararium shrine to the household gods – the Lares and Penates – usually in the form of a small niche in the style of a temple frontage, with a small altar in front.

materfamilias the senior female member of the family or household, usually the house owner's wife.

medianum corridor or court linking together the rooms in a **cenaculum** apartment.

nymphaeum a fountain, with architectural backdrop. In early times this might consist of a small mosaic within an architectural frame. In the case of public fountains and large houses the backdrop might be a **frons scenae** of alternating semi-circular and rectangular niches on one or two storeys. Each niche was flanked by columns, and could contain a statue. Usually located in the **peristyle** opposite the main reception or dining room.

oecus a reception room, normally interpreted as being at the centre of one peristyle portico. The precise application of the term to a particular room is the subject of some debate, and in some cases it can be synonymous with the term **triclinium**.

oppidum Latin term applied to very densely occupied pre-Roman settlements, or towns, in the Celtic world.

opus sectile a floor made out of pieces of different coloured marble.

opus signinum a mixture of tile and mortar used to make a floor. Also used in baths because of its water resistant properties.

opus spicatum a floor made out of tiles set on edge in a herringbone pattern.

orans an attitude of prayer adopted by early Christians. Both hands are raised in the air with palms open facing forwards.

palaestra a large open area for walking or exercising. Usually surrounded on four sides by colonnades.

paterfamilias the male head of the family.

peristyle an area enclosed by colonnades or **porticoes**, normally four-sided.

piano nobile a mediaeval term describing houses in which the main living rooms lay on an upper floor.

polycandelon a circular bronze fitting in which several glass lamps were placed. A late antique form of chandelier.

portico a roofed colonnade usually fronting a range of rooms.

Regia the traditional house of the Kings of Rome in the City of Rome below the Palatine hill.

salutatio the traditional morning greeting at which the clients met their patron. Normally took place in the **tablinum**.

sigma semicircular or cicular table used with the **stibadium** couch.

sportulae the rewards given to a poor client who attended the **salutatio** or dinner at a patron's house.

stadium the Greek running track, with one semicircular and one square end. This term was also applied to a large garden with a similar shape.

tablinum the traditional reception room for the **atrium** house. Setting for the **salutatio**.

triclinium traditional Roman dining room. The name derives from the three couches used in the room, which are often represented by plain mosaic panels.

valvae folding wooden partitions used for closing off rooms and windows.

venatio a form of mock hunt staged in the amphitheatre, and often represented in domestic mosaics.

Terms concerned with bathing can be found in Chapter 5.

Terms for rooms as used in the Egyptian papyri can be found in Chapter 3.

Notes

1. Introduction

1. Original excavations: A. Mau, 'Scavi di Pompeii 1894-5, Reg 6, Isola ad E della II', *Röm. Mitt.* 11 (1896), pp. 3-97, A. Sogliano, 'La casa dei Vettii in Pompeii', *Acad. dei Lincei* 8 (1898), cols 233-416. Amongst more recent studies T. Wirth, 'Zum Bildprogramm in der Casa dei Vettii', *Röm. Mitt.* 90 (1983), pp. 449-55.

2. The most important source on gardens at Pompeii is W. Jashemski, *The Gardens of Pompeii, Herculaneum, and the Villas Destroyed by Vesuvius* (New York 1979). Gardens are discussed more fully in Chapter 5.

3. P. Foss, 'Watchful lares: Roman household organization and the rituals of Roman domestic space', in R. Laurence and A. Wallace-Hadrill, ed., *Domestic Space in the Roman World: Pompeii and beyond* (Portsmouth 1997), pp. 196-218. See also H. Flower, *Ancestor Masks and Aristocratic Power in Roman Culture* (Oxford 1996).

4. E. Zanette, *Dizionario del dialetto di Vittoria Veneto, Bastiani* (Vittoria Veneto 1980), p. 295.

5. A. Wallace-Hadrill, 'The social structure of the Roman house', *PBSR* 56 (1988), pp. 79 and 82, discusses servants' quarters. For servants sleeping at the door of their masters see P. Veyne, 'The Roman Empire', in P. Veyne, ed., *A History of Private Life 1: from pagan Rome to Byzantium* (Cambridge 1987), p. 73, and S. Treggiari, *Roman Marriage: iusti coniuges from the time of Cicero to the time of Ulpian* (Oxford 1990), p. 416.

6. M. George, 'Servus and domus: the slave in the Roman house', in R. Laurence and A. Wallace-Hadrill, op. cit. n. 3, pp. 15-24.

7. Wallace-Hadrill, op. cit. n. 5. For detailed workings of the system of personal patronage see R. Saller, *Personal Patronage under the Early Empire* (Cambridge 1982), and A. Wallace-Hadrill, ed., *Patronage in Ancient Society* (London 1989).

8. For shops and lower-class housing see Chapter 3. A well preserved group of over 30 shops is reported in S. Crawford, *The Byzantine Shops at Sardis* (Cambridge 1990).

9. P. Garnsey and R. Saller, *The Roman Empire: economy, society and culture* (London 1987), chapter 6, pp. 107-25, provides a good recent picture of the relative standing of the various Roman social groups including slaves and peasants.

10. The last two were A.G. McKay, *Houses, Villas and Palaces of the Roman World* (London 1975), J. Percival, *The Roman Villa* (London 1975).

11. R. Stupperich, 'Some fourth century British mosaics', *Britannia* 11 (1980), pp. 289-302. R. Ling, 'Brading, Brantingham, and York: a new look at some fourth century mosaics', *Britannia* 22 (1991), pp. 147-58.

12. Stupperich, op. cit. n. 11, pp. 293-6. The site at Keynsham is discussed further below in Chapter 2.

13. Ling, op. cit. n. 11, pp. 148-53.

14. J.R. Clarke, *The Houses of Roman Italy 100 BC – AD 250* (Berkeley 1991), pp. 233-4.

15. For example M. Henig, *The Art of Roman Britain* (London 1995), p. 126, concludes that pattern books were used as far afield as Roman Britain.

16. Clarke, op. cit. n. 14, pp. 146 and 157.

17. There are numerous works which discuss mosaic schools, for example: K. Dunbabin, *The Mosaics of Roman North Africa: studies in iconography and patronage* (Oxford 1978); M. Spiro, *Critical Corpus of Mosaic Pavements of the Greek Mainland in the Fourth to Sixth Centuries with Architectural Surveys* (New York 1978); D.J. Smith, 'The mosaic pavements', in A.L.F. Rivet, ed., *The Roman Villa in Britain* (London 1969), pp. 71-126.

18. D.S. Peacock, *Pottery in the Roman World* (London 1982), pp. 120-8.

19. Henig, op. cit. n. 15, pp. 123-4, expresses similar doubts.

20. M. Millet, *The Romanisation of Roman Britain* (Cambridge 1990), is the clearest statement of the problem as applied to Britain.

21. G. Webster, ed., *Fortress into City* (London 1988), is a useful study discussing archaeological evidence linking town formation with the Roman military.

22. M. Benabou, *La résistance africaine à la romanisation* (Paris 1976); R. Hingley, *Romano-British Rural Settlement* (London 1989).

23. Clarke, op. cit. n. 14.

24. This is most obvious in the cities of Asia Minor, such as Ephesus and Side. Housing in a clearly Roman style is also known from Greece.

25. J. D'Arms, *Romans on the Bay of Naples: a social and cultural study of the villas and their owners* (Cambridge 1970).

26. A. Maiuri, 'Il palazzo di Tiberio detto "villa Iovis" a Capri', in *Atti del Congresso Nazionale di Studi Romani* (1933), pp. 156-71, id., *Capri* (Rome 1958), pp. 33-57, McKay, op. cit. n. 9, pp. 124-6.

27. This at least was the opinion of the slanderous Roman historian Suetonius and the anti-imperial Tacitus. The truth was probably more prosaic: B. Levick, *Tiberius the Politician* (London 1976).

28. *The Twelve Caesars* 3.60.

29. For the development of the Roman concept of a palace, see F. Millar, *The Emperor in the Roman World* (London 1977), pp. 18-22. Architectural trends are discussed in Chapter 2 below.

30. Pliny, *Letters* 2.17.20.

31. Pliny, *Letters* 9.16. *Letter* 3.19 about the purchase of a neighbouring farm emphasises the breadth of Pliny's agricultural concerns.

32. For elaboration of this point see the discussion in Chapter 3 below.

33. For Pompeii see Clarke, op. cit. n. 14, and for Britain J. Wacher, *The Towns of Roman Britain* (London 1995), pp. 33 and 318.

34. This is the definition used by E. Scott, *A Gazetteer of Roman Villas in Britain* (Leicester 1993), pp. 3-4. She also provides useful comment on the original Latin term.

35. Despite Pliny's statement to the contrary, see comments by A.N. Sherwin-White, *The Letters of Pliny* (Oxford 1966), pp. 186-9. Sherwin-White also doubts the common assumption that the villas were owned by Pliny himself.

36. B. Bergmann, 'Painted perspectives of a villa visit', in E. Gazda, ed., *Roman Art in the Private Sphere* (Ann Arbor 1991), pp. 49-70.

37. Sidonius Apollinaris, *Letters* 2.2.11-12.

38. This point is expressly made by Vitruvius, *On Architecture* 6.5. For commentary see R.P. Saller, 'Familia, domus, and the Roman family', *Phoenix* 38 (1984), pp. 351-55, T.P. Wiseman, 'Conspicui postes tectaque digna deo: the public image of aristocratic houses in the Late Republic and Early Empire', in *L'Urbs: espace urbain et histoire (1er siècle av. J.C. – IIIe siècle ap. J.C.)* (Rome 1987), pp. 393-413.

39. See for example A. Carrandini et al., *Sette Finestre: una villa schiavistica nell'etruria romana* (Modena 1985).

40. Y. Thébert, 'Private life and domestic architecture in Roman Africa', in P. Veyne, ed., *A History of Private Life 1: from pagan Rome to Byzantium* (Cambridge 1987), pp. 326-9.

41. Thébert, op. cit. n. 40, p. 326.

42. See Wacher, op. cit. n. 33, and B. Burnham and J. Wacher, *The Small Towns of Roman Britain* (London 1990).

43. H. Butler and H. Prentice, *Publications of the Princeton Archaeological Expedition to Syria 1904-5 and 1909, Division 2 Architecture* (Leiden 1919-20).

44. S. Ellis, *Graeco-Roman Egypt* (Princes Risborough 1992), pp. 23-8.

45. The precise origins of Roman housing in Celtic and Semitic traditions are subject to much debate, but serve here to give a broad context for discussion.

46. For the house and the family see Wallace-Hadrill, op. cit. n. 5. Traditional text-based studies of the family include S. Dixon, *The Roman Family* (Baltimore 1992), and S. Treggiari, op. cit. n. 5.

47. This is particularly clear in Gaul as seen through the letters of Sidonius Apollinaris and documented by R. Van Dam, *Leadership and Community in Late Antique Gaul* (California 1985).

48. See S. Ellis, 'The end of the Roman house', *AJA* 92 (1988), pp. 565-76, for a broader historical context.

2. Houses of Pretension

1. A. Wallace-Hadrill, *Housing and Society in Pompeii and Herculaneum* (Princeton 1994), pp. 4-5.

2. For the early excavations at Marzabotto see E. Brizio, 'Relazione degli scavi eseguiti a Marzabotto presso Bologna', *Mon. Ant.* (1891), cols 249-442. Later work includes G. Mansuelli, 'La casa etrusca di Marzabotto', *Röm. Mitt.* (1963), pp. 44-62.

3. Mansuelli, op. cit. n. 2, p. 56.

4. This is also the case with regard to similar sixth-century BC supposed 'atrium' houses recently excavated by Carrandini at the east end of the Roman Forum. Moreover these houses have not so far been the subject of detailed publication, and it would be premature to present interpretation in this work. See R. Ross Holloway, *The Archaeology of Early Rome and Latium* (London 1996), pp. 63-4.

5. The most important study is W. Hoepfner and E.-L. Schwander, *Haus und Stadt im klassischen Griechenland* (Munich 1994).

6. For Greek women in relation to domestic architecture, S. Walker, 'Women and housing in classical Greece: the archaeological evidence', in A. Cameron and A. Kuhrt, ed., *Images of Women in Antiquity* (Oxford 1983), pp. 81-91.

7. G. Vallet, F. Villard and P. Auberson, *Megara Hyblaea 1: le quartier de l'Agora archaïque* (Rome 1976), and id., *Megara Hyblaea 3: guide des fouilles* (Rome 1983).

8. ibid., pp. 81-4

9. H. Drerup, *Zum Ausstattungsluxus in der römischen Architektur: ein form-geschichtlicher Versuch* (Münster 1957), pp. 3-13.

10. Greek pottery dating from the eighth century BC has been found in an Archaic sanctuary below Sant' Omobono: *Il viver quotidiano in Roma arcaica* (Rome 1989), and R. Ross Holloway, op. cit. n. 4, pp. 68-70.

11. Principally early cemeteries in Rome: Holloway, op. cit. n. 4, pp. 170-1.

12. Although the general picture of the development of the Regia is becoming clearer, there is still much work to be done. See R. Ross Holloway, op. cit. n. 4, pp. 170-1, F. Coarelli, *Il Foro Romano 1: periodo arcaico* (Rome 1986), pp. 56-79, and C. Smith, *Early Rome and Latium* (Oxford 1996), pp. 174-8.

13. Smith, op. cit. n. 12, pp. 173-4.

14. S. Stoponni, ed., *Casa e palazzi d'Etruria* (1985), K.M. Phillips, *In the Hills of Tuscany: recent excavations at the Etruscan site of Poggio Civitate (Murlo, Siena)* (Philadelphia 1993), R.D. DePuma and J.P. Small, ed., *Murlo and the Etruscans: art and society in ancient Etruria* (Madison 1994), and Holloway, op. cit. n. 4, pp. 55-60.

15. For a concise summary of this discussion and comparison with Marzabotto see F. Prayon 'Architecture', in L. Bonfonte, ed., *Etruscan Life and Afterlife* (Warminster 1981), pp. 189-90.

16. Many of these aspects of the triclinium are covered in Chapter 4.

17. See R. Saller, 'Roman kinship: structure and sentiment', in B. Rawson and P. Weaver, ed., *The Roman Family in Italy* (Oxford 1997), pp. 31-2, maintaining that the legal rights of the paterfamilias were not so often enforced in practice.

18. S. Treggiari, *Roman Marriage: iusti coniuges from the time of Cicero to the time of Ulpian* (Oxford 1991), pp. 421-2.

19. For a good selection of arcae found in Pompeian atria, E. Pernice, *Hellenistische Tische, Zisternmündungen, Beckenduntersätze, Altäre und Truhen* (Berlin 1932), pp. 76-94.

20. R. Winkes, 'Pliny's chapter on Roman funerary customs in the light of the Clipeatae Imagines', *AJA* 83 (1979), pp. 481-4, P. Foss, 'Watchful lares: Roman household organization and the rituals of Roman domestic space', in R. Laurence and A. Wallace-Hadrill, ed., *Domestic Space in the Roman World: Pompeii and beyond* (Portsmouth 1997), pp. 196-218. For a full study of the use of ancestral images see H. Flower, *Ancestor Masks and Aristocratic Power in Roman Culture* (Oxford 1996), especially pp. 185-209 concerning houses.

21. A. Wallace-Hadrill, 'Rethinking the Roman atrium house', in Laurence and Wallace-Hadrill, op. cit. n. 20, pp. 219-40.

22. S.C. Nappo, 'The urban transformation at Pompeii in the late third century and early second centuries BC', in Laurence and Wallace-Hadrill, op. cit. n. 20, pp. 91-120.

23. V.J. Bruno and R.T. Scott, *Cosa IV: the Houses* (Rome 1993).

24. op. cit. n. 21, p. 238.

25. For example M. Wheeler, *Roman Art and Architecture* (London 1964), p. 128.

26. M.S. Retoloza, 'Distribucion y evolucion de la vivienda urbana tardorepublicana y altoimperial en Ampurias', in *La Casa Urbana Hispanoromana: ponencias y communicaciones* (Zaragoza 1991), pp. 19-34.

27. J. Guitart, P. Padros and C. Puerta, 'La casa urbana en Baetula', in *La Casa Urbana Hispanoromana*, pp. 35-47, supported by comments in S. Keay, *Roman Spain* (London 1988), p. 140.

28. The existence of an atrium in the House of the Silver Bust is claimed by A.G. McKay, *Houses, Villas and Palaces of the Roman World* (Southampton 1975), pp. 162-3, after A. Boëthius and J.B. Ward Perkins, *Etruscan and Roman Architecture* (Harmondsworth 1970).

29. C. Goudineau, 'Les fouilles de la Maison du Dauphin à Vaison-la-Romaine', *Gallia*, Suppl. 37 (1979).

30. Originally interpreted as a Greek colony, it has been reconsidered as an indigenous settlement of the second century BC: A.R. Congrès, 'Nouvelles fouilles à Glanum (1982-1990)', *JRA* 5 (1992), pp. 39-46.

31. H. Rolland, 'Fouilles de Glanum', *Gallia*, Suppl. 1 (1946), id., *Gallia Suppl.* 11 (1958), F. Chamoux, 'Les antiques de St. Rémy-en-Provence', *Phoibos* 6-7 (1951-3), pp. 97-111, McKay, op. cit. n. 28 pp. 159-61.

32. M. Sabrié, R. Sabrié and Y. Solier, *La maison à portiques du Clos de la Lombarde à Narbonne et sa décoration murale* (Narbonne 1987), M. Sabrié and R. Sabrié, 'La maison à portiques du Clos de la Lombarde à Narbonne et la décoration de trois pièces autour de l'atrium', *Revue Archéologique Narbonnaise* 22 (1989), pp. 237-86.

33. Information from Ian Ralston. See C. Goudineau and C. Peyre, *Bibracte et les Eduens: à la découverte d'un peuple gaulois* (Paris 1993), pp. 51-80.

34. Y. Thébert, 'Private life and domestic architecture in Roman North Africa', in P. Veyne, ed., *A History of Private Life*, Vol. I (Cambridge 1987), pp. 325-6.

35. R. Etienne, *Le quartier nord-est de Volubilis* (Paris 1960), pp. 121-2.

36. E. Dwyer, 'The Pompeian atrium house in theory and in practice', in E. Gazda, ed., *Roman Art in the Private Sphere* (Ann Arbor 1991), pp. 25-48.

37. op. cit. n. 7, pp. 45-7.

38. ibid., pp. 18-20.

39. T. Wiegand and H. Schrader, *Priene* (Berlin 1904), M. Schede, *Die Ruinen von Priene* (Berlin 1964). Hoepfner and Schwandner, op. cit. n. 5, pp. 210-16.

40. D.M. Robinson and J.W. Graham, *Excavations at Olynthus 8: the Hellenistic house* (Baltimore 1938), p. 160.

41. Ibid., pp. 63-8.

42. Hoepfner and Schwandner, op. cit. n. 5, pp. 82-9.

43. Right and left in this book are used in relation to someone standing in the main entrance to the house, facing in.

44. As for example the House of the Prince of Naples, discussed in the next chapter.

45. The idea of an atrium redesigned as a peristyle would seem to be suggested by the comments of McKay, op. cit. n. 28, p. 35, as well as J.B. Ward-Perkins and A. Claridge, *Pompeii AD 79* (London 1979), p. 48.

46. J.R. Clarke, *The Houses of Roman Italy 100 BC – AD 250* (Berkeley 1991), pp. 23-5.

47. J.-A. Dickmann, 'The peristyle and the transformation of domestic space in Hellenistic Pompeii', in Laurence and Wallace-Hadrill, op. cit. n. 20, pp. 121-36.

48. Clarke, op. cit. n. 46, p. 4.

49. Wallace-Hadrill, op. cit. n. 1, p. 20.

50. V.M. Strocka, *Casa del Labirinto* (Munich 1991).

51. McKay, op. cit. n. 28, p. 50.

52. As accepted by McKay, op. cit. n. 28, p. 51, and Clarke, op. cit. n. 46, p. 237. A. Wallace-Hadrill, *Houses and Society in Pompeii and Herculaneum* (Princeton 1994), pp. 18-19 sees the room as a tablinum, but also seemingly accepts it as an Egyptian oecus.

53. See below.

54. G. Hermansen, *Ostia: aspects of Roman city life* (Edmonton 1982), p. 19.

55. Wallace-Hadrill, op. cit. n. 1, pp. 51-2.

56. For this house see also V. Tran Tam Tinh, *La Casa dei Cervi a Herculaneum* (Rome, 1988).

57. Found in 1975 on the Jardin d'Hiver sites: C. Sintes, ed., *Du Nouveau sur L'Arles antique*, Revue d'Arles 1 (Arles 1987), p. 41.

58. A. Beltrán et al., *Colonia Victrix Iulia Lepida – Celsa (Velilla del Ebro) 1: la* *arquitectura de la Casa de los Delfines* (Zaragoza 1984), S. Keay, *Roman Spain* (London 1988), p. 135. For a more recent overview of Romanisation in Spain, A.T. Fear, *Rome and Baetica: urbanisation in southern Spain* (Oxford 1996), including pp. 206-12 on houses.

59. Keay, op. cit. n. 58, p. 69.

60. J.D. Redon et al., 'La Caridad (Caminreal, Teruel)', in *La casa urbana Hispano-romana*, op. cit. n. 26, pp. 81-129.

61. R. Agache, 'Nouveaux apports des prospections aériennes en archéologie pré-romaine et romaine de la Picardie', *Cahiers Arch. de la Picardie* 6 (1979), pp. 33-90.

62. D. Bayard and J.-L. Collart, ed., 'De la ferme indigène à la villa romaine: la romanisation des campagnes de la Gaule', *Revue Arch. de Picardie* 11 (1996) especially the papers by C. Haselgrove, 'La romanisation de l'habitat de l'Aisne d'après les prospections de surface et les fouilles récentes', pp. 109-20, and J.-L. Collart, 'La naissance de la villa en Picardie; la ferme gallo-romaine précose', pp. 124-32.

63. E. Wightman, *Gallia Belgica* (London 1985), pp. 88-9. For Trier, E. Wightman, *Roman Trier and the Treveri* (London 1970), and for Avenches, H. Bögli, 'Aventicum', *Bonner Jahrbücher* 172 (1972), pp. 175-94.

64. Wightman, op. cit. n. 63 (1985), p. 111, and id., op. cit. n. 63 (1970).

65. J. Metzler, J. Zimmer and L. Bakker, *Ausgrabungen in Echternach* (Luxembourg 1981).

66. Wightman, op. cit. n. 63 (1985), p. 111.

67. ibid.

68. See J. Wacher, *The Towns of Roman Britain* (London 1995), pp. 18 and 219 for municipal status, and p. 226 for Flavian housing.

69. S. Ellis, 'Classical reception rooms in Romano-British houses', *Britannia* 26 (1995), pp. 163-78.

70. B. Cunliffe, *Excavations at Fishbourne 1961-1969* (London 1971).

71. For the most recent excavations S.S. Frere, 'Roman Britain in 1986', *Britannia* 18 (1986), pp. 352-3. A summary of the role of Cogidubnus, the palace and supply base, is provided by Wacher, op. cit. n. 68, pp. 257-61.

72. D. Neal, A. Wardle and J. Huin, *Excavations of the Iron Age, Roman, and Mediaeval Settlement at Gorhambury, St Albans* (London 1990), pp. 56-7.

73. For an example of servants' quarters see the House of Menander at Pompeii, R. Ling, *The Insula of Menander at Pompeii 1: the structures* (Oxford 1997), for an example of family suites the House of the Triumph of Neptune at Acholla, S. Gozlan, *La maison du Triomphe de Neptune à Acholla (Botria, Tunis) 1: les mosaïques* (Rome 1992).

74. Martial, *Epigrams* 2.23, berates a friend for only inviting people to dine if he has bathed with them on a previous occasion.

75. M. Heleno, 'A villa lusitano-romana de Torre de Palma (Monforte)', *O Arqueólogo Português* 4 (1962), pp. 313-38; J. Gorges, *Les Villas Hispano-Romaines* (Paris 1979), pp. 465-6.

76. F. De Almeida, 'O mosaico dos cavalos (Torre de Palma)', *O Arqueólogo Português* 4 (1962), pp. 263-73.

77. Gorges, op. cit. n. 75, pp. 398-9.

78. ibid., pp. 481-2.

79. ibid., El Faro p. 307, Pago de Bruñel pp. 271-2, and Torre Llauder pp. 208-9. See also M. Prevosti et al., 'Recent work on villas around Ampurias, Gerona, Iluno and Barcelona (North-East Spain)', *JRA* 8 (1995), pp. 292-7, suggesting that the 'atrium' at El Faro is of Severan date.

80. *pace* Gorges, op. cit. n. 75, p. 208, where the word tablinum is used for a room at Torre Llauder without justification.

81. P. De Palol, 'Los dos mosaicos hispanicos de Aquiles, el de Pedrosa de la Vega y el de Santisteban de Puerto', *2 Congrès sur la mosaïque greco-romaine* (1975), pp. 227-37. Gorges, op. cit. n. 75, pp. 336-7.

82. J.M.R. Hidalgo, 'Dos ejemplos domesticos en Trajanopolis (Italica): las casas de los pajaros y de la exedra', in *La casa urbana Hispano-romana,* op. cit. n. 26, pp. 291-302.

83. The House of the Stags at Herculaneum, in particular shares the same elements of garden, open dining area, and view over the town walls: Tram Tan Tinh, op. cit. n. 56.

84. A. Pelletier, *Vienne Antique* (Lyon 1982-3). The general character of development at Vienne in comparison with other Gallic sites is described by R. Bedon, R. Chevallier and P. Pinon, *Architecture et Urbanisme en Gaule Romaine 1: l'architecture et la ville* (Paris 1988), pp. 358-62.

85. L. Joulin, 'Les établissements gallo-romaines de la plaine de Martres – Tolosanes', *Mémoires présentés par divers savants à L'Academie des Inscriptions et Belles-lettres* 11.1 (1901).

86. G. Fouet, 'La villa gallo-romaine de Montmaurin (Haute Garonne)', *Gallia*, Suppl. 20 (1969).

87. The original excavation was reported in E. Boeswillwald, R. Cagnat and A. Ballu, *Timgad: une cité africaine sous l'Empire romain* (Paris 1905), but has been much commented on since. House plans are re-published in R. Rebuffat, 'Maisons à peristyle d'Afrique du Nord: répertoire de plans publiés', *MEFR* 81 (1969), pp. 659-724. For a recent commentary see Thébert, op. cit. n. 34, pp. 330-2.

88. Rebuffat, op. cit. n. 87, p. 678.

89. R. Etienne, op. cit. n. 35 with additional material and notes in Rebuffat, op. cit. n. 87, pp. 667-71.

90. J. Baradez, 'La maison des fresques et la voie la limitant', *Libyca* 9 (1961), pp. 49-199.

91. L. Foucher, *Découvertes archéologiques à Thysdrus en 1961*, Tunis (not dated).

92. M. Alexander, M. Ennaifer et al., *Corpus de Mosaïques de la Tunisie 1.1 Utique Insula 1-3* (Tunis 1973), pp. 19-56.

93. For dating of Delos in general and the possibility of occupation after the first century BC see P. Bruneau, 'Contribution à l'histoire urbaine de Délos', *BCH* 92 (1968), pp. 633-709.

94. There is a huge literature on Delos, but for housing see in particular J. Chamonard, *Exploration Archéologique de Délos 8.2 Le quartier du théâtre* (Paris 1924), and P. Bruneau et al., *Exploration Archéologique de Délos 27 L'ilot de la Maison des Comédiens* (Paris 1970). Evidence is also summarised in Hoepfner and Schwandner, op. cit. n. 5, pp. 295-8.

95. Chamonard, op. cit. n. 94, pp. 139-52.

96. The final reports on excavations at Thasos have not yet published finds from the High Roman Empire, but a partial plan is published in G. Daux, 'Chronique des fouilles en 1953', *BCH* 78 (1954), pp. 192-3.

97. C. Kondoleon, 'Signs of privilege and pleasure: Roman domestic mosaics', in E. Gazda, ed., *Roman Art in the Private Sphere* (Ann Arbor 1991), pp. 105-15, and id., *Domestic and Divine* (Ithaca 1995).

98. G. Daux, 'Chronique des fouilles en 1964', *BCH* 89 (1965), pp. 792-8.

99. See for example that at the House of the Vettii discussed in the first chapter.

100. A variety of literary references are assembled by L. Nevett, 'Perceptions of domestic space in Roman Italy', in B. Rawson and P. Weaver, ed., *The Roman Family in Italy: status, sentiment, space* (Oxford 1997), p. 293, including Cicero *Pro Scaur.* 26.4 and Pliny *Letters* 5.1.6 and 5.3.11, concerning receiving friends 'in cubiculo'.

101. *Letters* 2.17.15-7, 4.2.5, 5.6.32-3, 9.36.3.

102. T. Ashby, 'The classical topography of the Roman campagna – 3 the Via Latina', *PBSR* 4 (1907), pp. 1-160.

103. Ibid., pp. 121-4, and *Notizie degli Scavi* (8th Series) 6 (1952), pp. 257-83.

104. See below for a preserved example at Domitian's palace in Rome.

105. G. Lugli, *Horace's Sabine Farm* (Rome 1931).

106. A. Boëthius and J.B. Ward Perkins, *Etruscan and Roman Architecture* (Harmondsworth 1970), p. 330.

107. A. Maiuri, *La Villa dei Misteri* (Rome 1931).

108. op. cit. n. 103.

109. *Notizie degli Scavi* (6th Series) 6 (1930), pp. 529-35.

110. A. Carrandini and S. Settis, *Una villa schiavistica nell'Etruria romana* (Modena 1985).

111. *Notizie degli Scavi* (7th Series) 2 (1942), pp. 43-69.

112. op. cit. n. 12, pp. 56-79.

113. *Roman History* 54.27, together with commentary of F. Millar, *The Emperor in the Roman World* (London 1977), pp. 19-20.

114. M. Steinby, *Lexicon Topographicum Romanum* 2 (Rome 1995), pp. 130-2.

115. Of course as indicated previously all Roman aristocrats had local power as patrons of their poorer clients.

116. The most up to date account of the imperial palaces is Steinby, op. cit. n. 114.

117. B. Tamm, *Auditorium and Palatium* (Stockholm 1963), pp. 64-5.

118. There is a very extensive literature on the palaces of Nero. Recent work on the building is described by L. Fabbrini, 'Domus Aurea, il piano superiore del quartiere orientale', *Atti della Pontificia Accademia Romana*, 3rd Series 14 (1982), p. 5ff, and id., 'Domus Aurea: una nuova lettura planimetrica del palazzo sul colle Oppio', in *Anal. Romana Inst. Danici Suppl* 10 (1983), p. 169ff, and especially L.F. Ball, 'A reappraisal of Nero's Domus Aurea', *JRA*, Suppl. 11 (1994), pp. 183-254. The historic background is given by M. Griffin, *Nero: the end of a dynasty* (London 1984), pp. 125-42.

119. Tacitus, *Annals* 15.42.

120. For early uses of the apse see F. Rakob, 'Ambivalente Apsiden – zur Zeichensprache der Römischen Architektur', *Röm. Mitt.* 94 (1987), pp. 1-28.

121. Ball, op. cit. n. 118, has recently demonstrated that while many architectural innovations in the domus Aurea are correctly assigned to Nero's reign many elements of the plan were determined by pre-existing structures.

122. Steinby, op. cit. n. 114, pp. 40-5.

123. Such as the House of the Stags at Pompeii – Tran Tam Tinh, op. cit. n. 47, or the House of Bacchus at Djemila/Cuicul – J. Lassus, 'La salle à sept absides de Djemila-Cuicul', *Ant. Afr.* 5 (1971), pp. 193-207, M. Blanchard-Lemée, 'La Maison de Bacchus à Djemila: architecture et décor d'une grande demeure provinciale à la fin d'antiquité', *Bulletin des Antiquaires de France* 17 (1981), pp. 131-42.

124. R. Lanciani, *The Ruins and Excavations of Ancient Rome* (London 1897), pp. 159 and 165-6.

125. See sections in this chapter on villas in Gaul, Spain and Italy.

126. There is a large literature on the palace, e.g. M. de Franceschini, *Villa Adriana: mosaici, perimetri, edifici* (Rome 1991), W. Macdonald and J. Pinto,

Hadrian's Villa and Its Legacy (New Haven 1995), especially p. 111 on the Canopus.

127. A. Hoffman, *Das Gartenstadion in der Villa Hadriana* (Mainz 1980).

128. M. Üblacker, *Das Teatro Marittimo in der Villa Hadriana* (Mainz 1985).

129. This is not to say that early classical beliefs were immoral. The strict moral tenets of Stoicism found favour amongst late Republican and early Imperial aristocrats, but were never widespread in the population of the empire as a whole.

130. The standard work on the palace is J. and T. Marasovic, *Diocletian Palace* (Zagreb 1970). More recently in English J.J. Wilkes, *Diocletian's Palace, Split* (Sheffield 1986).

131. E. Dyggve, *Ravennatum Palatium Sacrum. La basilica ipetrale per cerimonie. Studi sull' architettura dei palazzi della tarda antichita* (Copenhagen 1941).

132. D. Srejovic et al., *Gamzigrad: an imperial palace of late classical times* (Belgrade 1983), see also comments by Wilkes, op. cit. n. 130, pp. 67-70.

133. Constantinople: D. Talbot-Rice, ed., *The Great Palace of the Byzantine Emperors* (St Andrews 1959), records a pre-sixth-century AD peristyle. Thessalonika: M. Vickers, 'Observations on the octagon at Thessalonika', *JRS* 63 (1973), pp. 111-20. Sirmium: parts of the palace were recorded by N. Duval and V. Popovic during the 1970s, but detailed analysis is unpublished. Trier: preserves the famous Constantinian basilica, E. Wightman, op. cit. n. 63 (1970).

134. The best single source on the architecture of the houses is R. Stillwell, 'Houses of Antioch', *DOP* 15 (1961), pp. 45-57. The mosaics were originally published by D. Levi, *Antioch Mosaic Pavements* (Princeton 1947). Unpublished details can also be gleaned from the original excavation reports, cited here for individual houses, and the site notebooks in Princeton University.

135. R. Stillwell, *Antioch on the Orontes 3: the excavations of 1937-9* (Princeton 1941), pp. 27-31.

136. J. and J.Ch. Balty, ed., *Colloque Apamée de Syrie 29-31 mai 1980* (Brussels 1984), includes papers on all aspects of these houses by a wide range of scholars.

137. Stillwell, op. cit. n. 134, and F. Baratte, *Mosaïques paléochrétiennes du musée du Louvre* (Paris 1978), pp. 92-8.

138. This floor panel is figured, rather than being in plain mosaic as was normally the case for couch settings, but the shape of the panel leaves the location beyond doubt.

139. op. cit. n. 134.

140. Excavated by B. Walters. S.S. Frere, ed., 'Roman Britain in 1988', *Britannia* 20 (1989), pp. 315-17, and J. Toynbee, 'Apollo, beasts, and seasons; some thoughts on the Littlecote mosaic', *Britannia* 12 (1981), pp. 1-6.

141. S. Ellis, op. cit. n. 69, pp. 163-78.

142. There is an extensive literature on Woodchester. Recent work on the development of the villa is reported by G. Clarke, 'The Roman villa at Woodchester', *Britannia* 13 (1982), pp. 197-228.

143. S.S. Frere, 'The Bignor villa', *Britannia* 13 (1982), pp. 135-96.

144. A. Bulleid and D. Horne, 'The Roman house at Keynsham, Somerset', *Archaeologia* 25 (1926), pp. 109-38.

145. S. Drca et al., *Mediana* (Niš 1979).

146. E. Clifford, 'The Roman villa, Witcombe, Gloucestershire', *Transactions of the Bristol and Gloucestershire Archaeological Society* 73 (1954), D. Wilson, ed., 'Roman Britain in 1969', *Britannia* 1 (1970), pp. 294-5.

147. Apart from discussion of houses at Apamea and Littlecote in this chapter see S. Ellis, 'The end of the Roman house', *AJA* 92 (1988), pp. 565-76, and id., 'Power, Architecture and Decor: how the late Roman aristocrat appeared to his guests', in E. Gazda, ed., *Roman Art in the Private Sphere* (Ann Arbor 1991), pp. 117-34.

148. Ellis, op. cit. n. 174 (988) and (1991), and further discussion in Chapter 6.

149. See J. Wiseman, *Stobi: a guide to the excavations* (Belgrade 1973).

150. J-P. Darmon, *Nymfarum Domus* (Leiden 1980), pp. 20-1.

151. Wallace-Hadrill, op. cit. n. 1, Plate 3 and p. 190.

152. Clarke, op. cit. n. 46, passim especially pp. 14-19.

153. See Ellis, op. cit. n. 147 (1988).

3. Town and Country

1. G. Hermansen, *Ostia: Aspects of Roman city life* (Edmonton 1982), p. 24.

2. ibid., p. 22.

3. ibid., chapter 6.

4. R. Meiggs, *Roman Ostia* (Oxford 1973), p. 139 gives an eloquent description of the context of the development. See also J. Packer, *The Insulae of Imperial Ostia*, Memoirs of the American Academy of Rome 31 (Rome 1971), especially p. 16.

5. J.R. Clarke, *The Houses of Roman Italy 100 BC – AD 250* (Berkeley 1991), pp. 305-12, and pp. 354-8. See also B. Frier, *Landlords and Tenants in Imperial Rome* (Princeton 1980), pp. 8-13, including useful commentary on the surrounding buildings.

6. Hermansen, op. cit. n. 1, pp. 35-7.

7. J.S. Crawford, *The Byzantine Shops at Sardis* (Cambridge 1990).

8. J. Wacher, *The Towns of Roman Britain* (London 1995), pp. 63-6 discusses British markets. M. Alexander et al., 'Corpus des mosaïques de Tunisie', *Thuburbo Maius: les mosaïques de la region du forum* (Tunis 1980), pp. 13-14.

9. op. cit. n. 1, pp. 146-8. See also Packer op. cit. n. 4, pp. 6-7.

10. Hermansen, op. cit. n. 1, lists five Ostian taverns with floor mosaics alluding to their trade (pp. 143-5 and 172-4), as well as two with similar wall paintings (pp. 130-2 and 151-6).

11. V.M. Strocka, *Casa del Principe di Napoli (VI.15,7.8)* (Tübingen 1984), A. Wallace-Hadrill, *Housing and Society in Pompeii and Herculaneum* (Princeton 1994), pp. 47-50.

12. Wallace-Hadrill, ibid., p. 81, Table 4.2.

13. S.C. Nappo, 'Urban transformation at Pompeii, late 3rd and early 2nd c. BC', in R. Laurence and A. Wallace-Hadrill, ed., *Domestic Space in the Roman World: Pompeii and beyond* (Portsmouth 1997), pp. 91-120.

14. M. Alexander et al., *Corpus des mosaïques de Tunisie 1.1; Utique Insulae I-II-III* (Tunis 1973), pp. 95-100 for Lot 11.

15. Clarke, op. cit. n. 5, pp. 289-303.

16. M. Blanchard-Lemée, *Maisons à mosaïques du quartier central de Djemila (Cuicul)* (Aix-en-Provence 1975), pp. 175-80.

17. I have developed these ideas of planned and unplanned urban form in S. Ellis, 'Prologue to a study of urban form', in P. Rush, ed., *Theoretical Roman Archaeology: second conference proceedings* (Aldershot 1995), pp. 82-104.

18. For discussion of building regulations in the cities of Roman and Constantinople see Hermansen, op. cit. n. 1, pp. 212-18, and Frier, op. cit. n. 5, including distances between buildings and their height.

19. Blanchard-Lemée, op. cit. n. 16, pp. 23-106.

20. The house of Octavius Quartio (also known as the House of Loreius Tiburtinus): Clarke, op. cit. n. 5, pp. 198-201, and W. Jashemski, *The Gardens of Pompeii, Herculaneum and the Villas destroyed by Vesuvius*, Vol. 1 (New York

1979), pp. 45-7, Vol. 2 (New York 1993), pp. 78-83. For the Garden of the Fugitives see ibid. (1979), pp. 243-7, and (1993), pp. 69-70.

21. G. Boon, *Silchester: The Roman Town of Calleva* (1974), is the basic text, requiring further commentary from Wacher, op. cit. n. 8, pp. 271-9, and excavations by Fulford since the 1970s.

22. The most recent report is to be found in *Gallia Informations* (1992-3), pp. 108-11.

23. C. Allag et al., *Les fouilles du parking de la mairie à Besançon* (Besançon 1992), pp. 52-71.

24. S.S. Frere, *Verulamium Excavations* 1 (London 1973), pp. 13-23.

25. A. Carrandini, *Settefinestre: una villa schiavistica nell'Etruria romana* (Modena 1985).

26. A notable exception to this standpoint together with telling arguments against its original proponents is provided by Wallace-Hadrill, op. cit. n. 11, pp. 121-2.

27. P. Garnsey and R. Saller, *The Roman Empire: economy, society and culture* (London 1987), pp. 47-8, discuss the issues and assumptions surrounding the aristocracy's involvement in trade.

28. H. Butler, *Publications of an American Expedition to Syria in 1899-1900. Part 2 Architecture and other arts* (New York 1903), H. Butler and H. Prentice, *Publications of the Princeton Archaeological Expedition to Syria 1904-5 and 1909, Division 2 Architecture* (Leiden 1919-20).

29. G. Tchalenko, *Villages Antiques de la Syrie du Nord, le massif du Belus à l'époque romaine* (Paris 1953).

30. Butler and Prentice, op. cit. n. 28, pp. 190-3.

31. ibid., pp. 133-6.

32. Discussed in Chapter 5.

33. U. Holscher, *The Excavations of Medinet Habu 5 the post-Ramessid remains* (Chicago 1954).

34. Butler and Prentice, op. cit. n. 28, pp. 120-2.

35. ibid., pp. 141-2.

36. J.-P. Sodini et al., *Dehes Campagnes 1-3 (1976-8)* (Paris 1981).

37. B. de Vries, 'The Umm el-Jimal project 1972-7', *Bulletin of the American Schools of Oriental Research* 244 (1981), pp. 53-72.

38. G. Tate, *Les campagnes de la Syrie du Nord du 2e au 7e siècle: un exemple d'expansion démographique et économique à la fin de l'antiquité* (Paris 1992), pp. 87-168 places the first houses at the beginning of the third century AD. C. Strube, *Die 'Toten Städte': Stadt und Land in Nordsyrien während der Spätantike* (Mainz 1996), pp. 53-4 places a house at Bamuqqa in the first century AD, and three houses at Benebil in the second century.

39. For Umm Il Jimal see de Vries, op. cit. n. 37.

40. Butler and Prentice, op. cit. n. 28.

41. For example Butler and Prentice, op. cit. n. 28, inscription 1177 from Il Bara recording a house built by seven individuals including two architects, while inscription 1121 from Zerzita records construction through the efforts and kindness of Nonnos the deacon and his son Abramios.

42. The original excavation report is A. Boak and E. Peterson, *Karanis: Topographical and Architectural Report of Excavations during the seasons 1924-8* (Ann Arbor 1931), but this has been superseded by E. Husselman, *Karanis: excavations of the University of Michigan in Egypt 1928-35. Topography and Architecture* (Ann Arbor 1979).

43. The two most important works on houses from papyri are F. Luckhardt, *Das*

Privathaus in Ptolemaischen und Römischen Ägypten (Giessen 1914), and G. Husson, *Le vocabulaire de la maison privée en Egypte d'après les papyrus grecs* (Paris 1983). Also noteworthy is P. van Minnen, 'House-to-house enquiries: an interdisciplinary approach to Roman Karanis', *ZPE* 100 (1994), pp. 227-58, who attempts to relate the papyrus finds in Karanis to the house architecture.

44. R. Alston, 'Houses and households in Roman Egypt', in R. Laurence and A. Wallace-Hadrill, *Domestic Space in the Roman World: Pompeii and beyond* (Portsmouth 1997), p. 28.

45. M. Rodziewicz, *Les habitations romaines tardives d'Alexandria – Alexandrie 3* (Warsaw 1984). The house described in detail here is House D.

46. A. Boak, *Socnopaiou Nesos – the University of Michigan Excavations at Dime in 1931-2* (Ann Arbor 1935).

47. Medinet Habu: Holscher, op. cit. n. 33, Armant: Sir R. Mond and O. Myers, *Temples of Armant* (London 1940), Elephantine: P. Grossman, *Elephantine 2 – Kirche und spätantike Hausanlagen im Chrumtempelhof* (Mainz 1980).

48. Alston, op. cit. n. 44, p. 39.

49. C. Pellecoeur, ed., *Formes de l'habitat rural en Gaule Narbonnaise 1* (Juan Les Pins 1993).

50. V. Lelière in ibid.

51. J.-L. Fiches, *Les maisons gallo-romaines d'Ambrussum (Villetelle-Hérault): la fouille du secteur IV 1976-80* (Paris 1986).

52. A.R. Congrès, 'Nouvelles fouilles à Glanum (1982-1990)', *JRA* 5 (1992), pp. 39-55.

53. M. Compan et al. in op. cit. n. 49.

54. R. Hingley, *Rural Settlement in Roman Britain* (London 1989).

55. ibid., p. 31.

56. R. Leech, *Excavations at Catsgore 1970-3* (Bristol 1982).

57. H.S. Gracie, 'Frocester Court Roman Villa: First Report', *Trans. Bristol and Gloucs. Arch. Soc.* 89 (1970), pp. 15-86.

58. D. Gurney, *Settlement, Religion and Industry on the Fen-edge: three Romano-British sites in Norfolk* (Hunstanton 1986).

59. An example of this type is Lockleys: J.B. Ward-Perkins, 'The Roman villa at Lockleys, Welwyn', *Ant. J.* 18 (1938), pp. 339-76, and comments of S. Ellis, 'Classical reception rooms in Romano-British houses', *Britannia* 26 (1995), pp. 163-78.

60. op. cit. n. 57, p. 43.

61. D.S. Neal 'Upper storeys in romano-British villas' in P. Johnson and I. Haynes ed., *Architecture in Roman Britain* (York 1996), pp. 33-53.

62. op. cit. n. 57, pp. 59-65.

63. M.G. Jarrett and S. Wrathmell, *Whitton: an Iron Age and Roman farmstead in South Galmorgan* (Cardiff 1981), pp. 90-5. The significance of the slow change in building style was noted by H. Mytum, 'Rural settlement of the Roman period in North and East Wales', in D. Miles, ed., *The Romano-British Countryside: studies on rural settlement and economy* (Oxford 1982), pp. 313-35.

64. W. Stanley, 'Porth Dafarch, Holyhead', *Archaeologia Cambrensis* 35 (1878).

65. A.H.A. Hogg, 'Din Lligwy', *Arch. J.* 132 (1975), pp. 285-6.

66. G. Barker et al., *Farming the Desert: the UNESCO Libyan Valleys Archaeological Survey,* 2 vols (Paris 1996).

67. J. Wahl, 'Castelo de Lousa, ein Wehrgehöft caesarisch-augustischer Zeit', *Mad. Mitt.* (1985), pp. 149-76.

68. R.B. Hitchner, 'The Kasserine archaeological survey 1982-6', *Ant. Afr.* 24 (1988), pp. 7-41.

69. S. Ellis, 'Town housing in the Mediterranean region AD 400-700', unpublished DPhil, Oxford University (1984).

70. L. Anselmino et al., *Il castellum del Nador: storia di un fattoria tra Tipasa e Caesarea (I-VI sec dc)* (Rome 1989).

71. ibid., pp. 23-5.

72. The site was no. 255 of the Kasserine survey.

73. See Ellis, op. cit. n. 69, unpublished dissertation, and S. Ellis, 'The end of the Roman house', *AJA* 92 (1988), pp. 565-76, for characteristics of subdivision, which can be identified as a specific architectural style.

74. e.g. Juvenal, *Satires* 3; Martial, *Epigrams* 1.86.

75. The classic presentation of this interpretation is A. Carrandini, *Sette Finestre: una villa schiavistica nella campagna* (Modena 1985).

76. This has been amply demonstrated by W. Jashemski, op. cit. n. 20, and is discussed below in Chapter 5.

77. Examples of the 1990s approach are M. Millet, *The Romanisation of Roman Britain* (Cambridge 1990), and D. Mattingley, *Roman Tripolitania* (London 1996).

78. E. Blake, 'Negotiating Nuraghi: settlement and the construction of ethnicity in Roman Sardinia', in K. Meadows, C. Lemke and J. Heron ed., *TRAC96: Proceedings of the Sixth Annual Theoretical Roman Archaeology Conference* (Oxford 1997), pp. 113-19.

79. Ellis, op. cit. n. 75.

80. For the latter see the Freudenhaus at Ephesus, and the House of Neptune at Thuburbo Majus amongst others – Ellis, op. cit. n. 75.

81. J. Russell, 'Excavations at Anemurium 1973', *Türk Arkeoloji Dergisi* 23 (1975), pp. 121-39.

82. J. Baradez, 'Nouvelles fouilles à Tipasa', *Libyca* 9 (1961).

4. Decoration

1. E. Dwyer, *Pompeian Domestic Sculpture: a study of five Pompeian houses and their contents*, American Academy at Rome (Rome 1980), followed by J.R. Clarke, *The Houses of Roman Italy 100 BC – AD 250* (Berkeley 1991), who puts great emphasis on this aspect of his work.

2. A. Mau, *Die Geschichte der dekorativen Wandmalerei in Pompeji* (Leipzig 1882).

3. A. Laidlaw, *The First Style in Pompeii: painting and architecture*, American Academy (Rome 1985).

4. R. Ling, *Roman Painting* (Cambridge 1991), p. 21.

5. A. De Franciscis, 'La villa romana di Oplontis' in B. Andrae and H. Kyrieleis, ed., *Neue Forschungen in Pompeji* (Recklinghausen 1975), and Clarke, op. cit. n. 1.

6. Ling, op. cit. n. 4, pp. 42-7.

7. e.g. Clarke, op. cit. n. 1, pp. 125-6.

8. ibid., pp. 65-6.

9. ibid., pp. 68-9.

10. ibid., pp. 69-72.

11. ibid., p. 71; for recent work on the Domus Aurea see L.F. Ball, 'A reappraisal of Nero's Domus Aurea', *JRA*, Suppl. 11 (1994), pp. 183-254.

12. Clarke, op. cit. n. 1, pp. 72-7.

13. ibid., pp. 278-82 and 286-8.

14. ibid., pp. 283-5.

15. ibid., pp. 301-3.

16. ibid., pp. 308-12.

17. ibid., pp. 320-39, and J.R. Clarke, 'The decor of the house of Jupiter and Ganymede at Ostia Antica: private residence turned gay hotel?', in E. Gazda, ed., *Roman Art in the Private Sphere* (Ann Arbor 1991), pp. 89-104.

18. Clarke, op. cit. n. 1, pp. 349-54. A similar approach is adopted in some late paintings at the House of the Yellow Walls: ibid., pp. 354-8.

19. ibid.

20. Ling, op. cit. n. 4.

21. Clarke, op. cit. n. 1, p. 339.

22. Fragments of red and green plaster were for example found at the site of Whitton discussed in the previous chapter: M.G. Jarrett and S. Wrathmell, *Whitton: an Iron Age and Roman farmstead in South Galmorgan* (Cardiff 1981), p. 231.

23. M. Henig, *The Art of Roman Britain* (London 1995), p. 89.

24. A. Barbet, *La peinture murale romaine, les styles décoratifs pompéiens* (Paris 1985), as well as a large number of more specific articles.

25. N. Davey and R. Ling, *Wall-painting in Roman Britain*, Britannia Monographs 3 (1982), pp. 123-31.

26. H. Chew, ed., *Peintures romaines en Narbonnaise*, Réunion des Musées Nationaux (Paris 1995), p. 44.

27. F. Dumasy-Mathieu, *La villa du Liégeaud et ses peintures: La Croisille-sur Briance (Haute-Vienne)* (Paris 1991), pp. 100-76.

28. Henig, op. cit. n. 23, p. 68.

29. Ling, op. cit. n. 4, p. 174.

30. ibid., p. 191.

31. CNRS, *La peinture murale romaine de la Picardie à la Normandie* (Dieppe 1982), pp. 97-9.

32. C. Meates, *The Roman Villa at Lullingstone, Kent*, 2 vols (Maidstone 1979, 1987).

33. C. Kraeling, *The Christian Buildings. The Excavations at Dura Europos conducted by Yale University and the French Academy of Inscriptions and Letters. Final Report 8.2* (New York 1967).

34. C. Rüger, 'Vorbericht über die Arbeiten in Centcelles 4', *Mad. Mitt.* 10 (1969), pp. 251-75, P. de Palol, *Arte Paleocristiano en España* (Barcelona undated), pp. 58-71.

35. A. Carrandini, A. Ricci and M. De Vos, *Filosofiana: La villa di Piazza Armerina* (Palermo 1982), R. Wilson, *Piazza Armerina* (London 1983).

36. V.M. Strocka, *Die Wandmalerei der Hanghäuser in Ephesos* (Vienna 1977).

37. *Digenis Akritas* 7.60 as discussed in D. Hull, *Digenis Akritas: the Two-Blood Border Lord. The Grottaferata Version* (Athens 1972), and S. Ellis, 'Power architecture and decor: how the late Roman aristocrat appeared to his guests', in E. Gazda, ed., *Roman Art in the Private Sphere* (Ann Arbor 1991), pp. 117-34.

38. O. Callot, 'Les décors en stucs du batiment dit de L'Huilerie à Salamine', in *Salamine de Chypre Histoire et Archéologie: état de récherches* (Lyons 1978), pp. 341-73, and G. Argoud, O. Callot and B. Helly, *Salamine de Chypre XI: une résidence Byzantine L'Huilerie* (Paris 1980).

39. Ling, op. cit. n. 4, pp. 19-21 on the problems of perspective caused by setting 'emblema' paintings in the floor.

40. S. Aurigemma, *I mosaici di Zliten* (Rome 1926).

41. D. Parrish, *Season Mosaics of Roman North Africa* (Rome 1984).

42. S. Gozlan, *La maison du Triomphe de Neptune à Acholla (Botria), Tunisie 1 – Les mosaïques* (Rome 1992).

43. S. Ellis, 'Late Antique dining: architecture, furnishings and behaviour', in

R. Laurence and A. Wallace-Hadrill, ed., *Domestic Space in the Roman World: Pompeii and beyond* (Portsmouth 1997), pp. 41-51.

44. Henig, op. cit. n. 23, pp. 123-4, neatly summarising a wide range of work by D.J. Smith. For a general sythesis on British mosaics see R. Ling, 'Mosaics in Roman Britain: discoveries and research since 1945', *Britannia* 28 (1997), pp. 259-95.

45. Henig, op. cit. n. 23, p. 124, see also comments of Ling, op. cit. n. 44, pp. 267-8.

46. D.J. Smith, 'Roman mosaics in Britain: a synthesis', in R. Farioli Campanati, *3 colloquio internazionale sul mosaico antico* (Ravenna 1984), pp. 357-80, is the principal work on the Corinium mosaic schools.

47. K. Branigan, *The Roman Villa in South-West Britain* (Bradford-on-Avon 1977), p. 55, Ling, op. cit. n. 4, pp. 280-1.

48. K. Dunbabin, *The Mosaics of Roman North Africa* (Oxford 1978) remains the best work.

49. On Rudston see D. Neal, *Roman Mosaic in Britain* (London 1981), pp. 92-8. On North African influence in British mosaics see D. Johnston, 'Some possible North African influences in Romano-British mosaics', in P. Johnson, R. Ling and D. Smith, ed., *Fifth International Colloquium on Ancient Mosaics held at Bath, England, on September 5-12 1987* (Portsmouth 1994), pp. 295-306.

50. J.R. Clarke, *Roman Black-and-White Figural Mosaics* (New York 1979).

51. ibid., p. 45.

52. Dunbabin, op. cit. n. 48, pp. 109-23.

53. J. Lassus, 'La salle à sept absides de Djemila-Cuicul', *Ant. Afr.* 5 (1971), pp. 193-207, M. Blanchard-Lemée, 'La Maison de Bacchus à Djemila: architecture et décor d'une grande demeure provinciale à la fin d'antiquité', *B. Ant. F.* 17 (1981), pp. 131-42, with additional comment by S. Ellis, 'Power, architecture and decor: how the late Roman aristocrat appeared to his guests', in E. Gazda, ed., *Roman Art in the Private Sphere* (Ann Arbor 1991), pp. 117-34.

54. For Antioch see D. Levi, *Antioch Mosaic Pavements* (Princeton 1947).

55. R. Stillwell, *Antioch on the Orontes 3: the excavations of 1937-9* (Princeton 1941), Plate 71, showing the Buffet Supper.

56. This would appear to have been first noticed by R. Brilliant, 'Mythology' in K. Weitzmann, ed., *The Age of Spirituality: Late Antique and Early Christian Art, Third to Seventh Century* (Princeton 1979), p. 129.

57. Identification of the hero and villa owner in domestic mosaics has been suggested by Y. Thébert, 'Private life and domestic architecture in Roman North Africa', in P. Veyne, ed., *A History of Private Life* Vol I (Cambridge 1987), pp. 388-9, and by Ellis, op. cit. n. 53.

58. Ellis, op. cit. n. 53, and more recently S. Ellis, 'Late Antique houses in Asia Minor', in S. Isager and B. Poulsen, ed., *Patron and Pavements in Late Antiquity* (Odense 1997), pp. 38-50.

59. E. Gazda, 'A marble group of Ganymede and the Eagle', in J. Humphrey, ed., *Excavations at Carthage conducted by the University of Michigan* 6 (Ann Arbor 1981), pp. 125-78.

60. For the palace of Lausus see Ellis, op. cit. n. 53. The interpretation of Orpheus derives from work of Martin Henig, op. cit. n. 22, p. 154, and S. Scott, 'The power of images in the late Roman house', in R. Laurence and A. Wallace-Hadrill, ed., *Domestic Space in the Roman World: Pompeii and beyond* (Portsmouth 1997), pp. 53-68.

61. For assessment in relation to architecture and decor see Dwyer, op. cit. n. 1.

62. D. Brinkerhoff, *A Collection of Sculpture in Classical and Early Christian Antioch* (New York 1970).

63. E. Bartman, 'Decor et duplicatio: pendants in Roman sculptural display', *AJA* 92 (1988), pp. 211-25, and more generally E. Bartman, 'Sculptural collecting and display in the private realm', in E. Gazda, ed., *Roman Art in the Private Sphere* (Ann Arbor 1991), pp. 71-88.

64. Ellis, op. cit. n. 53, pp. 128-9.

65. Henig, op. cit. n. 23, p. 76.

66. See E. Salza Prina Ricotti, *L'arte del convito nella Roma Antica* (Rome 1983), pp. 59-62, discussing Varro 3.17.5-6 – fish were to be admired rather than eaten.

67. Many such fountains are recalled in the modern names of Roman houses given by the archaeologists who discovered them – the House of the Cascade at Utica, or the House of the Mosaic Fountain at Pompeii.

68. Examples within dining rooms are common at Stobi, see J. Wiseman, *Guide to the Excavations at Stobi* (Belgrade 1973).

69. A good example of a monumental public nymphaeum is that perserved at Side: A. Mansel, *Side* (Ankara 1978), while the houses at Stobi (Wiseman, op. cit. n. 68) include several large nymphaea.

70. Meates, op. cit. n. 32.

71. J.B. Ward-Perkins 'The Christian architecture of Apollonia', in J. Humphrey, ed., *Apollonia the Port of Cyrene: excavations conducted by the University of Michigan 1965-1967* (Tripoli 1976), pp. 267-92.

72. For example G. Hanfmann, 'The continuity of Classical art: culture, myth and faith', in K. Weitzmann, ed., *The Age of Spirituality: a symposium* (Princeton 1980), pp. 85-6 on Bellerophon and the Chimera, and Henig, op. cit. n. 23, p. 155 on lion and huntsman.

73. Most notably Dunbabin, op. cit. n. 48, p. 216 on Bellerophon.

74. S. Ellis, 'Classical reception rooms in Romano-British houses', *Britannia* 26 (1995), pp. 163-78.

75. A. Wallace-Hadrill, *Housing and Society in Pompeii and Herculaneum* (Princeton 1994), pp. 30-1.

76. See Ellis, op. cit. n. 74 after Ling.

77. B. Bergmann, 'Painted perspectives of a villa visit: landscape as status and metaphor', in E. Gazda, ed., *Roman Art in the Private Sphere* (Ann Arbor 1991), pp. 49-70.

78. From Smirat, Dunbabin, op. cit. n. 48, pp. 67-9.

79. From El Djem, Dunbabin, op. cit. n. 48, pp. 78-9.

80. op. cit. n. 75, pp. 30-1.

81. Ling, op. cit. n. 4, pp. 135-6.

82. Clarke, op. cit. n. 1, pp. 113-23, De Franciscis, op. cit. n. 5, and Ling, op. cit. n. 4, pp. 27-31.

83. See Bergmann, op. cit. n. 77.

84. Bergman, op. cit. n. 77, discussing Statius, as well as Pliny, Sidonius and Ausonius.

85. Above all T. Sarnowski, *Les représentations de villas sur les mosaïques africaines tardives* (Warsaw 1978), also N. Duval, 'La représentation du palais dans l'art du Bas Empire', *Atti del 6 Congresso Int di Arch. Cristiana* (Rome 1965), pp. 481-4.

86. Ling, op. cit. n. 4, pp. 145-7 considers that realistic villa representations first came into vogue in the Third Style.

87. Dunbabin, op. cit. n. 48, pp. 119-21.

88. Within the artistic tenets of late antiquity it would not be too surprising if the house owners were actually transposing their urban house to a rural scene, demonstrating in one view their urban and rural wealth.

5. Furniture

1. E. Salza Prina Ricotti, *L'arte del convito nella Roma antica* (Rome 1983), p. 50.

2. S. Treggiari, *Roman Marriage: iusti coniuges from the Cicero to the time of Ulpian* (Oxford 1991), p. 421.

3. E. Pernice, *Hellenistische Tische, Zisternmündungen, Beckenduntersätze, Altäre und Truhen* (Berlin 1932), pp. 76-94.

4. P. van Minnen, 'House-to-house enquiries: an interdisciplinary approach to Roman Karanis', *ZPE* 100 (1994), pp. 227-58, discusses an archive from houses at Karanis, but a number of the papyri were discovered under the threshold block of the door. This could be a case of hiding things under the doormat, or more likely plugging a draft with some rags.

5. Varro, *Latin Language* 5.125.

6. J. Berry, 'Household artefacts: towards a re-interpretation of Roman domestic space', in R. Laurence and A. Wallace-Hadrill, ed., *Domestic Space in the Roman World: Pompeii and beyond* (Portsmouth 1997), pp. 183-95, records the finding of one such table in situ in house I.8.17 in Pompeii with a pot, a bronze jar and a bronze bowl below it. The location of the cartibulum is also grudgingly accepted by P. Allison, 'Artefact distribution and spatial function in Pompeian houses', in B. Rawson and P. Weaver, ed., *The Roman Family in Italy* (Oxford 1997), p. 334.

7. A. McKay, *Houses, Villas and Palaces of the Roman World* (Southampton 1975), p. 136.

8. Berry, op. cit. n. 6, p. 188 house 1.8.17 – cart, Fig. 1 house 1.9.12 – amphorae.

9. Allison, op. cit. n. 6.

10. Contra J.-A. Dickmann, 'The peristyle and the transformation of domestic space in hellenistic Pompeii', in R. Laurence and A. Wallace-Hadrill, ed., *Domestic Space in the Roman World: Pompeii and beyond* (Portsmouth 1997), pp. 121-36.

11. *Letters* 2.17.5 and 5.6.19.

12. A. De Franciscis, 'La villa romana di Oplontis', in B. Andrae and H. Kyrieleis, ed., *Neue Forschungen in Pompeji* (Recklinghausen 1975).

13. Allison, op. cit. n. 6, pp. 337-8, notes the frequency of cupboards in the triclinia of Pompeian houses, and S. Ellis, 'Late antique dining: architecture, furnishings, and behaviour', in R. Laurence and A. Wallace-Hadrill, ed., *Domestic Space in the Roman World: Pompeii and beyond* (Portsmouth 1997), p. 46, notes their frequency in the triclinia of late antique houses.

14. K. Dunbabin, 'Convivial spaces: dining and entertainment in the Roman villa', *JRA* 9 (1996), pp. 66-80, is the best summary of these changes.

15. The most important article on sigma tables remains G. Roux, 'Tables chrétiennes en marbre découvertes à Salamine', *Salamine de Chypre*, 4 (1973), pp. 133-96. For the overall setting of the furniture, G. Åkersatröm-Hougen, *The Calendar and Hunting Mosaics of the Villa of the Falconer in Argos* (Stockholm 1974).

16. Ellis, op. cit. n. 13, p. 49.

17. ibid., p. 47.

18. E. Salza Prina Ricotti, 'The importance of water in Roman garden triclinia', in E. MacDougall, ed., *Ancient Roman Villa Gardens* (Washington DC 1987), pp. 135-84, Dunbabin, op. cit. n.14.

19. Ellis, op. cit. n. 13.

20. Roux, op. cit. n. 15.

21. Amongst modern authors stressing the theatrical element in Roman dinners, see J. Rossiter, 'Convivium and villa in late antiquity', in W. Slater, ed.,

Dining in a Classical Context (Ann Arbor 1991), pp. 121-48, and S. Ellis, 'Power, architecture and decor: how the late Roman aristocrat appeared to his guests', in E. Gazda, ed., *Roman Art in the Private Sphere* (Ann Arbor 1991), pp. 117-34.

22. G. Hanfmann, 'Excavations at Sardis 1959', *BASOR* 157 (1960), pp. 8-43, J. Waldebaum, *Metalwork from Sardis* (Cambridge 1983), S. Ellis, 'Lighting in Late Roman houses', in S. Cottam et al., ed., *Proceedings of the Fourth Annual Theoretical Roman Archaeology Conference Durham 1994* (1995), pp. 65-71.

23. The house and the shops opposite were originally assumed to have been destroyed by the Sassanian invasion of AD 616, but doubt has now been cast on this interpretation.

24. Dunbabin, op. cit. n. 14.

25. Hanfmann, op. cit. n. 22.

26. Ricotti, op. cit. n. 1.

27. Ellis, op. cit. n. 13, following work of Marlia Mundell.

28. See Chapters 1 and 2 and below in this chapter.

29. See Allison, op. cit. n. 6 for wooden cupboards, and Ellis, op. cit. n. 13 for cupboards in the wall.

30. Ellis, op. cit. n. 13.

31. Ricotti, op. cit. n. 1.

32. The loaves are however sometimes an artist's mistake for the circular cusps, or cuts which often decorated the sides of the sigma table.

33. E. Condurachi et al., *Histria I* (Bucharest 1954). The first to identify the room as a dining room was N. Duval, 'L'archéologie en Roumanie à propos de deux livres récents de I. Barnea', *RA* (1980), pp. 313-40.

34. M. Blanchard-Lemée, *Maisons à mosaïques du quartier central de Djemila (Cuicul)* (Aix-en-Provence 1975), pp. 23-106.

35. J.S. Crawford, *The Byzantine Shops at Sardis* (Cambridge 1990), pp. 99-101.

36. See Chapter 3 for further discussion of 'shops' as houses.

37. J. Liversidge, *Furniture in Roman Britain* (London 1955). For a recent comment see M. Henig, *The Art of Roman Britain* (London 1995), pp. 134-5.

38. Liversidge, op. cit. n. 37, pp. 8, 37-9, 47 and 51.

39. T. Solley, 'Romano-British side-tables and chip carving', *Britannia* 10 (1979), pp. 169-78, and K. Branigan, *The Roman Villa in South-West England* (Bradford-on-Avon 1977), pp. 63-5.

40. Liversidge, op. cit. n. 38, recognises such candelabra from London and York.

41. The evidence is set out in S. Ellis, 'Classical reception rooms in Romano-British houses', *Britannia* 26 (1995), pp. 163-78, with mosaic panels from Dewlish and Lullingstone.

42. Liversidge, op. cit. n. 38, pp. 28-33 and 57-8.

43. McKay, op. cit. n. 7, fig. 60, after B.F. Cook, 'The Boscoreale cubiculum: a new installation', *Bulletin of the Metropolitan Museum of Art* (1964), pp. 166-83.

44. L. Nevett, 'Perceptions of domestic space in Roman Italy', in B. Rawson and P. Weaver, ed., *The Roman Family in Italy: status, sentiment, space* (Oxford 1997), p. 293.

45. See papers by L. Nevett, M. George and P. Allison, in B. Rawson and P. Weaver, ed., *The Roman Family in Italy: status, sentiment, space* (Oxford 1997), all stressing the mobility of Roman furniture and variations in rooms function.

46. For the houses at Herculaneum see in the first place A. Maiuri, *Ercolano: I nuovi scavi (1927-1958)*, 2 vols (Rome 1958), pp. 407-16 for the House of Opus Craticum plus J.R. Clarke, *The Houses of Roman Italy 100 BC – AD 250* (London 1991), pp. 257-63.

47. Maiuri, op. cit. n. 46, p. 41.

48. Allison, op. cit. n. 6, pp. 335-6.

49. P. Foss, 'Watchful lares: Roman household organization and the rituals of Roman domestic space', in R. Laurence and A. Wallace-Hadrill, ed., *Domestic Space in the Roman World: Pompeii and beyond* (Portsmouth 1997), pp. 196-218.

50. See Chapter 1 for the House of the Vettii.

51. R. Goodchild, 'The Palace of the Dux', in J. Humphrey, ed., *Apollonia the Port of Cyrene: excavations conducted by the University of Michigan 1965-1967*, Suppl. to Libya Antiqua 4 (Tripoli 1976), pp. 245-56, also S. Ellis, 'The Palace of the Dux and related houses', in G. Barker, J. Lloyd and J. Reynolds, ed., *Cyrenaica in Antiquity* (Oxford 1985), pp. 15-25.

52. Ricotti, op. cit. n. 1, p. 10, S. Ellis, op. cit. n. 13, pp. 49-50.

53. G. Hermansen, *Ostia: aspects of Roman city life* (Edmonton 1982), and B. Frier, *Landlords and Tenants in Imperial Rome* (Princeton 1980), see also Chapter 3 above.

54. For Karanis see above Chapter 3. For the meal of the holy man see for exmple Mark the Deacon, *Life of Porphyry* 98.

55. This is above all the work of Penelope Allison and Joanne Berry. P. Allison, 'Artefact assemblages: not "the Pompeii premise" ', in E. Herring, R. Whitehouse and J. Wilkins, ed., *Papers of the Fourth Conference of Italian Archaeology: new developments in Italian Archaeology Part 1* (London 1992), pp. 49-56, Allison, op. cit. n. 6, and Berry, op. cit. n. 6.

56. Berry, op. cit. n. 6.

57. Allison, op. cit. n. 6, and Berry, op. cit. n. 6.

58. Berry, op. cit. n. 6, p. 193.

59. A. Carrandini, A. Ricci and M. De Vos, *Filosofiana: La villa di Piazza Armerina* (Palermo 1982), R. Wilson, *Piazza Armerina* (London 1983).

60. R. Ling, *The Insula of Menander at Pompeii 1: The Structures* (Oxford 1997).

61. W. Jashemski, *The Gardens of Pompeii, Herculaneum, and the Villas Destroyed by Vesuvius*, 2 vols (New York 1979 and 1993).

62. ibid. (1979), p. 32.

63. See the papers by M. LeGlay, J. de Alarçao and Etienne, and Cunliffe in E. MacDougall and W. Jashemski, ed., *Ancient Roman Gardens* (Washington DC 1981).

64. Jashemski, op. cit. n. 61 (1979): pp. 233-8 vegetable plots (House of the Ship Europa), pp. 24-30 orchards (House of Polybius), pp. 201-18 ('Foro Boario') and pp. 228-32 vineyards.

6. The House and the Family

1. A. Carrandini et al., *Sette Finestre: una villa schiavistica nell'etruria romana* (Modena 1985).

2. A. Wallace-Hadrill, 'The social structure of the Roman house', *PBSR* 56 (1988), and his later expansion of this work, A. Wallace-Hadrill, *Housing and Society in Pompeii and Herculaneum* (Princeton 1994).

3. This is also very much the model of circulation used by John Clarke whose study of Pompeii, *The Houses of Roman Italy, 100 BC – AD 250* (Berkeley 1991), has often been cited in this work.

4. B. Hillier and J. Hanson, *The Social Logic of Space* (Cambridge 1984).

5. ibid., pp. 108-9 and 151-2.

6. ibid., pp. 102 and 154.

7. The most complex of these houses would appear to be the 'Palace' above the theatre at Ephesus, the Palace of the Dux at Apollonia, and the Theodosian Palace at Stobi. The former two houses are discussed in S. Ellis, 'The end of the Roman house', *AJA* 92 (1988), pp. 565-76, and the last is described in J. Wiseman, *Guide to the Excavations at Stobi* (Belgrade 1973). The analysis referred to can only be regarded as tentative, and needs to be applied to a much wider range of housing.

8. M. Grahame, 'Public and private in the Roman house: investigating the social order of the Casa del Fauno', in R. Laurence and A. Wallace-Hadrill, ed., *Domestic Space in the Roman World: Pompeii and beyond* (Portsmouth 1997), pp. 137-64.

9. R. Saller, *Personal Patronage in the Roman Empire* (Cambridge 1982), follows the development of patronage and the salutatio amongst the Roman aristocracy, also C. Darmon, *The Mask of the Parasite* (Ann Arbor 1998).

10. This process was also influenced by the abandonment of public meeting places; see Ellis, op. cit. n. 7, who describes several houses with audience chambers.

11. S. Ellis, 'Power architecture and decor: how the late Roman aristocrat appeared to his guests', in E. Gazda, ed., *Roman Art in the Private Sphere* (Ann Arbor 1991), pp. 117-34. For the House of Bacchus at Djemila see J. Lassus, 'La salle à sept absides de Djemila-Cuicul', *Ant. Afr.* 5 (1971), pp. 193-207, M. Blanchard-Lemée, 'La Maison de Bacchus à Djemila: architecture et décor d'une grande demeure provinciale à la fin d'antiquité', *Bulletin des Antiquares de France* 17 (1981), pp. 131-42.

12. S. Ellis, 'Classical reception rooms in Romano-British houses', *Britannia* 26 (1995), pp. 163-78.

13. P. Laslett, *The World We Have Lost* (Cambridge 1983) is the classic account of pre-modern social structures. One of the first acknowledged structures was identified in the Languedoc region of France: J.-L. Flandrin, *Les amours paysannes (XVIe-XIXe siècle)* (Paris 1975). The most recent attempt to question this nuclear structure is D. Martin, 'The construction of the ancient family: methodological considerations', *JRS* 86 (1996), pp. 40-60.

14. R. Saller and B. Shaw, 'Tombstones and Roman family relations in the Principate: civilians, soldiers, and slaves', *JRS* 74 (1984), pp. 124-56.

15. See K. Hopkins, *Death and Renewal* (Cambridge 1983).

16. See for example the firm supporting statements of P. Garnsey and R. Saller, *The Roman Empire: economy, society and culture* (London 1987), pp. 141-3.

17. Papyrus BGU 115.

18. R. Alston, 'Houses and households in Roman Egypt', in R. Laurence and A. Wallace-Hadrill, ed., *Domestic Space in the Roman World: Pompeii and beyond* (Portsmouth 1997), p. 33 suggests an average size of 5.4, while the most comprehensive demographic analysis, R. Bagnall and B. Frier, *The Demography of Roman Egypt* (Cambridge 1994), p. 68, suggests 5.3 people, and that this was the maximum size for high mortality societies.

19. Bagnall and Frier, p. 60.

20. ibid., pp. 66-7.

21. ibid., pp. 69-71.

22. ibid., p. 64. For a similar argument, see K. Bradley, 'Remarrying and the structure of the upper class Roman family', in B. Rawson, ed., *Marriage, Divorce and Children in Ancient Rome* (Oxford 1991), pp. 79-98.

23. P. Gallivan and P. Wilkins, 'Familial structures in Roman Italy: a regional approach', in B. Rawson and P. Weaver, ed., *The Roman Family in Italy: status, sentiment, space* (Oxford 1997) pp. 239-79. In particular their results need to be adjusted for underestimation of numbers of children. This would take account of the fact that few children in each family were commemorated with an inscription.

24. F. Pirson, 'Rented accommodation at Pompeii: the Insula Arriana Polliana', in R. Laurence and A. Wallace-Hadrill, ed., *Domestic Space in the Roman World:*

Pompeii and beyond (Portsmouth 1997), pp. 165-81, gives a good idea of the problems of identifying different properties and households in Pompeii.

25. See Chapters 2 and 3 above.

26. There is now a very considerable literature on the place of Roman women in the household. Among the major works are S. Dixon, *The Roman Mother* (London 1988), id., *The Roman Family* (Baltimore 1992), and S. Treggiari, *Roman Marriage: iusti coniuges from the time of Cicero to the time of Ulpian* (Oxford 1991).

27. P. Ariès, *L'enfant et la vie familiale sous L'Ancien Régime* (Paris 1960).

28. For information on Roman children see the works of Dixon cited in n. 26, and B. Rawson, 'Children in the Roman familia', in B. Rawson, ed., *The Family in Ancient Rome: new perspectives* (Oxford 1986), pp. 170-200.

29. J. Crook, *Life and Law at Rome* (London 1967), pp. 143-4.

30. Juvenal, *Satire* 3.

31. B. Frier, *Landlords and Tenants in Imperial Rome* (Princeton 1980).

32. J.T. Smith, 'Villas as the key to social structure', in M. Todd, ed., *Studies in the Romano-British Villa* (Leicester 1978), pp. 149-85, and id., *Roman Villas: a study in social structure* (London 1997), but against which the telling critique of S. Clarke, 'The social significance of villa architecture in Celtic north-west Europe', *Oxford Journal of Archaeology* 9 (1990), pp. 337-53.

33. This is directly stated by Vitruvius, *On Architecture* 6.5.

34. See, for example, texts cited by E. Salza Prina Ricotti, *L'arte del convito nella Roma antica* (Rome 1983), pp. 62-4.

35. S. Scott, 'The power of images in the late Roman house', in R. Laurence and A. Wallace-Hadrill, ed., *Domestic Space in the Roman World: Pompeii and beyond* (Portsmouth 1997), pp. 53-67.

36. S. Ellis, 'The end of the Roman house', *AJA* 92 (1988), pp. 565-76.

37. J.B. Ward-Perkins, 'The Christian architecture of Apollonia', in J. Humphrey, ed., *Apollonia the Port of Cyrene: excavations conducted by the University of Michigan 1965-1967*, Suppl. 4 to Libya Antiqua (Tripoli 1976), pp. 267-92.

38. Discussed in Chapter 4.

39. See in particular M. Millet and S. Keay, *The Ager Tarraconensis* (Portsmouth 1997).

40. Thus third-century pottery is hard to date, coinage is poor in quality, and it would appear that there was reduced building activity in many parts of the Empire.

41. Ellis, op. cit. n. 36.

42. R. Wilson, *Piazza Armerina* (London 1983).

43. See comments on subdivision at the end of Chapter 3 above, and S. Ellis, 'Power-broking and the re-use of public buildings in late antiquity', *Acts of the 13th International Congress of Early Christian Archaeology Split-Salona 1994* (forthcoming).

7. Conclusions

1. S. Treggiari, *Roman Marriage: iusti coniuges from the time of Cicero to the time of Ulpian* (Oxford 1990), and many other recent works.

2. P. Ariès, *L'enfant et la vie familiale sous L'Ancien Régime* (Paris 1960).

3. S. Ellis, 'Late Antique dining: architecture, furnishings and behaviour', in R. Laurence and A. Wallace-Hadrill, ed., *Domestic Space in the Roman World: Pompeii and beyond* (Portsmouth 1997), pp. 41-51.

4. S. Ellis, 'Late Antique houses in Asia Minor', in S. Isager and B. Poulsen, ed., *Patron and Pavements in Late Antiquity* (Odense 1997), pp. 38-50.

Index of Sites

General Index